After the Death of Childhood

After the Death of Childhood

Growing Up in the Age of Electronic Media

David Buckingham

polity

The right of David Buckingham to be identified as author of this work has been asserted in accordance with the Copyright, Designs and Patents Act 1988.

First published in 2000 by Polity Press in association with Blackwell Publishing Ltd

Reprinted 2000, 2003

Editorial office:
Polity Press
65 Bridge Street
Cambridge CB2 1UR, UK

Marketing and production:
Blackwell Publishing Ltd
108 Cowley Road
Oxford OX4 1JF, UK

Published in the USA by
Blackwell Publishing Inc.
350 Main Street
Malden, MA 02148, USA

ISBN 0–7456–1932–0
ISBN 0–7456–1933–9 (pbk)

A catalogue record for this book is available from the British Library.

Library of Congress Cataloging-in-Publication Data
Buckingham, David, 1954–
    After the death of childhood : growing up in the age of electronic media / David Buckingham.
        p.   cm.
    Includes bibliographical references and index.
    ISBN 0-7456-1932-0 (alk. paper) — ISBN 0-7456-1933-9 (pbk. : alk. paper)
    1. Mass media and children.   2. Digital media—Social aspects.
    3. Children—Social conditions.   4. Children's rights.   I. Title.
    HQ784.M3 B83 2000
    302.23—dc21   99-047595

Typeset in 10.5 on 12 pt Palatino
by Ace Filmsetting Ltd, Frome, Somerset
Printed in Great Britain by MPG Books Ltd, Bodmin, Cornwall

This book is printed on acid-free paper.

For more information on polity, please visit our website: http://www.polity.co.uk

Contents

Acknowledgements

This book is in many respects a summation – or at least a provisional summation – of an area of research that has preoccupied me for more than fifteen years. As such, it draws upon work that has been published elsewhere, and in some places directly reworks and incorporates material from earlier books and articles. Nevertheless, the book was conceived as a coherent project from the start, and it includes a substantial amount of new material.

I would like to thank the many people who have worked with me on the numerous empirical research projects on which this book is based, notably Mark Allerton, Sara Bragg, Hannah Davies, Valerie Hey, Sue Howard, Ken Jones, Peter Kelley, Gunther Kress, Gemma Moss and Julian Sefton-Green. Particular thanks are due to Peter Kelley for his work on the statistical data presented in chapter 4. I would also like to thank the many organizations that have funded these projects: the Economic and Social Research Council, the Broadcasting Standards Council, the Nuffield Foundation, the Spencer Foundation and the Arts Council of England.

I owe a special debt to Professor Elihu Katz and the Annenberg School for Communication in Philadelphia for awarding me a fellowship that enabled me to begin working on the book; and to the Institute of Education for providing a supportive working environment. I would also like to thank other international colleagues with whom I have debated these issues, or whose research has informed and supported my own, particularly Elisabeth Auclaire, Kirsten Drotner, JoEllen Fisherkeller, Horst Niesyto, Geoff Lealand and Joe Tobin. Thanks also to the many groups of students, academics and teachers who have been on the receiving end of some of these arguments over the past few years, and have helped me to reformulate and develop my ideas: these include my M.A. students on the Children's Media Culture course at the Institute of Education, as well as audiences in France, Germany, Norway, Denmark, Finland, Luxembourg, Canada, Australia, the United States and Britain.

Finally, fond thanks to Celia Greenwood, Clemency Ngayah-Otto and Julian Sefton-Green for their careful reading of the manuscript; and to my junior research assistants Nathan and Louis Greenwood, who have always displayed a healthy independence from their father's ideas. This book is dedicated to them.

Introduction

1

In Search of the Child

The claim that childhood has been lost has been one of the most popular laments of the closing years of the twentieth century. It is a lament that has echoed across a whole range of social domains – in the family, in the school, in politics, and perhaps above all in the media. Of course, the figure of the child has always been the focus of adult fears, desires and fantasies. Yet in recent years, debates about childhood have become invested with a growing sense of anxiety and panic. Traditional certainties about the meaning and status of childhood have been steadily eroded and undermined. We no longer seem to know where childhood can be found.

The place of the child in these debates is profoundly ambiguous, however. On the one hand, children are increasingly seen as threatened and endangered. Thus, we have seen a succession of high-profile investigations into child abuse, both in families and in schools and children's homes. There are frequent press reports about child murders and the scandal of neglected 'home alone kids'; and public hysteria about the risk of random abduction by paedophiles has steadily intensified. Meanwhile, our newspapers and television screens show scenes of the very different childhoods of children in developing countries: the street children of Latin America, the child soldiers in Africa and the victims of sex tourism in Asia.

On the other hand, children are also increasingly perceived as a threat to the rest of us – as violent, anti-social and sexually precocious. There has been growing concern about the apparent collapse of discipline in schools, and the rise in child crime, drug-taking and teenage pregnancy. As in the 1970s, the threat of an uncontrollable underclass of young people, caught in the liminal space between school and work, has begun to loom large – although this time around, the delinquents are even younger. The sacred garden of childhood has increasingly been violated; and yet children themselves seem ever more reluctant to remain confined within it.

The media are implicated here in contradictory ways. On the one hand, they serve as the primary vehicle for these ongoing debates about the changing nature of childhood – and in the process, they undoubtedly contribute to the growing sense of fear and panic. Yet on the other hand, the media are frequently blamed for *causing* those problems in the first place – for provoking indiscipline and aggressive behaviour, for inflaming precocious sexuality, and for destroying the healthy social bonds which might prevent them from arising in the first place. Journalists, media pundits, self-appointed guardians of public morality – and increasingly academics and politicians – are incessantly called on to pronounce on the dangers of the media for children: the influence of violent 'video nasties', the 'dumbing down' of children's television, the explicit sexuality of teenage magazines and the easy availability of pornography via the internet. And the media are now routinely condemned for 'commercializing' childhood – for transforming children into rapacious consumers, seduced by the deceptive wiles of advertisers into wanting what they do not need.

Meanwhile, the media themselves display an ambivalent fascination with the very *idea* of childhood. Hollywood movies have become preoccupied with the figure of the child-like adult (*Forest Gump*, *Toys*, *Dumb and Dumber*) and the adult-like child (*Jack*, *Little Man Tate*, *Big*). Advertising images display a similar ambivalence, from the notorious black devil/white angel of the campaign for Benetton clothing to the waif-like supermodels of the Calvin Kline ads. Meanwhile, the resurgence of the Disney Corporation points to the global marketability of conventional 'children's culture' to both adults and children – although, ironically, *Kids*, Larry Clark's controversial documentary-style film of casual sex and drugs among younger teenagers in New York, is also owned by a Disney subsidiary.

And then there is the figure of Michael Jackson – in the words of his biographer, 'the man who was never a child and the child who never grew up'.[1] From the children's crusade represented in his 'Heal the World' video, through his obsession with the imagery of Disney and Peter Pan, to the scandals surrounding allegations about his sexual abuse of children, Jackson epitomizes the intense uncertainty and discomfort that has come to surround the notion of childhood in the late modern era.

The responses of politicians and policy-makers to this sense of cri-

sis have been largely authoritarian and punitive. To be sure, there
has been a renewed emphasis on children's rights in recent years, in
the wake of the United Nations Convention on the Rights of the Child;
although in practice, this has often been interpreted as simply a matter of children's right to protection by adults. In most other respects,
there has been increasing enthusiasm for more disciplinary social
policies. Thus, we have seen the introduction of curfews and the
building of new children's prisons. In Britain, state benefit for young
people has been withdrawn; and there have been 'hit squads' to reassert discipline in schools. Such policies appear to be designed not
so much to protect children from adults as to protect adults from
children.

In relation to the media, the official response has also been predominantly a disciplinary one. In the wake of growing moral panics
about the influence of sex and violence in the media, governments in
many countries have introduced tighter censorship legislation; and
in North America we have seen the introduction of the V-chip, a
technical device fitted to all new television sets that will apparently
filter out 'violent' material. Meanwhile, there is growing interest in
the potential of blocking software, programs with symptomatically
anthropomorphic titles like 'Net Nanny' and 'Cyber Sitter' that promise to restrict children's access to proscribed sites on the internet. Yet
despite this search for a 'technological fix', national governments
appear ever more incapable of regulating the commercial corporations that now control the global circulation of media commodities –
not least those aimed at the children's market.

Nevertheless, interpretations of these changes in childhood – and
of the role of the media in reflecting or producing them – have been
sharply polarized. On the one hand, there are those who argue that
childhood as we know it is disappearing or dying, and that the
media – particularly television – are primarily to blame. From this
perspective, the media are seen to have erased the boundaries between childhood and adulthood, and hence to have undermined the
authority of adults. On the other hand, there are those who argue
that there is a growing generation gap in media use – that young
people's experience of new media technologies (and particularly of
computers) is driving a wedge between their culture and that of their
parents' generation. Far from erasing the boundaries, the media are
seen here to have reinforced them – although now it is adults who
are believed to have most to lose, as children's expertise with technology gives them access to new forms of culture and communication that largely escape parental control.

To some extent, these arguments can be seen as part of a more

general anxiety about social change which has accompanied the advent of a new millennium. The metaphor of 'death' is everywhere
around us – not least on bookshelves, where books about the death
of childhood sit alongside those about the death of the self, of society, of ideology, and of history. Such debates often seem to permit
only a narrow choice between grandiose despair and breathless optimism.

In the first part of this book, I review these contrasting arguments
in more detail, and seek to challenge the totalizing rhetoric that characterizes them. As I shall indicate, both positions are based on essentialist views of childhood and of communications media – and indeed
of the relationships between them. Yet for all their limitations, these
arguments point to two significant assumptions which form the basis of my analysis here. Both implicitly and explicitly, they suggest
that the notion of childhood is itself a social, historical construction;
and that culture and representation – not least in the form of electronic media – are one of the main arenas in which that construction
is developed and sustained.

Constructing childhood

The idea that childhood is a social construction is now commonplace
in discussions of the history and sociology of childhood; and it is
even being increasingly accepted by some psychologists.[2] The central premise here is that 'the child' is not a natural or universal
category, which is simply determined by biology. Nor is it something which has a fixed meaning, in whose name appeals can
unproblematically be made. On the contrary, childhood is historically, culturally and socially variable. Children have been regarded
– and have regarded themselves – in very different ways in different
historical periods, in different cultures and in different social groups.
Furthermore, even these definitions are not fixed. The meaning of
'childhood' is subject to a constant process of struggle and negotiation, both in public discourse (for example, in the media, in the academy or in social policy) and in interpersonal relationships, among
peers and in the family.

This is not to imply that the biological individuals whom we might
collectively agree to call 'children' somehow do not exist, or that we
cannot describe them. Rather, it is to say that these collective definitions are the outcome of social and discursive processes. There is a
kind of circularity here. Children are defined as a particular category,
with particular characteristics and limitations, both by themselves

and by others – by parents, teachers, researchers, politicians, policy-makers, welfare agencies, and (of course) by the media. These definitions are codified in laws and policies; and they are embodied within particular forms of institutional and social practice, which in turn help to *produce* the forms of behaviour which are seen as typically 'child-like' – and simultaneously to generate forms of resistance to them.[3]

Schooling, for example, is a social institution that effectively constructs and defines what it means to be a child – and indeed a child of a particular age. The separation of children by biological age rather than 'ability', the highly regulated nature of teacher/student relationships, the organization of the curriculum and the daily timetable, the practice of grading – all in various ways serve to reinforce and to naturalize particular assumptions about what children are and should be. And yet these definitions are, for the most part, only made explicit in specialized forms of institutional and professional discourse from which children themselves are largely excluded.

Of course, these various definitions and discourses are not necessarily consistent or coherent. On the contrary, we should expect them to be characterized by resistance and contradiction. The school and the family, for instance, appear to lay out clear definitions of the rights and responsibilities of both adults and children. Yet as teachers and parents know only too well, children routinely challenge and renegotiate these definitions, not always directly but often through what amounts to a form of guerrilla warfare. Furthermore, the expectations of these institutions are often themselves contradictory. On the one hand, for example, parents and teachers will routinely exhort children to 'grow up', and to behave in what they perceive as a mature and responsible way; while on the other, they will deny children privileges on the grounds that they are not yet old enough to deserve or appreciate them. And at the same time, becoming – and being perceived to be – an adult necessarily involves suppressing elements of one's behaviour which others might deem to be inappropriately 'childish'.

'Childhood' is thus a shifting, relational term, whose meaning is defined primarily through its opposition to another shifting term, 'adulthood'. Yet even where the respective roles of children and adults are defined in law, there is considerable uncertainty and inconsistency. Thus, the age at which childhood legally ends is defined primarily (and crucially) in terms of children's *exclusion* from practices which are defined as properly 'adult', most obviously, paid employment, sex, drinking alcohol and voting. Yet in each case, children are seen to attain majority at a different age. In the UK, for example, they can pay taxes at the age of sixteen, yet they cannot receive state benefits until they are seventeen, and they cannot vote until they are eighteen. They are entitled to have heterosexual sex at the age of sixteen; yet they cannot witness explicit images of such behaviour on film until they are eighteen. And yet, of course, real children engage in many of these activities well before they are legally entitled to do so.

Representing childhood

Broadly speaking, the definition and maintenance of the category 'childhood' depends on the production of two main kinds of discourses. First, there are discourses *about* childhood, produced by adults primarily *for adults* – not only in the form of academic or professional discourse, but also in the form of novels, television programmes and popular advice literature. Indeed, 'scientific' or 'factual' discourses about childhood (for example, those of psychology, physiology or medicine) are often intimately connected with 'cultural' or 'fictional' ones (such as philosophy, imaginative literature, or painting). Second, there are discourses produced by adults *for children*, in the form of children's literature, television and other media – which, despite the label, are rarely produced by children themselves.

Thus, the period in which our characteristic modern definition of childhood emerged – the second half of the nineteenth century – was characterized by an explosion of such discourses. During this period, children were gradually and systematically segregated from the world of adults, for example through the raising of the age of consent, the introduction of compulsory education, and attempts to eradicate child labour. Children were gradually moved out of the factories, off the streets and into the schools; and a whole range of new social institutions and agencies sought to oversee their welfare in line with a broadly middle-class domestic ideal, and thereby to ensure the 'health of the nation'.[4]

This demarcation of childhood as a distinct stage of life – and the removal of children from what Harry Hendrick has termed 'socially significant activity'[5] – was both justified by and reflected in discourses of both kinds. The work of the Romantic poets and Victorian novelists, for example, placed a central emphasis on the innate purity and natural goodness of children. For writers as diverse as Dickens and Wordsworth, the figure of the child became a powerful symbol in their critique of industrialism and social inequality. Childhood became, according to the historian Hugh Cunningham, 'a substitute for religion'.[6] It was also at this time that the scientific study of children – most notably in the form of paediatrics and developmental psychology – began to be established;[7] and such work quickly found its way into popular advice literature directed at parents.

Meanwhile, this period is also often seen as the Golden Age of children's literature: the work of writers such as Lewis Carroll, Edward Lear and J. M. Barrie reflected the widespread fascination and longing for childhood – not to mention the unresolved tensions around children's sexuality – which were characteristic of the time.[8] At the same time, the origins of more 'vulgar' (and indeed 'violent') forms of popular literature aimed at children – and particularly at working-class boys – can also be traced to this period; as can the first wide-scale marketing of toys and educational materials designed for use in the home.[9]

Of course, this is not to say that 'children' were somehow conjured into existence by these means, or indeed that such discourses and representations had not previously existed. It is merely to note that broader historical shifts in the social status of children are often accompanied by this kind of proliferation in discourse. As we shall see, similar developments occurred in the sixteenth and seventeenth centuries, and are also taking place at the present time.

Inevitably, the audiences for these two types of discourse are bound to overlap. Children are often extremely interested in certain forms of discourse *about* childhood, particularly where this touches on the most obviously forbidden forms of adult behaviour. And adults play a significant part in mediating texts *to* children, for example by buying and reading books for them, or by accompanying them to the cinema. Certain kinds of texts – the contemporary 'family' films of Walt Disney or Steven Spielberg, for example – could be seen precisely to unite these two audiences: they tell both adults and children very powerful and seductive stories about the relative meanings of childhood and adulthood. As in a good deal of nineteenth-century literature, the figure of the child here is at once a symbol of hope and a means of exposing adult guilt and hypocrisy. Such films often define the meaning of childhood by projecting its future loss: both for adults and for children, they mobilize anxieties about the pain of mutual separation, while offering reassuring fantasies about how it can be overcome.[10]

These cultural representations of childhood are thus often contradictory. They frequently say much more about adults' and children's fantasy investments in the *idea* of childhood than they do about the realities of children's lives; and they are often imbued with nostalgia for a past Golden Age of freedom and play. However, these

representations cannot be dismissed as merely illusory. Their power
depends on the fact that they also convey a certain truth: they must
speak in intelligible ways, both to children's lived experiences and
to adult memories, which may be painful as well as pleasurable.

As Patricia Holland argues, these representations of childhood are
part of a continuous effort on the part of adults to gain control over
childhood and its implications – not only over actual children, but
also over our own childhoods, which we are constantly mourning
and constantly reinventing. Such imagery, she argues,

> displays the social and psychic effort that goes into negotiating the diffi-
> cult distinction between adult and child, to keep childhood separate from
> an adulthood that can never be fully achieved. Attempts are made to es-
> tablish dual and opposing categories and hold them firm in a dichotomy
> set against the actual continuity of growth and development. There is an
> active struggle to maintain childhood – if not actual children – as pure
> and uncontaminated.[11]

As Holland emphasizes, these cultural constructions of childhood
serve functions not merely for children, but also for adults. The idea
of childhood serves as a depository for qualities which adults regard
both as precious and as problematic – qualities which they cannot
tolerate as part of themselves; yet it can also serve as a dream world
into which we can retreat from the pressures and responsibilities of
maturity.[12] Such representations, Holland argues, reflect 'the desire
to use childhood to secure the status of adulthood – often at the expense of children themselves'.[13]

Childhood, power and ideology

This view of childhood as a social and cultural construction is thus
to some extent a relativist one. It reminds us that our contemporary
notion of childhood – of what children are and should be – is comparatively recent in origin, and that it is largely confined to Western
industrialized societies. The majority of the world's children today
do not live according to 'our' conception of childhood.[14] To judge
these alternative constructions of childhood – and the children whose
lives are lived within them – as merely 'primitive' is to display a
dangerously narrow ethnocentrism. Likewise, this perspective causes
us to question the notion that the modern age was one in which the
innate 'needs' of children were truly recognized for the first time.
On the contrary, such definitions of children's unique characteristics
and needs are themselves culturally and historically produced; and

they necessarily imply particular forms of political and social organization.

Furthermore, this view of childhood reminds us that any description of children – and hence any invocation of the idea of child*hood* –
cannot be neutral. On the contrary, any such discussion is inevitably
informed by an *ideology* of childhood – that is, a set of meanings which
serve to rationalize, to sustain or to challenge existing relationships
of power between adults and children, and indeed between adults
themselves.[15]

This is most apparent when one considers how the figure of the
child is invoked by social movements, ranging from the broadly progressive to the distinctly reactionary. In his analysis of the moral
panics that have characterized British social life over the past two
decades, Philip Jenkins identifies a 'politics of substitution' which
has been practised by moral entrepreneurs of both left and right.[16] In
a climate of growing uncertainty, invoking fears about children provides a powerful means of commanding public attention and support: campaigns against homosexuality are redefined as campaigns
against paedophiles; campaigns against pornography become campaigns against child pornography; and campaigns against immorality and Satanism become campaigns against ritualistic child abuse.
Those who have the temerity to doubt claims about the epidemic
proportions of such phenomena can therefore easily be stigmatized
as hostile to children.

However, this is not to imply that such concerns are necessarily
illegitimate or false. On the contrary, they would not be so widely
felt if they did not in some way build on pre-existing anxieties – which,
as Jenkins indicates, are themselves a response to fundamental social changes, for example in the nature of the family. Nevertheless,
invoking the figure of the threatened child clearly serves particular
functions, both for campaigning groups and for government. The
wave of concern around child abuse in the 1980s, for example, fur-
thered the political ambitions both of Christian evangelical groups
and of feminists, whose influence came to dominate social work and
welfare agencies. Yet it also enabled the government to distract attention from the more intractable economic and social problems of
the time; and as a result, the extent to which children themselves can
be seen to have benefited from such campaigns is certainly debatable.

Of course, moral panics of this kind are not the only arena in which
the notion of childhood is invoked in this way. The discourse of environmentalism, for example, is often implicitly addressed to children, on the grounds that they represent 'the future' and are somehow

'closer to nature'. The figure of the child within feminism, or in the history of the Labour movement, is equally highly charged. The child is often seen as the most helpless victim of social policies that are primarily directed against women, or against the working classes; and here again, the call to protect children acts as a powerful means of mobilizing support.[17] For those with a wide range of motivations, adult politics are often carried out in the name of childhood.

Likewise, the production of texts *for* children – both in the modern electronic media, and in more traditional forms like children's literature – can also be seen to sustain particular ideologies of childhood. Such activity has traditionally been characterized by a complex balance between 'negative' and 'positive' motivations. On the one hand, producers have been strongly informed by the need to protect children from 'undesirable' aspects of the adult world. Indeed, in some respects, texts for children could be characterized primarily in terms of what they are *not* – that is, in terms of the *absence* of representations that are seen to constitute a negative moral influence, most obviously in the form of sex and violence.[18] On the other hand, there are also strong pedagogical motivations: such texts are frequently characterized by the attempt to educate, to provide moral lessons or 'positive images', and thereby to model forms of behaviour that are seen to be socially desirable. Cultural producers, policy-makers and regulators in this field are thus concerned not only to protect children from harm, but also to 'do them good'.

In both domains, adult definitions of childhood are thus simultaneously repressive *and* productive. They are designed both to protect and control children – that is, to keep them confined to social arenas and forms of behaviour which will not prove threatening to adults, or in which adults will (it is imagined) be unable to threaten *them*. Yet they are seeking not just to prevent certain kinds of behaviour, but also to teach and encourage others. They actively produce particular forms of subjectivity in children, just as they attempt to repress others. And, as I have suggested, they serve similar functions for adults themselves.

Yet, perhaps inevitably, adults have always monopolized the power to define childhood. They have laid down the criteria by which children are to be compared and judged. They have defined the kinds of behaviour which are appropriate or suitable for children at different ages. Even where they have purported merely to describe children, or to speak on their behalf, adults have unavoidably established normative definitions of what *counts* as child-like. To be sure, children can and do 'speak for themselves', although they are rarely given the opportunity to do so in the public domain, even on matters which directly concern them. The contexts in which they can speak, and the responses they can invoke, are still largely controlled by adults; and their ability to articulate alternative public constructions of 'childhood' remain severely circumscribed. Even arguments for 'children's rights' are predominantly made by adults, and in adult terms.

Of course, children may resist, or refuse to recognize themselves in, adult definitions – and in this respect, adult power is very far from absolute or uncontested. Nevertheless, their space for resistance is largely that of interpersonal relationships, amid the 'micropolitics' of the family or the classroom. Furthermore, children may be actively complicit in sustaining these definitions of what is 'adult' or 'child-like', if only by default: age differences, and the meanings that are attached to them, are a primary means through which power relationships are enacted, not only between adults and children, but also between children themselves. Children will routinely put other children 'in their place' by mocking or condemning them for their 'babyish' tastes or behaviour; and they will often strenuously attempt to distance themselves from such accusations. Such distinctions between 'adult' and 'child' are mutually policed on both sides. As we shall see, this has significant implications for research into children's relationships with the media – an arena which they sometimes perceive as uniquely their own.

Childhood as exclusion

This analysis points towards a rather less benign view of the construction of childhood than that which is typically invoked in debates about the 'death of childhood'. To be sure, definitions of childhood are diverse and often contradictory. At any given historical moment, or within any given social or cultural group, it is possible to trace many conflicting definitions – some of which may be residues of older conceptions, while others are perhaps newly emergent. Nevertheless, in the recent history of industrialized countries, childhood has essentially been defined as a matter of *exclusion*. For all the post-Romantic emphasis on children's innate wisdom and understanding, children are defined principally in terms of what they are *not* and in terms of what they *cannot* do. Children are not adults; and hence they cannot be allowed access to the things which adults define as 'theirs', and which adults believe they are uniquely able to comprehend and to control. By and large, children are denied the right to self-determination: they must rely on adults to represent their interests, and to argue on their behalf. 'Childhood', as it is predominantly conceived, is in this respect actively disempowering for children.

This is largely a consequence of the way in which children are defined as in some way not social – or, more accurately, as *pre*-social. Thus, the academic discipline which has until recently enjoyed exclusive claim to the study of children is that of psychology. It is a discipline which (at least in its most influential and dominant forms) interprets the study of human interaction in terms of the individual psyche or personality; and it defines the ways in which children change over time as a teleological process of development towards a preordained goal. Children are constructed here as isolated individuals, whose cognitive development proceeds through a logical sequence of 'ages and stages' towards the achievement of adult maturity and rationality. If childhood is thus defined as a process of becoming, adulthood is implicitly seen as a finished state, in which development has effectively ceased. Those who do not attain this state are judged in terms of individual pathology, and hence identified as suitable cases for treatment.[19]

While this approach has been increasingly questioned (not least within psychology itself), the dominant psychological construction of children clearly sanctions a view of them as essentially lacking or incomplete. Children's behaviour is assessed in terms of the extent to which it is or is not 'appropriate' to their biological age. The index of 'maturity' and 'immaturity' becomes the standard against which they are measured, and come to measure themselves. And these differences are themselves defined in terms of what are seen to be specifically adult qualities: rationality, morality, self-control and 'good manners'.

This is not, of course, to imply that adulthood is necessarily always privileged above childhood in these discourses – at least overtly. Children may be defined in terms of their lack of rationality, social understanding or self-control; yet, by the same token, they can also be extolled (in however patronizing a way) for their lack of artifice, self-consciousness and inhibition. There is, of course, a whole self-help industry which is premised on the claim that adults need to get in touch with their 'inner child' – claims that implicitly reinforce romantic notions of childhood as a site of truth and purity.[20]

Nevertheless, what remains disturbing for so many adults are the consequences of children 'crossing the line'. Manifestations of 'precocious' behaviour threaten the separation between adults and children, and hence represent a challenge to adult power. It is at this point that liberal discourses of child development, with their emphasis on nurturance and natural growth, begin to crack. Children's psychological health, it seems, positively requires us to police the line between adults and children, in the home, in the school and in the wider arena of public culture. This process is thus not just a matter of the *separation* between children and adults: it also entails an active *exclusion* of children from what is seen to be the adult world.

This attempt to exclude children applies most obviously to the domains of violence and sexuality, of the economy and of politics. And the significance of the electronic media in this context is, of course, that they provide one of the primary sources of knowledge about these things. Both in relation to the media, and in these other social domains, this leads to a situation in which the fundamental dilemmas are seen to be those of *access* and *control*. As I shall indicate, such dilemmas are becoming ever more acute as a result of new technology, and of the global proliferation of electronic media. Renewed calls for control are emerging precisely because the possibility of control is steadily passing away.

However, my position here is not a liberationist one. In principle, I would not deny children's prolonged biological dependency on adults; nor would I contest the idea that individuals do indeed develop and change as they grow older. 'Maturity' is certainly a relative term, but it is not entirely unconnected with biological age. Furthermore, the exclusion I have identified is not simply about the imposition of some monolithic form of 'adult power'. On the contrary, it is achieved with the active complicity of children themselves; and it functions equally to exclude *adults* from what are seen to be the appropriate domains of children. Furthermore, while I have emphasized the changing social constructions of childhood, I am not thereby implying that these constructions are a falsification of the essence of childhood, or a kind of artificial imposition on the 'natural' child. Nor am I suggesting that this natural essence would somehow be released if the sources of power were to be magically removed. In these respects, the call for 'children's liberation' seems to be characterized by a kind of Romanticism which is very similar to that of the protectionist arguments it has sought to oppose.

Nevertheless, I would argue that the dominant construction of children as pre-social individuals effectively prevents any consideration of them as social beings, or indeed as citizens. Defining children in terms of their exclusion from adult society, and in terms of their inability or unwillingness to display what we define as 'adult' characteristics, actively *produces* the kinds of consciousness and behaviour which some adults find so problematic. The differences which are observed to exist between adults and children justify the segregation of children; but this segregation then gives rise to the behaviour that justifies the perception of differences in the first place.

As I have implied, culture and representation are crucial aspects of this process, both for children and for adults. For a whole variety of reasons, the electronic media play an increasingly significant role in defining the cultural experiences of contemporary childhood. Children can no longer be excluded from these media and the things they represent; nor can they be confined to material that adults perceive to be good for them. The attempt to *protect* children by restricting their access to media is doomed to fail. On the contrary, we now need to pay much closer attention to how we *prepare* children to deal with these experiences; and in doing so, we need to stop defining them simply in terms of what they lack.

An outline of the book

In the two chapters that follow, I discuss two contrasting analyses of the changing nature of childhood, and of the role of the media in children's lives. On the one hand, there is the 'death of childhood' thesis, most popularly associated with the work of Neil Postman – the view that television and other electronic media have at least blurred the boundaries between childhood and adulthood, if not completely erased them. On the other hand, there is an argument that has become increasingly popular among enthusiasts for the so-called 'communications revolution' – the idea that children and young people are being liberated and empowered by the new electronic media. As I shall indicate, there are some striking similarities – and indeed some shared weaknesses – in these apparently very different arguments.

My critique of these positions raises a series of fundamental questions, which are dealt with much more directly in the second part of the book. These are, most obviously, to do with the changing nature of *childhood* – both in terms of our ideas about childhood, and in terms of the realities of children's lives. They are also to do with the changing nature of the *media* – not just at the level of technology, but also in terms of the form and content of media texts, and the interactions between media producers and their audiences. And they are, finally, to do with how we understand children's *relationships* with the media, whether we conceive of this in terms of 'uses' or 'effects', as 'active' or 'passive', or as an essentially psychological or social phenomenon. My own position on these issues is laid out in turn in chapters 4, 5 and 6.

Cutting across these questions are a number of more specific concerns to do with the place of electronic media in contemporary society. These are issues that take on a particular form, and in some cases a particular intensity, in relation to children; although they have a broader significance too. They are all areas that, in different ways, are predominantly defined in terms of *exclusion* – that is, as areas of 'adult' life to which, it is argued, children should not be given access. These are, first, issues to do with *morality*, which typically focus on representations of sex and violence. Secondly, there are issues to do with the place of *commerce*, and the relations between the market and the public sphere. These lead into the third key area, which is that of *citizenship* – that is, children's relationships with broadly 'political' debate and activity. These three themes are addressed in the third part of the book, in chapters 7, 8 and 9 respectively.

While emphasizing the complexities and difficulties of these issues, my intention is also to point towards the consequences of my arguments for future policy, not just in relation to the media themselves, but also in terms of children's experiences and rights as an audience. These more specific projections begin to surface towards the end of each of the chapters in part III, and are drawn together and developed more fully in my concluding chapter. These arguments, and some of the specific examples that are drawn on throughout the book, are bound to relate partly to the situation in the UK; and there are obvious difficulties in generalizing from the specific social and cultural characteristics of one national context to those of others. Nevertheless, I believe that many of the broader arguments here will have an international resonance.

Despite its provocative title, then, this book is not another lament for the death of childhood; nor is it simply a celebration of what might succeed it. On the contrary, it seeks to provide the basis for a more realistic, and more comprehensive, understanding of the experience of children growing up in the age of electronic media. We need this understanding if we are to help them cope with the challenges of the present, let alone of the future.

Part I

2

The Death of Childhood

The notion that children are growing up deprived of childhood has become a staple theme in popular psychology. Over the past three or four decades, it is argued, there has been a radical change in how society treats children, and in how children themselves behave. Critics point to evidence of growing levels of violent crime and sexual activity among the young, and to the steady disintegration of family life; and they argue that the safety and innocence which characterized previous generations' experience of childhood has been lost forever.

Two books, both published in the US in the early 1980s, were among the first to raise these concerns: David Elkind's *The Hurried Child* (1981) and Marie Winn's *Children without Childhood* (1984). The very similar slogans on the covers of these books neatly encapsulate the argument: 'Growing Up Too Fast Too Soon' (Elkind) and 'Growing Up Too Fast in the World of Sex and Drugs' (Winn). Yet while these writers appear to be describing similar phenomena, their analysis of the causes of those phenomena are rather different.

As a child psychologist, Elkind's starting point is the 'stress' which he argues characterizes contemporary children's lives. He points to growing levels of psychological disturbance brought on by divorce; the rise in teenage pregnancy and venereal disease; and the increasing numbers of young people seeking escape through drug-taking, crime, suicide and religious cults. Children, he argues, are now being 'hurried' through childhood by their parents and schools, and by the media. Parents, stressed and frustrated by their own working lives, are increasingly displacing their anxieties on to their children, pressurizing them to succeed academically and in organized sports at ever earlier ages, paralysing them with the fear of failure. Mean-while, schools have become product-oriented, obsessed with grad-ing and drilling children in 'basic skills'. Parents are being urged to transform the home into an extension of the school, by providing formal, programmed instruction for their children, rather than the more informal learning of the past.

The media both reflect and produce this 'hurrying' of children. Television, Elkind argues, lacks the 'intellectual barriers' of older media, since it does not require children to learn to interpret it. By simplifying their access to information, it opens them to experiences that were once reserved for adults: 'scenes of violence or of sexual intimacy that a young child could not conjure up from a verbal description are presented directly and graphically upon the tele-vision screen.'[1] On one level, this means that human experience be-comes 'homogenized'; although since children themselves do not necessarily understand what they watch, television creates a kind of 'pseudosophistication', which in turn leads adults to treat children as more grown up than they really are. Elkind makes similar argu-ments about contemporary children's books, where the focus on the poor, the disabled, the sick and the emotionally troubled is seen to present a further pressure on children to grow up before their time. Meanwhile, he condemns rock music as emotionally regressive and as an incitement to masturbation and the use of illicit drugs.

The key problem, according to Elkind, is that children are exposed to these experiences before they are 'emotionally ready' to handle them:

> Hurried children are forced to take on the physical, psychological, and social trappings of adulthood before they are prepared to deal with them. We dress our children in miniature adult costumes (often with designer labels), we expose them to gratuitous sex and violence, and we expect them to cope with an increasingly bewildering social environment – di-vorce, single parenthood, homosexuality.[2]

By contrast, Elkind proposes that growing up needs to proceed slowly, at its own pace. Following Piaget's model of child develop-ment, he argues that children will only truly learn when they are *ready* to do so. Forcing them to skip developmental stages will make it much harder for them to establish a secure sense of their personal identity, and hence leave them unprepared for the difficulties of ado-lescence.

Marie Winn's *Children without Childhood* echoes many of Elkind's concerns. She too points to a growing epidemic of social problems affecting children; and while she is careful not to exaggerate these, she argues that there has been a general 'loss of control' on the part of parents and an overall 'decline in child supervision'. While problems such as drug-taking and teenage pregnancy have, she argues, always existed among lower social classes, they are now becoming widespread among middle-class children. Like Elkind, Winn is dismayed at the blurring of boundaries between adults and children, and the fact that 'children look, talk and behave in ways that do not seem very childlike.'[3] Using extensive amounts of anecdotal testimony, she argues that most parents are either unconcerned, ignorant or fatalistic in the face of their own powerlessness to alter this situation.

Like Elkind, Winn accuses the media of 'indoctrinating children into the secrets of adult life' – by which she means primarily sex and violence. While she shares his concerns about the 'new realism' in children's books, and the focus on 'gang rape, homosexuality and sadistic violence' in movies, her primary anxiety is about television:

> [Parents] have little chance of controlling their children's exposure to every variety of adult sexuality, every permutation and combination of human brutality and violence, every aspect of sickness, disease and suffering, every frightening possibility for natural and man-made disaster that might impinge on an innocent and carefree childhood. There is always the television set waiting to undo all their careful plans.[4]

Nevertheless, Winn's concern about television – which is extensively developed in her earlier book, *The Plug-in Drug*[5] – is not only to do with content. Regardless of *what* they watch, she argues, television deprives children of play, and of other forms of healthy interaction. It is used by too many parents simply as a 'babysitter'.

Despite their similarities, the diagnoses of these two authors, and hence their prescriptions for change, are rather different. Winn's position is essentially that of a moral conservative. She is dismayed at the decline of the traditional nuclear family, the growing financial independence of women, the 'loosening of sexual standards' and the diminished role of organized religion. She regrets the move towards coeducation, the disapproval of 'spanking' children and the increasing public visibility of homosexuality. In these respects, her book clearly belongs to the moral backlash against 1960s 'permissiveness' which characterized the 1980s of Ronald Reagan and Margaret Thatcher.

By contrast, the problem for Elkind seems to be not so much permissiveness, but the lack of it. While he shares some of Winn's broader moral concerns, he bemoans the move away from earlier child-rearing practices based on the notion of 'self-expression'. While this approach may have led to 'spoiled children', who remain children for too long, the pendulum has now swung too far in the other direction: 'hurried children' are subjected to far too much pressure and discipline by adults.

However, Winn and Elkind are united in their desire to move back to an earlier era – to what Winn without apparent irony calls 'the Golden Age of Innocence', an era in which (she tells us) 'innocence truly *was* bliss, once upon a time.'[6] Both writers seem to locate this period in the earlier part of this century, or in the previous one. Nevertheless, both are aware that this Golden Age was itself a particular stage in a longer history of childhood. Winn, for example, compares the 'uncivilized' approach to child-rearing in the Middle Ages with the emphasis on protectiveness and careful nurture which emerged during the nineteenth century. Children, she notes, were gradually separated from the adult world in order that they could be prepared for their future roles in an increasingly complex industrial society: 'Slowly and painfully, children were helped to acquire such graces as co-operation, tactfulness, and social sensitivity, skills they would need someday in the new kinds of work available to adults in towns and cities.'[7] In this era, Winn argues, children displayed 'a relatively docile acceptance of their role as dependent beings who didn't have many choices about their lives or even their daily behaviour'[8] – and, as a result, they came to behave in ways which came to be seen as characteristically child-like.

Now, by contrast, children are much less deferential to those in authority. Their 'critical powers', according to Winn, have been 'too early awakened'.[9] They are aware that adults are not always to be trusted or respected simply because they are adults. Children, it seems, are even claiming the right to choose what clothes they will wear!

Significantly, both writers acknowledge that the developments they describe could be seen as part of broader moves towards equality in society which have occurred in the wake of the Civil Rights movement and the rebirth of feminism. Yet it is with children that both are seeking to draw the line. Rather than extending equality to children, Elkind argues, we need to give them time apart from the adult world to learn and grow. It is not discrimination, he suggests, to emphasize children's 'special needs'; on the contrary, 'it is the only way that true equality can be attained.'[10]

For Winn, the implication here is clear: parents should be actively reinforcing these boundaries between adults and children. They should be doing less *preparing*, and more *protecting*. Parents have to reassert their authority, and thereby restore to children their right 'to be a child'. Elkind's analysis is perhaps less overtly coercive, although it is equally normative. Rather than emphasizing the responsibilities of parents to keep their children innocent, Elkind implies that this will occur naturally if children are not forced to grow up before they are 'ready'. In this account, therefore, psychological norms stand in for – and inevitably support – social norms. While both writers recognize the existence of historical change, they ultimately fall back on the notion of childhood as a 'natural' phenomenon, which is implicitly seen as timeless.

Literacy myths

Despite the differences between them, the arguments developed in these books represent a powerful mind-set in contemporary popular thinking about childhood which appears to unite those of contrasting political and moral persuasions. They embody a growing sense of anxiety about social change, and particularly about the changing power relationships between adults and children, which is characteristic of much journalistic commentary on child-rearing. Yet, as we shall see throughout this book, several of the themes they discuss have also featured – albeit in somewhat more cautious terms – in academic studies of childhood, and particularly of children's relationships with the media.

   In pursuing these ideas, I turn now to four works written by academics: Neil Postman's *The Disappearance of Childhood* and Joshua Meyrowitz's *No Sense of Place*, both published in the early 1980s; and Barry Sanders's *A is for Ox* and Shirley Steinberg and Joe Kincheloe's collection *Kinderculture*, both published in the mid-1990s. Again, the subtitles or cover slogans are symptomatic: 'How TV is changing children's lives' (Postman); *The Impact of Electronic Media on Social Behaviour* (Meyrowitz); *The Collapse of Literacy and the Rise of Violence in an Electronic Age* (Sanders); and *The Corporate Construction of Childhood* (Steinberg and Kincheloe). As these titles suggest, all four books provide a peculiarly one-dimensional analysis of the *causes* of these developments. Where Elkind and Winn attempt to explain contemporary changes in childhood by means of more general arguments about approaches to child-rearing, these authors all identify a singular villain of the piece: namely, the electronic media.

Postman's book is the earliest and most popularly written of the four. Like Elkind and Winn, he offers a range of different kinds of evidence to prove that childhood – or at least the distinction between adults and children – is disappearing. He points to the demise of children's traditional games and distinctive styles of dress; the increasing homogenization of children's and adults' leisure pursuits, language, eating habits and tastes in entertainment; and the increase in child crime, drug-taking, sexual activity and teenage pregnancy. He is particularly dismayed by the erotic use of children in commercials and movies, the prevalence of 'adult' themes in children's books and what he sees as the misguided emphasis on 'children's rights'.

Nevertheless, like the other authors discussed here, Postman is under no illusions that childhood is a timeless phenomenon. Following the work of the French historian Philippe Ariès,[11] he traces the 'invention' and evolution of childhood since the Middle Ages. In his own words, this is a story of 'how the printing press created childhood and how the electronic media are "disappearing" it'.[12] As this statement implies, Postman attributes a determining significance to technologies and the human attributes which they (somehow automatically) require or cultivate. Print, he argues, effectively created our modern notion of individuality; and it was this 'intensified sense of self' that led to the 'flowering of childhood'. Print required an apprenticeship in literacy, and hence the invention of schools, to check children's 'exuberance' and to cultivate 'quietness, immobility, contemplation [and] precise regulation of bodily functions'.[13] Yet the printing press and the school not only created the child: in the process, they also created 'the modern concept of the adult'. Adulthood became, in Postman's terms, a symbolic, not just a biological, achievement.

Like Winn, Postman sees the advantage of print as its ability to preserve adult 'secrets' from those who have not yet acquired literacy. Television, by contrast, is a 'total disclosure medium', which renders information 'uncontrollable'. The 'dark and fugitive mysteries' of adult life (and particularly of sex) are, he suggests, no longer hidden from children. Television effectively abolishes shame, a quality which Postman sees as a prerequisite for the existence of childhood.

However, Postman's view of the differences between these media is primarily concerned not with their content, but with their implications for cognition. Following Harold Innis and Marshall McLuhan,[14] he argues that print is essentially symbolic and linear, and hence cultivates abstraction and logical thinking:

Almost all the characteristics we associate with adulthood are those that are (or were) either generated or amplified by the requirements of a fully literate culture: the capacity for self-restraint, a tolerance for delayed gratification, a sophisticated ability to think conceptually and sequentially, a preoccupation with both historical continuity and the future, a high valuation of reason and hierarchical order.[15]

By contrast, Postman argues, television is a visual medium. It requires no special skills to interpret, nor does it cultivate any. It offers no propositions, and it does not have to conform to rules of evidence or logic: it is essentially irrational.

The implications of these technological changes for relations between adults and children were thus straightforward. Through print and schooling, Postman argues, 'adults found themselves with unprecedented control over the symbolic environment of the young, and were therefore able and required to set forth the conditions by which a child was to become an adult.'[16] In the age of television, this power and control has accordingly become impossible to exert.

Only just below the surface of Postman's text is a form of moral conservatism which has much in common with that of Marie Winn. What seems particularly troubling for him about the 'television age' is the demise of 'good manners'. While Postman distances himself from what he sees as the 'arrogance' of the so-called Moral Majority, he explicitly shares its desire to 'turn back the clock'. He supports 'its attempts to restore a sense of inhibition and reverence to sexuality' and to establish schools that will insist on 'rigorous standards of *civilité*'; and he urges parents to impress on their children the value of 'self-restraint in manners, language and style' and the need for 'deference and responsibility to elders'.[17] Nevertheless, Postman is not especially optimistic about the chances of survival: he assigns a 'monastic' role to those parents who would limit their children's exposure to the media, teach them good manners, and hence 'resist the spirit of the age'.

The tone of Joshua Meyrowitz's *No Sense of Place* is much less polemical, and much more scholarly, than *The Disappearance of Childhood*; and although it appeared two years later, Meyrowitz implies that Postman and others were popularizing ideas which he himself had originally developed.[18] Like the other writers I have been discussing, Meyrowitz proposes that childhood and adulthood are becoming merged as a consequence of changes in communications media. However, Meyrowitz's argument is much broader than Postman's. The essential difference between television and older media, according to Meyrowitz, is that television makes 'backstage'

behaviour visible to all. It reveals facts that contradict dominant social myths and ideals. In effect, it makes it impossible for powerful
groups to keep 'secrets', and hence undermines much of the basis of
their authority. In this way, television has blurred the boundaries,
not just between adults and children, but also between men and
women, and between individual citizens and their political representatives.

At the same time, Meyrowitz is much more agnostic than Postman. His descriptions of contemporary changes in childhood, while
they overlap in several respects with those we have considered so
far, are much more even-handed. Thus, while he notes the rise in
child crime, he also points to the move away from paternalistic approaches to child-rearing, and to the new emphasis on children's
welfare and children's rights. Likewise, he describes children's books
as 'an informational ghetto', arguing that the new communications
media make it possible for children to communicate directly with
each other in a way that could not be achieved in earlier times. Ultimately, Meyrowitz's aim is not to judge whether such changes are
good or bad, or whether they represent an unnatural deviation from
'proper' adults' and children's roles. Indeed, he strongly refutes
universalist accounts of child development, of the kind to which
Elkind and others ultimately adhere: he argues that 'the child' and
'child psychology' are social constructions, which reflect some very
specific (and increasingly questionable) cultural values. The notion
of childhood 'innocence', he suggests, does not reflect an essential or
natural state of being: on the contrary, it was deliberately produced
in order to justify the social separation between adults and children.[19]

Likewise, Meyrowitz has little sympathy with arguments about
the *cognitive* implications of different media. While he does make a
clear distinction between print and television, he defines this in terms
of the *social uses* of these media. Print, he argues, has a tendency
to segregate children and adults, because it requires a prolonged
apprenticeship in literacy; while television tends to reintegrate
them, because its basic symbolic forms – pictures and sounds – are
immediately accessible. Regardless of the specific messages it carries, television changes the pattern of information flow into the home,
challenging the control of adults and allowing the young child to be
vicariously 'present' at adult interactions: 'Television removes barriers that once divided people of different ages and reading abilities
into different social situations. The widespread use of television is
equivalent to a broad social decision to allow young children to be
present at wars and funerals, courtships and seductions, criminal
plots and cocktail parties.'[20]

Like Winn and Postman, therefore, Meyrowitz argues that television undermines adults' attempts at 'secrecy', although he does not seem to share their moralistic alarm at this situation. Controlling children's access to media – Postman's preferred response – is likely to prove difficult, he suggests. With television, the practice of parental control has to become overt and visible, in a way that it did not need to be with print. Furthermore, television alerts children to the existence of 'backstage' behaviour, even if it does not always show it explicitly; and it also frequently shows children how adults attempt to conceal such behaviour from them. Thus, it is not just that television reveals 'secrets': it also reveals 'the secret of secrecy', and hence renders adults open to the charge of hypocrisy.[21]

If Meyrowitz thus implicitly rejects the technological determinism of Postman, he replaces this by what might be (rather clumsily) termed 'information-system determinism'. The crucial difference between television and print, he suggests, is in the possibilities that literacy offers for 'the separation of adult and child information-systems'. In other words, it is not the cognitive processes, or indeed the content, that make the difference: it is the fact that print allows children to be separated from adults, and television does not. As the distinctions between information systems for children and adults become blurred, Meyrowitz argues, this will inevitably lead to far-reaching changes in social behaviour.

Barry Sanders's *A is for Ox* is a more recent development of these themes, and it is in many ways the most apocalyptic. Like Neil Postman, Sanders states his central thesis in bold terms. 'Human beings as we know them', he writes, 'are the products of literacy.'[22] Yet, as young people show less interest in 'the culture of the book', and as rates of literacy fall, the idea of the 'critical, self-directed human being' is rapidly disappearing. Those who are illiterate, Sanders argues, are incapable of abstract, critical thought, or of distancing themselves from their own immediate experience. They cannot develop a sense of individual consciousness, only a kind of tribal, 'group consciousness'. Their world is one of self-destructive violence, 'a world marked by pain and death, a world filled with despair and drop-outs, teenage suicides, gang killings, broken homes, and homicides'.[23]

The primary cause of this epidemic of youth violence, predictably enough, is television (and to a lesser extent, home computers). Yet, as with the other writers discussed here, the problem is not so much that particular forms of television content produce 'copycat' behaviour – although Sanders clearly believes that such effects do occur. The problem is more with the kinds of consciousness television is seen to produce. In a novel twist to the argument, Sanders argues

that the primary victim of television is not so much literacy as orality
– and particularly the practice of oral story-telling in the home. Watching television rather than talking destroys children's ability to develop their own voices and imaginative powers. Of course, television
does contain oral language, yet it is a false orality, 'an auditory and
visual lie'. In destroying 'true' orality, television also destroys the
foundation for literacy, since it is on the prior existence of orality
that the development of literacy depends.

Sanders's vision of the relation between print literacy and television is akin to a Manichean struggle between good and evil. Literacy is effectively equated with the notion of selfhood, and thereby
with life itself. Thus, Sanders suggests, illiterate gang members do
not possess selfhood, and hence place no value on human life. 'Oral
cultures', he argues, 'do not operate with the same concept of "murder" as literate ones. One cannot "take" someone else's life, because
a demarcated, fully articulated internalized life exists only in literacy.'[24] Violence thus becomes a kind of compensation for what is
lost by those who do not possess literacy; while literacy 'civilizes'
individuals, transforming them into 'consenting members of the body
politic'. On the other hand, the negative effects of television are dev-
astating:

> [Television] debilitates young people . . . short-circuits the natural, em-
> otional development they need to become healthy human beings . . .
> strangles the development of their own voices, and denies them their
> imaginative powers . . . washes the child clean of his or her own images
> . . . weakens the will . . . [and] delivers one of the most debilitating psy-
> chological blows in denying the youngster the chance to turn inside him-
> self or herself and to have a silent conversation with that budding social
> construct, the self.[25]

In the light of this apocalyptic analysis, it is perhaps not surprising that Sanders's conclusions are so bleak. The 'crisis' he identifies
can only be resolved, it would seem, by 'a wholesale revision of the
way we live our lives'. For Sanders, schools are clearly part of the
problem, rather than a potential solution: in the age of 'electronic
mass culture', he argues, schools have turned literacy into a commodity, through imposing arbitrary standards of correctness and
mechanized forms of instruction. Thus, he suggests that literacy instruction, at least in the preschool, should be replaced by a comprehensive emphasis on the oral arts. Sanders's other concrete
suggestion, however, is rather less radical, and is one he shares with
several of the other authors considered here. Every mother, he asserts, should return to the home. It is the nuclear family which will

be the guarantee of literacy, just as literacy will guarantee the survival of childhood, and ultimately of society itself.

If the conclusions of Sanders, Postman and Winn are essentially conservative, the final text I want to consider here illustrates the appeal of this argument to some on the political left. In their edited book *Kinderculture*, Shirley Steinberg and Joe Kincheloe develop what purports to be a more politically radical account of the 'death of childhood'. Like Postman and others, these authors claim that 'traditional notions of childhood as a time of innocence and adult-dependency have been undermined', not so much by changing family structures or child-rearing practices, but 'by children's access to popular culture during the late twentieth century'.[26] Similarly, they argue that it is by virtue of the *knowledge* the media provide that adult authority has been challenged: 'As postmodern children gain unrestricted knowledge about things once kept secret from nonadults, the mystique of adults as revered keepers of secrets about the world begins to disintegrate.'[27]

However, the central villain of the piece here is not so much the media themselves as corporate capital – even if, in practice, the two seem to be regarded as indistinguishable; and the central concern is not so much with the cognitive consequences of the media as with their role as purveyors of *ideology*. Despite the authors' explicit rejection of old-style conspiracy theories, their account of ideology is most obviously derived from the analyses of 'mass society' developed during the 1930s and 1940s. Both the media and their audiences are seen here as effectively homogeneous. The media, it is argued, are responsible for securing the consent of the masses to an unjust social order, through a process of delusion or deception. They offer a form of false pleasure that destroys the capacity for imagination and critical thought, and hence the possibility of resistance. While this theory is most commonly identified with the work of the Frankfurt School – that is, with the political left – it also has much in common with the arguments of cultural conservatives.[28] In Steinberg and Kincheloe's account, it is also easily aligned with more traditional notions of 'media effects', for example in relation to the influence of screen violence.[29]

Nevertheless, this argument takes on a particular form when it comes to *children*, who are presumed to be particularly vulnerable to ideological manipulation. Thus, the media are seen here as agents of a one-dimensional ideology that 'occupies the human psyche'. It is an ideology that operates not for 'the social good' or the 'well-being of kids', but merely for 'individual gain'. It supports 'free market' principles and right-wing notions of 'family values'; it is militaristic, patriarchal, class-biased and racist; and it systematically dehistoricizes and ignores oppression and inequality. Above all, this ideology is irresistible: it ceaselessly 'bombards' and 'manipulates' children, leaving them abandoned, confused and disoriented. 'Corporate kinderculture', the editors argue, 'colonizes American consciousness in a manner that represses conflicts and differences . . . Given their power to sink their tentacles deep into the private lives of children, the corporate producers of kinderculture constantly destabilize the identity of children.'[30] As this quotation implies, there is assumed to be a natural state of childhood here – a stable identity that is located in children's 'private lives' – that is systematically denied and perverted by the capitalist media. The damage here is as much psychic as it is social. Young people, we are told, are 'cognitively impaired' by their experience of the media, and 'lose the faith that they can make sense of anything'.[31]

As a result, it is only adults – in this case, 'critical childhood professionals' – who are seen to be able to counter this ideological barrage. Steinberg and Kincheloe, and several of their contributors, argue for such individuals to adopt a form of 'critical pedagogy' – in effect, a form of counterindoctrination. The aim of this pedagogy is equally one-dimensional: it is to enable children to 'oppose', to 'challenge' and to 'resist' the seductive pleasures of popular culture, and thereby to conform to the 'critical consciousness' espoused by their teachers.[32] Ultimately, while these authors' preferred solutions are very different from the conservative emphases of Postman and Sanders, they too seem to favour a renewal of adult authority.

A postmodern condition?

The very notion of the 'death of childhood' is, of course, symptomatic of its times. Despite the differences between them, all these writers are responding to what they identify as a peculiarly contemporary malaise; and the nature of their responses reflects a combination of panic and nostalgia which is characteristic of the closing decades of the twentieth century.

In this context, it does not seem unwarranted to define 'childhood' as itself a fundamentally *modernist* idea. As several of these writers indicate, the separation of children from adults began at the time of the Renaissance, and gathered pace with the expansion of capitalist industrialism. The demarcation – and indeed the study – of childhood as a distinct stage of life depended on children's removal from the workforce and the streets, and their containment within the institutions of compulsory schooling. To define children as inherently 'irrational' justified the introduction of a lengthy period in which they could be trained in the arts of self-control and disciplined behaviour. In these respects, our contemporary notion of childhood could be seen as part of the Enlightenment project, with its emphasis on the development of rationality as a means to ensure the stability of the social order.[33]

From this perspective, the 'death of childhood' might then be seen as a symptom of *post*modernity, a reflection of the fate which awaits us as the 'dream of reason' finally collapses. While none of the writers considered here would have much sympathy with postmodernism, at least some of their arguments have much in common with the work of theorists such as Baudrillard. The blurring of boundaries, the demise of selfhood, the dominance of visual culture, the death of the social – all of these are ideas which frequently recur in the rhetoric of postmodernism. What distinguishes the work of these writers (with the exception of Meyrowitz), however, is that the postmodern world is one they observe not with ambivalent fascination but with unrestrained horror.

Of course, it would be tempting simply to dismiss many of these arguments as empty hyperbole. Indeed, in summarizing them, I have deliberately avoided some of their more spectacular eccentricities; and in some cases, this has involved considerable restraint on my part. Nevertheless, the 'death of childhood' thesis deserves to be taken seriously. However overstated and occasionally hysterical it may appear, it does point to some fundamental historical changes, and to many of the broader issues that are at stake in them. Before outlining the rather different perspective which is developed in this book, therefore, it is important to confront the limitations of this approach. How do these arguments about the 'death of childhood' compare with what is known about the changing nature of children's lives? How adequately do they take account of the historical evidence? And how justified are the theoretical assumptions on which they are based?

History as representation

The history of childhood is ultimately a history of representations. As numerous historians have pointed out, there is very little available evidence on which one might base a history of *children* themselves. Like women, children have to a great extent been 'hidden from history' – and this coincidence is, of course, far from accidental. On one level, this produces significant methodological problems. To what

extent can we read cultural representations of childhood as reflections
of the realities of children's lives? The work of Philippe Ariès, for example, which is often credited with identifying the 'invention' of childhood,[34] has been challenged on precisely these grounds. Ariès's thesis
is based primarily on an analysis of how children were represented –
or, more often, simply *not* represented – in medieval and Renaissance
paintings. On this basis, he traces the ways in which children were
gradually identified as a distinctive group, with their own pastimes
and styles of dress, in the late sixteenth and early seventeenth centuries. According to his critics, however, such evidence is highly inadequate. Demographic data, for example, suggest that his analysis only
applies to the children of the upper classes; and the limited contemporary accounts that do exist significantly challenge his argument that
affective ties between adults and children, and explicit programmes
of child-rearing, were largely absent in medieval times.[35] Ultimately,
Ariès's data may reveal more about changing conventions of artistic
representation than they do about changing social realities.

More recently, historians of childhood have actively recognized their
reliance on representations – and in this respect, their work has come to
focus more explicitly on the evolution of adult *ideas* about childhood
than on the realities of children's lives. Carolyn Steedman, for example,
analyses the figure of 'Mignon', who recurs in popular culture throughout the nineteenth century, and who seems to personify a notion of
'human interiority' or subjectivity associated with childhood which (she
argues) came into being at this time.[36] Hugh Cunningham's history of
'the children of the poor' is subtitled *Representations of Childhood since
the Seventeenth Century*, and traces the ways in which working-class
children were gradually led to conform to middle-class definitions of a
'proper' childhood.[37] Valerie Walkerdine analyses the mid twentieth-
century figure of 'little orphan Annie' in the context of other representations of working-class girls, arguing that it both articulates and resolves
broader anxieties about knowledge and innocence which reflect the
social and political tensions of the period.[38] Likewise, Patricia Holland
traces the evolution of contemporary constructions of childhood over
the past three decades through a reading of adult representations in
advertisements, photographs and other media artefacts.[39]

In different ways, all these writers point to the significance of cultural representations of childhood as a basis for changes in social
policy. Images of childhood – both as sinful and polluted and as innocent and pure – were consciously used by the social reformers
of the nineteenth century; while equally stereotypical images of
children as natural and free have been part of the visual rhetoric
of 'children's liberation' in more recent times. Yet these writers also

argue that such representations function as a means whereby adults work out their own unresolved conflicts about childhood. Such images and texts are thus not only embodiments of *ideas* about childhood, but also a vehicle for adults' ambivalent *feelings* about children, and about their own childhoods – feelings of fear, anxiety, pity, nostalgia, pleasure and desire. As such, they tell us much more about adults than they do about children.

These historical studies clearly show that the fear that children will become prematurely adult – that they will be deprived of 'childhood' – has a long history. Indeed, writers like Marie Winn and Neil Postman explicitly draw on one of the most seductive post-Romantic *fantasies* of childhood: the notion of a pre-industrial Golden Age, an idyllic Garden of Eden in which children could play freely, untainted by corruption. The persistence of such fantasies should in itself give us cause to question contemporary assertions about the 'death of childhood'. A particular *idea* of childhood may well be disappearing; but it is much harder to identify the consequences of this in terms of the realities of children's lives.

Certainly, one can challenge the validity or representativeness of the evidence on this point. Winn's book, for example, is replete with anecdotes about the children of affluent parents who repair to their country homes at weekends, leaving their teenagers unsupervised in the city; while Sanders appears to take journalistic accounts of Los Angeles gangs as *prima facie* evidence of the attitudes of young people in general. Furthermore, it is important to distinguish between fundamental changes and those that might prove merely superficial. For example, does the fact that adults now wear similar clothes to children (at least in *some* social contexts) necessarily mean that they have become more 'child-like'? Do the similarities between children's and adults' eating habits or tastes in music automatically imply that the differences between them have disappeared?

Of course, this is not to deny that material changes may have occurred. It is simply to recognize the partiality and the rhetorical functions of evidence, both about the past and about the present. This is most obviously the case with popular texts that rely primarily on anecdotes or journalistic sources, such as those of Winn and Sanders. Yet it is also apparent where the evidence takes the seemingly more 'objective' form of social statistics.[40] Crime figures, for example, are subject to a wide range of interpretations, and cannot be taken as a straightforward reflection of the incidence of particular types of behaviour. As I shall argue in chapter 6, academic research also relies on theoretical and rhetorical constructions of childhood that inevitably determine what *counts* as evidence in the first place.

Nevertheless, historians have increasingly challenged the optimistic narrative of the 'invention' of childhood on which these arguments are based. Lloyd de Mause is probably the most influential exponent of the view – shared by writers such as Postman and Winn – that the modern conception of childhood was an essentially humane and civilized development.[41] According to de Mause, the 'infanticidal' mode of child-rearing which characterized the Middle Ages gradually gave way to our modern 'helping' mode, as neglect and cruelty were replaced with care and attention. Yet this account has been questioned by many subsequent writers. Carmen Luke, for example, argues that what is now interpreted as adult indifference towards children (for example, in practices such as swaddling) had a great deal to do with material constraints.[42] In this respect, she argues, de Mause implicitly judges the past from the perspective of contemporary notions of 'human nature'. At the same time, de Mause's account tends to sanction a complacency about the present which neglects the continuing incidence of child abuse, and of routine practices such as corporal punishment.

Similar arguments could be made about the more recent history of childhood. Here again, it would seem, the emphasis on abrupt change has led to a neglect of the substantial evidence of continuity. Thus, for example, Winn suggests that working-class children were effectively 'given' a childhood by removing them from the workforce and the dangers of the streets, and placing them in schools. As Cunningham argues, this version of history is a kind of heroic romance, in which working-class children are seen to be rescued from a life of savagery through the intervention of middle-class philanthropists.[43] Yet in addition to neglecting the role of working-class agitators, this story clearly ignores the continuing existence of child labour in some of the most marginal and exploited areas of the economy.[44] It also offers a highly benign analysis of the role of schooling, which neglects its function as a means of disciplining – rather than simply enlightening – the 'dangerous classes'. Despite the civilizing rhetoric that surrounded it, compulsory schooling in fact tended to encourage the same degree of regimentation, repetition and discipline as the factories from which children were removed.[45]

Beyond technological determinism

A more detailed historical analysis also leads us to challenge the kind of technological determinism that characterizes these arguments. As I have indicated, assertions about the 'death of childhood' typically rest on an opposition between print and electronic media, particularly television. Most overtly in the work of Postman, print is seen to be responsible for the creation of our contemporary conception of childhood; and television is what is destroying it. From this perspective, technology is seen as autonomous from other social forces, exercising its influence irrespective of the contexts and purposes for which it is used.

As Carmen Luke indicates, the notion that the printing press somehow created 'childhood' is at least a major oversimplification.[46] She points out that the modern notion of childhood emerged much earlier in Germany than it did in France, and that this was largely because of *theological* differences. The reading public in Germany was much larger, as a result of the Lutheran emphasis on giving all believers access to the scriptures in the vernacular. The printing press led to the emergence of a standardized language, and to a 'systematization of discourses', not least those concerned with pedagogy and child-rearing; and this led in turn to the implementation of compulsory schooling, and a growing emphasis on parental care and attention. The teaching of print literacy in schools during this period was part of a broader range of authoritarian strategies designed to cultivate obedience, self-discipline and religious conformity. As this implies, Ariès's analysis of the 'invention of childhood' may be specific to France, and should not be translated to the rest of Europe. Furthermore, Luke's account suggests that the advent of our modern conception of childhood was not an automatic consequence of the invention of the printing press – nor indeed was the Reformation. On the contrary, the modern conception of childhood arose as a result of a complex network of interrelationships between ideology, government, pedagogy and technology, each of which tended to reinforce the others; and as a result, it developed in different ways, and at different rates, in different national contexts.

Indeed, if we trace the history back well before the advent of the printing press and of literacy, there is clear evidence that children were indeed defined and addressed as a distinct social group. Plato's *Republic*, for example, contains very definite prescriptions about the stories and representations to which children should and should not be exposed; as indeed does the Hebrew Talmud.[47] Furthermore, if childhood is merely a consequence of print literacy, it is hard to interpret the explicit marking of boundaries between childhood and adulthood – 'rites of passage' – in non-literate societies.

The opposition between print and electronic media also rests on a set of empirical claims which have been widely challenged. The notion that rates of literacy are falling, for example, is extremely questionable – although here again, it is hard to establish definitive evidence, since what 'counts' as literacy (and hence what is being measured) has shifted significantly over time.[48] The notion that television has somehow supplanted the reading of books is even more dubious. Study after study has shown that television displaces 'functionally equivalent' activities such as reading comics or listening to the radio, rather than the reading of books. If anything, it would seem that there was not much reading going on before television, and there is still not much today.[49] Likewise, one might well challenge the claim that the young people who are provoking so much concern among adults are those who are most likely to be exposed to the electronic media. The gang members whom Sanders takes to be emblematic of contemporary youth are, one suspects, much *less* likely to be spending time at home watching TV than other young people; and despite his claims, they are certainly less likely to possess home computers. And there is, to say the least, considerable debate among researchers about the causal relationship between rates of drug-taking or sexual activity or violent crime and the viewing of television, or even the viewing of particular *types* of television.[50]

Ultimately, the claims of Postman and others rest on a view of media audiences as an undifferentiated mass. Children, in particular, are implicitly seen to be passive and defenceless in the face of media manipulation. Audiences are not seen here as socially differentiated, or as capable of responding critically to what they watch. Television, because of its inherently 'visual' nature (one wonders what happened to the soundtrack), is effectively seen to bypass cognition entirely. It requires no intellectual, emotional or imaginative investment: it simply imprints itself on children's consciousness. Again, no empirical basis is offered for these assertions: they seem so self-evident, it is as though none were considered necessary. And yet, as we shall see in chapter 6, such claims are directly refuted by most contemporary research on the relationship children have with television.

The claim that print and television *produce* different forms of consciousness is, by its very nature, harder to refute. Nevertheless, anthropological and psychological studies of literacy have increasingly questioned the idea that the ability to read and write has inherent cognitive benefits irrespective of the social contexts in which it is acquired or used.[51] On the other hand, many critics have argued that electronic media require particular kinds of 'literacy' – that is, particular skills which must be learned in order to interpret them.[52]

Such assertions are, predictably, open to considerable dispute; although ultimately the crucial issue is what one means by 'literacy' in the first place. Postman and others are directly opposed to a reductive definition of literacy, which would see it simply in terms of the mechanics of encoding and decoding print. While they do not use the term, their argument is about a kind of 'cultural literacy', which amounts to a set of qualities which are seen as in some way 'civilized' or even essentially 'human'.[53] This broadening of the notion of literacy is certainly important and productive. Yet it seems quite contradictory then to confine literacy to a particular *technology* – that of the printed book – and indeed to suggest that it is this technology which actually *produces* it.

The limits of protection

Ultimately, the 'death of childhood' thesis offers very limited grounds for positive intervention or change. Postman and Sanders in particular seem to lapse into a kind of grandiose fatalism about the future. Their response to the various crises they describe is to call for the television sets and computers to be turned off, and for the clocks to be stopped. Their prescriptions for change are also largely conservative: they involve a reassertion of traditional morality, of hierarchical family structures and gender roles, and of conventional forms of child-rearing. And yet, as they propose such ideas, it is as though they recognize that their time has already passed.

Even Steinberg and Kincheloe, for all their self-proclaimed radicalism, seem to share this essentially conservative, pessimistic stance. While they acknowledge that these changes may prove 'liberating' for children, their overall analysis is one in which children are effectively supine in the face of growing corporate control. Only Meyrowitz seems able to avoid this kind of fatalism – albeit largely by virtue of his agnostic stance, and his refusal to see these changes as some kind of distortion of a 'natural' childhood.

Significantly, all these proposals are addressed to parents: they are injunctions to *parents* to take greater steps to protect or control their children, or to help them resist the influence of the media. Children themselves are granted little or no independent agency here. As in their relations with the electronic media, children are implicitly seen to be passive recipients of adult attempts at control or manipulation. Their struggle for autonomy – and hence their resistance to adult authority – is the problem. It cannot provide any basis for a solution. In denying children's active role in creating their own culture, and in conceiving of them as simply passive victims, the 'death of childhood' thesis thus effectively guarantees its own despair.

For all these criticisms, however, the arguments I have considered in this chapter do raise some complex and difficult questions which cannot simply be wished away. They alert us to some significant contemporary changes, both in our notions of childhood, and in children's relationships with the media – even if the account they provide is ultimately simplistic and one-dimensional. Above all, they indicate that the issue of children and the media is not just a local matter, but one which goes to the heart of contemporary debates about culture and communications. They raise a series of fundamental questions to do with literacy, morality, citizenship and the relations between culture and commerce – questions that are for various reasons particularly acute in relation to children, but also possess a much more general relevance.

In part II of the book, I outline my own analysis of these developments in detail. Before doing so, however, I need to consider a rather different account of these themes. It is an account which outwardly seems quite opposed to the pessimistic, conservative analysis of the 'death of childhood' thesis – although it is one that, I shall argue, suffers from similar limitations.

3

The Electronic Generation

The relationship between childhood and the electronic media has often been perceived in essentialist terms. Children are typically seen to possess inherent qualities that are somehow uniquely related to the inherent characteristics of particular communications media. In most instances, of course, that relationship is defined as negative: electronic media are seen to have a singular power to exploit children's vulnerability, to undermine their individuality and to destroy their innocence. The 'death of childhood' thesis advanced by Neil Postman and others, considered in chapter 2, represents a particularly forceful version of this argument. It speaks directly to many adults' fears and desires about childhood – and indeed to an idealized nostalgia for their own past. And yet it gives rise to an all-embracing pessimism, a form of grandiose despair which is ultimately paralysing.

More recently, however, a much more positive construction of this relationship has begun to emerge. Far from being passive victims of the media, children are seen here to possess a powerful form of 'media literacy', a spontaneous natural wisdom that is somehow denied to adults. In particular, new media technologies are seen to provide children with new opportunities for creativity, for community and for self-fulfilment. While some have voiced concern about this growing generation gap in media use,[1] others have celebrated these new media as a means of 'empowerment' or even 'liberation' for children. Far from urging adults to reassert their authority over the young, advocates of this view typically call on adults to 'listen to' – and 'catch up with' – their children.

In some respects, these more optimistic arguments – which will be reviewed in detail in this chapter – can be seen as a consequence of technological change. These arguments focus primarily on children's relationships with *digital* media technologies – with computers, and with the new 'interactive' forms of culture and communication they make available. In some cases, they are based on a direct opposition between these new media and the 'old' medium of television, which was seen as the primary cause of the 'death of childhood'. From this perspective, computers are uniformly good for children, just as television was uniformly bad.

Yet this distinction is not only about technology. In fact, several of the writers discussed in the previous chapter have sought to extend their arguments about the baleful influence of the media from television to computers. In *A is for Ox*, Barry Sanders blames home computers along with television for the destruction of 'true orality' and the rising tide of violence that has followed in its wake. Meanwhile, Neil Postman's book *Technopoly* condemns computers – as well as the use of technology in industry, medicine and most other spheres of social life – in much the same terms as his earlier books condemned television.[2] Explicitly acknowledging his debt to the Luddites, Postman accuses this technology of dehumanizing, of destroying natural forms of culture and communication in favour of a mechanistic bureaucracy. Like television, computers are seen to undermine rationality, morality and social coherence, and to generate confusion and chaos. Despite his technological determinism, Postman seems to perceive little difference between these 'old' and 'new' technologies.

As we shall see, some of the writers whose work is considered in this chapter also refuse to make absolutist distinctions between technologies *per se*. Nevertheless, they do suggest that the contemporary media favoured by the young have fundamentally different qualities from those of their parents' generation. These new media are seen as democratic rather than authoritarian; diverse rather than homogeneous; participatory rather than passive. In this respect, they are seen to engender new forms of consciousness among young people that take them beyond the restricted imaginations of their parents and teachers. If these writers do not all see *technologies* as determining consciousness, they nevertheless seem to believe that *media* do.

Nightmares and utopias

In developing these more optimistic arguments, the advocates of the 'electronic generation' must inevitably struggle against the much more negative views that often dominate public debate. In fact, the advent of new forms of culture and communication has often been greeted by an almost schizophrenic response. On the one hand, these new forms are seen to have enormous positive potential, particularly in terms of learning; while on the other, they are frequently seen to be harmful to those who are regarded as particularly vulnerable. In both cases, it is children – or perhaps more accurately, the *idea* of childhood – which is the vehicle for many of these aspirations and concerns.

This kind of ambivalence was certainly apparent in the early years of television. Amid current fears about the impact of screen violence, it is interesting to recall that television was initially promoted to parents as an *educational* medium.[3] Likewise, in the 1950s and 1960s, television and other new electronic technologies were widely seen to embody the future of education: they were described as 'teaching machines' that would bring new experiences and new forms of learning from the real world into the classroom.[4] Even here, however, hopes of a utopian future were often balanced against fears of loss and cultural decline. The notion that television might replace the teacher was powerfully promoted by some, yet it also provoked predictable anxiety and concern. Likewise, in the home, television was seen both as a new way of bringing the family together, and as something which would undermine natural family interaction.[5] The medium was extolled as a means of nurturing children's emotional and educational development, and simultaneously condemned for taking them away from more wholesome or worthwhile activities.

Contemporary responses to digital technology are equally ambivalent. On the one hand, there is a highly pessimistic account of the impact of computers on children's lives. This account focuses not on their *educational* potential, but on their role as a medium of *entertainment* – and it implicitly depends on an absolute distinction between the two. Many of the anxieties that are regularly rehearsed in relation to television now appear to have been carried over to this new medium. Thus, computers are frequently seen to be a bad influence on children's behaviour. Computer games, for example, are accused of causing imitative violence – and, it is argued, the more 'realistic' graphic effects become, the more likely they are to encourage 'copycat' behaviour.[6] These technologies are also believed to be bad for your brain – and indeed for your body. Thus, there are numerous clinical studies of phenomena such as 'Nintendo elbow' and the epileptic fits allegedly caused by computer games; while research is increasingly invoked in order to prove the dangers of computer 'addiction', and its negative effects on imagination and academic achievement.[7] Computers are also held to be bad for your social life: they apparently cause people to become anti-social, destroying normal human interaction and family togetherness. The phenomenon of the 'Otaku' or 'stay-at-home tribe' in Japan is seen as emblematic of the ways in which young people come to prefer the distance and anonymity of virtual communication to the reality of face-to-face interaction.[8] Finally, digital media are also regarded as bad for your politics and morality. Games playing is seen as a highly gendered activity which reinforces traditional stereotypes and negative role models;[9] while there is a rising tide of concern about the availability of pornography on the internet, and its capacity to corrupt the young.[10]

On the other hand, however, there is a form of visionary utopianism – albeit one that focuses primarily on *education* rather than *entertainment*. Thus, it is argued that computers bring about new forms of learning which transcend the limitations of older methods, particularly 'linear' methods such as print and television. And it is children who are seen to be most responsive to these new approaches: the computer somehow releases their natural creativity and desire to learn, which are apparently blocked and frustrated by old-fashioned methods.[11] Such utopianism is increasingly popular in the area of literacy and the arts. Some authors, for example, argue that digital technology will bring about a new form of democratic literacy. It will bring the means of expression and communication within everyone's reach, and thereby (in the words of Richard Lanham) 'enfranchise the public imagination in genuinely new ways'.[12] Meanwhile, the creative potential offered by these technologies is often seen to render formal training in artistic techniques redundant: the computer, it is argued, will make artists of us all. Far from destroying 'natural' human relationships and forms of learning, digital technology will liberate children's innate spontaneity and imagination.[13]

This utopian rhetoric is strongly reflected in advertising for computers and software, particularly that aimed at parents and teachers.[14] Ads for Apple Macs or Microsoft, for example, work hard to counter popular views of technology as somehow unnatural or inhuman, and therefore threatening. They focus not on the scientific specifications, but on the magical promise of the technology: the computer is represented here as a window on to new worlds, a way of developing children's intuitive sense of wonder and their thirst for knowledge. 'Where', they ask, 'do you want to go today?' As I shall indicate, there are interesting parallels between the utopianism of some academic (and quasi-academic) writing about computers and the rhetoric of the sales pitch. Yet this tone is also increasingly adopted by politicians and policy-makers, who are keen to represent the 'information superhighway' as the solution to all the problems of contemporary schooling.

These arguments are effectively two sides of the same coin. Without wishing to sweep aside concerns about the negative impact of such technologies – or indeed to deny their enormous potential – I would argue that these apparently contrasting positions share similar weaknesses. As with debates around television, both positive and negative arguments draw on essentialist notions both of childhood and of technology. In effect, they connect a *mythology* about childhood with a parallel mythology about technology. Thus, children are seen to possess a natural, spontaneous creativity, which is somehow (perhaps paradoxically) released by the machine; and, at the same time, they are seen as vulnerable, innocent and in need of protection from the damage that the technology will inevitably inflict on them.

So, on the one hand, the computer becomes a convenient scapegoat, a bad object on to which we can off-load our worries and frustrations – whether they are about violence, immorality, commercialism, sexism or the demise of 'family values'. Equally, on the other hand, the computer can serve as a panacea, a bearer of hopes and dreams, a magical agent that will unlock the wisdom and virtue that have previously remained hidden away. Yet whether we perceive these changes as good or bad, they are understood to follow inexorably from the implementation or availability of the technology. The technology is seen to transform our social relationships, to alter our mental functioning, to change our basic conceptions of knowledge and culture – and, crucially in this context, to transform what it means to learn, and to be a child.

Ultimately, therefore, both positions are characterized by a kind of technological determinism.[15] From this perspective, technology is seen to emerge from a neutral process of scientific research and development, rather than from the interplay of complex social, economic and political forces – forces which in fact play a crucial role in determining which technologies are developed and marketed in the first place. Technology is then seen to have effects, to bring about social and psychological changes, irrespective of the ways in which it is used and of the social contexts and processes into which it enters. As in the debates about the printing press and about television considered in the previous chapter, the computer is predominantly seen as an autonomous force that is somehow independent of human society, and acts on it from the outside.

The new generational rhetoric

My emphasis in this chapter is primarily on the utopian side of this argument. I intend to consider four key books which focus specifically on the implications of new media technologies for children and young people: Don Tapscott's *Growing Up Digital*, Seymour Papert's *The Connected Family*, Jon Katz's *Virtuous Reality* and Douglas Rushkoff's *Playing the Future*.[16] All were published in the mid or late 1990s. With the exception of Papert's, these books are not written by academics, unlike the 'death of childhood' texts considered in chapter 2. Like the majority of those texts, however, these are essentially 'popular' books, polemics written for a general rather than an academic readership.

Here again, the subtitles are symptomatic: *The Rise of the Net Generation* (Tapscott); *Bridging the Digital Generation Gap* (Papert); *How Kids' Culture Can Teach Us to Thrive in an Age of Chaos* (Rushkoff). Only Katz's reveals a more sardonic, and somewhat less fervent, edge: *How America Surrendered Discussion of Moral Values to Opportunists, Nitwits and Blockheads like William Bennett*, a blurb which will receive further explanation below.

In many respects, these books provide a mirror image of the 'death of childhood' thesis considered in chapter 2. While Postman and others perceive the media as agents of some all-embracing social decline, these authors see them as agents of an equally comprehensive form of social progress. While Postman and others see the media as an enormously powerful, negative influence on children, these authors see children as the powerful ones, and the media as the means of their empowerment. And if Postman wishes to return to a traditional notion of childhood, in which children are taught once more to know their place, these authors all trade in a kind of generational rhetoric, in which children and young people are seen as agents of a much broader transformation in society as a whole.

Don Tapscott's *Growing Up Digital* is the most substantial of these books, and the most relentlessly optimistic. The argument here is based on two sets of binary oppositions, between technologies (television versus the internet) and between generations (the 'boomers' versus the 'net generation'). Thus, television is seen as passive, while the net is active; television 'dumbs down' its users, while the net raises their intelligence; television broadcasts a singular view of the world, while the net is democratic and interactive; television isolates, while the net builds communities; and so on. Just as television is the antithesis of the net, so the 'television generation' is the antithesis of the 'net generation'. Like the technology they now control, the values of the 'television generation' are increasingly conservative, 'hierarchical, inflexible and centralized'. By contrast, the 'N-Geners' are 'hungry for expression, discovery and their own self-development': they are savvy, self-reliant, analytical, creative, inquisitive, accepting of diversity, socially conscious, globally oriented – and the list goes on.

Ultimately, however, these generational differences are seen to be *produced* by technology, rather than as a result of other social, historical or cultural forces. Unlike their parents, who are portrayed as incompetent 'technophobes', children are seen to possess an intuitive, spontaneous relationship with digital technology. 'For many kids,' we are told, 'using the new technology is as natural as breathing.'[17] It is this technology that is seen as the means of their empowerment. Children have become 'active', but only because technology has permitted them to do so:

> [Children today] have new powerful tools for inquiry, analysis, self-expression, influence, and play. They have unprecedented mobility. They are shrinking the planet in ways their parents could never imagine. Unlike television which was done *to* them, they are the actors in the digital world.[18]

As this implies, Tapscott is an unashamed technological determinist. In each area he considers – individual psychology, schooling, the workplace, family life, the market – digital technology is seen to result in inevitable (and inevitably positive) changes, as the new values of the 'N-Gen' displace those of the 'technophobic, old-style-thinking boomers'. Digital technology, Tapscott argues, guarantees structural changes – democratization, freedom of choice and expression, openness, innovation, collaboration. It develops a new human authenticity characterized by independence of thought, trust, honesty, sharing, self-confidence and a healthy scepticism about authority. And it will eventually bring about a 'generational explosion', a 'social awakening' that will overthrow traditional hierarchies of knowledge and power.

Tapscott's evidence is drawn partly from market research, and partly from using the internet itself. The text is interspersed with speech bubbles containing decontextualized 'soundbites' from young people gathered during online chat sessions, all of whom seem to agree with Tapscott that 'kids are building a new culture.'[19] We are told little about these young people, other than their age and where they live. They clearly are a self-selected, unrepresentative group; but whether they represent a vision of the future for *all* young people is a crucial question.

In fact, Tapscott does acknowledge some of the limitations of the 'digital revolution', albeit somewhat late in the day. He points out that the widening gap between the 'technology rich' and the 'technology poor' both reflects and accentuates broader inequalities in US society; and he argues that this gap will not be bridged simply by providing more equipment, but that a more fundamental investment in infrastructure and human expertise is required. Yet, on the other hand, Tapscott appears to take the 'logic' of capitalism for granted: the internet, he argues, is 'a creature of market forces', and in offering choice and control to its users, it is seen as inherently 'democratizing'.[20] Likewise, he generalizes about the workforce of the future by focusing on what will only ever be an entrepreneurial elite. Potential concerns about the impact of new technologies on unskilled labour, or about their role in the control and surveillance of the workforce, for example, are simply ignored. For all his insistence on the social awareness of his generation of 'young navigators', Tapscott's new era seems to represent the apotheosis of consumerism – an era guaranteed by customized advertising, a 'flexible' labour force and the relentless drive for profit through 'innovation'.

Seymour Papert is one of the authorities cited by Tapscott, and appears to enjoy (and indeed to cultivate) a guru-like status in this field. *The Connected Family* is intended as a self-help book for parents, and manages to combine the homespun common sense of advice literature with occasional Zen-like inspirational mottoes. Arguments that some readers might be forgiven for finding banal and patronizing are clearly intended to possess a child-like profundity. As Papert's colleague Nicholas Negroponte proclaims in his foreword to the book, 'Seymour is the emancipated child.'[21]

Like Papert's earlier, symptomatically titled *The Children's Machine*,[22] *The Connected Family* combines a faith in the natural wisdom of children with an equal faith in the liberating potential of digital technology as a means of learning. He begins thus:

> Across the world there is a passionate love affair between children and computers. I have worked with children and computers in Africa and Asia and America, in cities, in suburbs, on farms and in jungles. I have worked with poor children and rich children; with children of bookish parents and with children from illiterate families. But these differences don't seem to matter. Everywhere, with few exceptions, I see the same gleam in their eyes, the same desire to appropriate this thing. And more than wanting it, they seem to know that in a deep way it already belongs to them. They know that they can master it more easily than their parents. They know they are the computer generation.[23]

Embedded in these hushed, almost mystical tones is a denial of cultural differences and social inequalities that is symptomatic of Papert's essentialist approach. There is, it appears, a kind of natural essence of childhood – an innate knowledge, a spontaneous fluency, a thirst for learning – that is somehow automatically released by this technology. Children, it would seem, just intuitively *know* how to use computers; and the computer's mode of operation somehow magically coincides with their natural mode of learning. As the final sentence here suggests, Papert sees this in terms of *generational* difference: like Tapscott, he represents parents and teachers as fearful and incompetent in their relations with computers, and yet reluctant to hand over control.

In general, the children of Papert's 'computer generation' are younger than Tapscott's 'N-Geners', but his analysis of the benefits of the technology for their learning is very similar. Papert claims allegiance to a form of cognitive psychology, influenced by Piaget; and his emphasis is accordingly on individualized, 'self-directed' learning, which proceeds at the child's natural pace. Problems only arise, he argues, when parents, teachers and software designers seek to impose the old-fashioned assumptions and learning methods that derive from their own schooldays. Papert is thus highly critical of the 'instructional', back-to-basics software packages which are heavily promoted in the market, particularly those which attempt to 'deceive' children into believing that they are simply playing a game.

As this implies, Papert does not ignore some of the negative aspects of the contemporary enthusiasm for computers. He acknowledges that using the internet can be slow and frustrating, that some commercial software is badly designed, and that most uses of computers in schools are limited and unimaginative. But these are all, he implies, temporary phenomena, merely reflecting the fact that it is adults who still control these media. When children are given free rein, it would seem that only positive consequences can follow: reluctant learners are transformed into straight-A students, families become more caring and communicative, teachers discover new worlds of learning – all by virtue of their access to technology.

Jon Katz's *Virtuous Reality* is characterized by a similar optimism, although (as his subtitle suggests) more of its energy is expended on critique. After the breathless sales talk of Tapscott and Papert, Katz's acerbic wit is positively refreshing. Where Tapscott seeks to assuage parental anxieties about the moral corruption that is seen to arise from digital media – most obviously in the form of online pornography – Katz is more forthright in attacking the new moral authoritarianism that dominates contemporary debates about youth in the

United States (and indeed in Britain). He sees blocking software and the V-chip, for example, as fundamental attacks on children's freedom – although he takes comfort from their likely ineffectiveness. He is scathing about the lucrative moralistic homilies produced by former US Secretary of Education and White House drug czar William Bennett, and about the desire of other 'mediaphobes' to blame the media for what they perceive as all the ills of the world.

While some of Katz's targets are easy ones, his position on perennial questions of media effects represents a significant challenge to dominant views, particularly in the United States. Thus, he challenges the idea that sexual content in the media is necessarily harmful for children; and he argues that blaming the media for violent crime is simply a way of distracting attention from its more fundamental (and more intractable) causes. He reminds us of the fact that new technologies have effectively undermined the possibility of centralized control; and that a great deal of children's (and youth) culture is by definition bound to be subversive. Our aim, he argues, should not be to prevent children gaining access to such material, but to enable them to cope with it.

Like Tapscott and Papert, Katz is relentlessly optimistic about the young, and scathing about their 'boomer' parents. The boomers are, he asserts, increasingly conservative: they cannot understand the 'information revolution' or the 'rebellious' character of contemporary youth culture, and hence resort to ever more desperate attempts to control and censor it. By contrast, it is their children who are now more liberal and more socially aware. They are, Katz argues, less accepting of established authority; they value interactivity rather than passivity; they appreciate diversity and outspokenness; and they don't like media that take themselves too seriously. They are 'citizens of a new order'.

Katz's argument here is explicitly informed by notions of 'children's rights', a theme which (as we shall see in subsequent chapters) is currently undergoing a resurgence. Unlike the protectionist rhetoric that often surfaces in such debates, Katz's emphasis is explicitly political. He looks back to Tom Paine, both for a model of the kind of controversial popular journalism which he argues has been overcome by corporate conservatism, and for a set of arguments about human rights. The internet, Katz argues, is 'the embodiment of everything (Paine) believed'. It is finally enabling children to move out of adult control:

> Not only is this new machinery making the young more sophisticated, altering their ideas of what culture and literacy are, it is transforming them – connecting them to one another, providing them with a new sense of

political self . . . As digital communications flash through the most heavily fortified borders and ricochet around the world independent of government and censors, children can for the first time reach past the
suffocating boundaries of social convention, past their elders' rigid notions of what is good for them.[24]

Yet while he is keen to proclaim a 'children's revolution', Katz's
model contract between parents and children provides a more realistic (even conservative) balance of rights and responsibilities. Children, he argues, have 'a moral right of access' to media culture; but
they also need to negotiate with parents' conditions, for example
about privacy, and with their expectations about school performance and behaviour.[25]

Despite his overall optimism, Katz does not subscribe to the essentialist view of media technologies espoused by Papert and
Tapscott. Unlike Tapscott, he also knows that the word 'media' is a
plural noun. Katz's opposition is not between television and digital
media, but between 'new' and 'old' cultural forms. Thus, he is particularly incisive on the failure of traditional news journalism to keep
pace with what he sees as young people's changing orientation towards information. He is positive about 'interactivity', not merely in
digital media, but also in talk shows, cable television and rap music
– which he collectively describes as 'one of the great creative explo-
sions of modern culture.'[26] Yet Katz does not argue that the new
should simply replace the old. For example, he regards the
'interactivity' of the new media as potentially empowering and democratizing, and as a challenge to centralized control; but he also
argues that it is important to retain the positive aspects of 'old' media, such as newspapers and television, for their ability to create a
common culture and to provide the 'coherence, rationality and context' that can help us find our way through the barrage of information. This is not, he insists, an either/or choice between one
information culture and another. Here again, Katz's approach is
rather more measured than his occasional bursts of generational
rhetoric might lead one to expect.

By contrast, Douglas Rushkoff's *Playing the Future* employs the
rhetoric with wild abandon. Here again, the argument is based on
a binary opposition between the new media generation – the
'screenagers', as he calls them – and their parents – the 'boomers'. As
they have grown older, Rushkoff argues, the boomers have simply
returned to the authoritarian values they attempted to overturn in
the 1960s. It is the young who are now the key hope for social evolution. While the boomers are aligned with linearity, and with the com-

fortable certainties of dualistic morality, the screenagers embrace discontinuity, turbulence and complexity. Young people, Rushkoff argues, have the 'natural adaptive skills' that enable them to deal with the problems of postmodernity; they alone can understand 'the secret workings of technology'. Adults will have to abandon their function as role models and educators, and accept the fact that they must 'catch up' with their children. If they maintain their allegiance to 'the sinking, obsolete institutions of the past', he warns, they will simply 'go down with the ship'.[27]

Like Katz, Rushkoff does not obviously espouse the kind of technological determinism adopted by Tapscott and Papert. His 'generation gap' is not primarily a matter of technology, but of the differences between 'old' and 'new' media. Like Katz, Rushkoff characterizes these new media – not just the internet, but also cable television, computer games, MTV, role-playing and fashion subcultures – as inherently more 'interactive' and hence more democratic than the hierarchical 'monoculture' that preceded them. These media, he argues, permit young people to become cultural producers in their own right, and hence to evade the control of their 'parental gatekeepers'.

Of all these writers, Rushkoff is the most obviously sympathetic to these new forms of young people's media culture. He ranges widely across a whole range of media, from pogs and *Power Rangers* to vampire subcultures, mosh pits and body piercing, celebrating 'individuality, weirdness, inconsistency, openness and even mutation'.[28] He provides a particularly interesting analysis of the romantic, 'pagan spirituality' of contemporary children's and youth culture, arguing that this represents both a reaction against technological domination, and an instinctive ability to evolve along with it.

According to Rushkoff, these new modes of being are not only apparent in the media forms young people favour, but also in their different orientation towards them. The characteristic mode of the screenager is that of channel surfing, rather than passive obedience to linear 'programming'. Like Tapscott, Rushkoff argues that the screenagers have developed new cognitive skills that enable them to cope with the surfeit of information by processing it much more quickly. Their use of media is characterized not by slavish obedience but by a form of collective irony or 'distanced participation': they refuse to be persuaded or drawn into the role of passive viewers.

As his subtitle suggests, Rushkoff's approach is informed by 'chaos theory' – as indeed is his characteristic mode of argument. He regards this process of adaptation as a matter of 'the evolution of the species', which can be explained in terms of metaphors drawn from the natural world: social and historical processes are seen as apparently random sequences of discontinuous events. Rushkoff repeatedly insists that (as with fractals) there are 'bigger patterns' or 'underlying structures' amid the apparently random turbulence, although he never adequately explains what they are. His argument is constantly 'zapping' from one theme to another via dubious analogies and leaps of logic, in a manner reminiscent of Marshall McLuhan. The more diverse the material becomes, and the more rapidly the argument proceeds, the more it seems that 'embracing chaos' is indeed the only solution.

As such, Rushkoff appears to demand consent, not by means of argument and evidence, but by a kind of act of faith. Optimism appears to be compulsory here. Young people, we are told, will naturally evolve towards the next stage of humanity. The media are our 'partners in cultural evolution', and technology is 'more accurately reflecting our desires and priorities every day'.[29] Like Tapscott, Rushkoff is enthusiastic about the ways in which new technology is transforming the workplace. Technology, he asserts, will bring about the end of mindless labour; and the 'screenager world view' will transform corporate culture, making it more democratic and socially responsible, and encouraging a new honesty and sense of community. Similarly, Rushkoff implicitly accepts the notion that, in bringing about an 'interactive free-for-all' of new media forms, the market has also brought increased consumer choice and hence a new responsiveness to the cultural needs of audiences. This is, he asserts, 'a culture left to its own devices'. Yet Rushkoff's 'free-flowing fractal system' implicitly represents democratic anarchism as a justification of free-market liberalism. In his conclusion, the market becomes effectively a 'force of nature': 'our media promotes [*sic*] free communication,' he enthuses, 'our economy promotes choice.'[30]

The limits of optimism

The energetic optimism of these books is, on one level, highly attractive. Like the nostalgia of the 'death of childhood' authors, it has a direct emotional appeal that is hard to resist. It would be comforting to agree with Tapscott and others that young people are not greedy, materialistic and anti-social; and that they will eventually overthrow the hierarchical bureaucracies of government, making way for an egalitarian, free society. This argument represents a powerful challenge to the stigmatization of young people and the reliance on

authoritarian social policies that have become increasingly popular
with governments on both sides of the Atlantic.

In relation to the media, these arguments also provide a valuable
alternative to the assumptions that typically inform public debate.
Rather than conceiving of children as passive consumers of all-powerful media, these authors emphasize their critical sophistication and
competence. In some cases quite courageously, they also challenge
the simplistic moralism that dominates public debates about the influence of 'sex and violence'. Children and young people are defined
here, not as dupes or victims, but as active agents in their dealings
with the media.

And yet, as I have implied, this optimism too often slides into a
form of wishful thinking that flies in the face of the facts. Unlike the
historical accounts considered in the previous chapter, futurology of
this kind obviously cannot be expected to deal only in representative evidence. Tapscott's soundbites from internet chat rooms or
Papert's anecdotes about four-year-old web surfers are intended precisely as predictions of a new generation in the making: they are by
definition untypical. Yet accentuating the positive in this way inevitably raises questions about what is omitted.

Thus, these authors largely ignore the awkward empirical questions about how these technologies are designed, produced and
marketed, and how they are actually used by real children. One might,
for example, point to the dominance of the computer market by a
small number of immensely profitable multinational corporations;
the growing horizontal and vertical integration of the entertainment
industries; and the massive acceleration in planned obsolescence of
computer hardware. The claim that new media necessarily provide
greater 'diversity' or 'freedom of choice' – as opposed to simply an
increase in *quantity* (and hence in profitability) – is far from proven
here. Likewise, one's enthusiasm about the democratic possibilities
of the internet might be tempered by considering its increasing use
in the surveillance of consumer behaviour, the global dominance of
'developed' countries in internet traffic, and the *un*democratic character of many so-called 'online communities'. There is little evidence
as yet that the internet is any more democratic – or that it has actually generated greater amounts of political activity and change – than
comparable older technologies such as radio, telephones or photo-
copiers. Finally, optimism about the potential of computers in education should also be set against declining state investment, the
growing involvement of commercial corporations in schooling, and
the increasing pressure on parents to compensate for what are seen
as the failings of public education. Evidence about the bestselling

software titles or about the actual uses of computers in classrooms would suggest that this new technology has largely reinforced traditional methods of learning rather than challenged them.[31]

In terms of young people's uses of these new media, several key terms remain undefined here. For example, the notion of 'interactivity' – and the related distinction between 'active' and 'passive' – is applied quite indiscriminately to media texts and experiences of very different kinds: an online chat room is 'interactive' in a very different way from a 'beat-em-up' computer game, which is different again from a television talk show or a rave party. Furthermore, children do not 'naturally' know how to use computers: like adults, their experiences are frequently ones of confusion, boredom and frustration. The proliferation of new media, and the characteristics of the internet in particular, require significant new skills in terms of how we locate, select and evaluate information. At present, the creative, educational and communicative benefits of these technologies are only realized by a small elite – and that elite, like other elites, is predominantly white, male and middle class. Both globally and within technologically wealthy countries, there is a growing polarization between the 'information rich' and the 'information poor'; and this is not simply to do with the unequal distribution of equipment, but also of the cultural and technological 'capital' that is required to *learn* to use it creatively and effectively.[32]

To be fair, there is some recognition of these problems in the books considered here. Both Tapscott and Katz, for example, acknowledge the increasing inequalities in access to technology, which rather give the lie to Papert's essentialist view of children's 'love affair'; but their recognition of the potential dangers of this situation is effectively lost in the onward rush of optimism. Likewise, Papert acknowledges the limited ways in which computer technology is currently used in homes and schools, and some of the weaknesses of the software; but the blame for this is simply laid at the door of some generalized group of conservative 'adults', who will eventually have to cede control to the new generation.

Ultimately, all these authors tend to neglect the real social contexts in which technologies are produced and used, and the social differences that characterize them. Their essentialist position leads them to argue in absolutist terms about the differences between generations, as though 'generations' were somehow self-contained and homogeneous. Just as 'adults' and 'parents' are condemned as uniformly conservative and backward looking, so 'children' or 'young people' are seen to adapt naturally and effortlessly to changes of all kinds. This essentialist view of childhood is reinforced by an essen-

tialist view of technology (or of media). New media, and particularly digital media, are described as inherently 'interactive', and hence
as 'democratic', irrespective of the ways in which they are used. All
these writers list the psychological attributes of the 'electronic generation' as though these were simply inevitable consequences of their
relationship to technology. Most obviously in Rushkoff's case, technology becomes tantamount to a form of biology.

As a result, these authors largely conceive of social change as an
inevitable consequence of the passing of time – or, in Rushkoff's terms,
as a process of natural evolution. What is largely taken for granted
here is the role of the market. While some of these authors, notably
Papert, express occasional regrets about the influence of the market,
this is seen as something that is bound to pass away as the conservative values of the older generation give way to the democratic ones
of the new. In other instances, notably in Rushkoff's book, the market is positively celebrated as a kind of natural force for good. The
market will, it is argued, inevitably come to fulfil the promise of the
technology, since both effectively embody the essential human values of the young.

Like the grandiose despair of the 'death of childhood' authors,
therefore, this generalized optimism displays significant limitations
when it comes to implications for policy. For all his morale-boosting
rhetoric, Tapscott is alone in suggesting some concrete ways in which
children's access to technology can be equalized, mainly through
community-based charitable projects of various kinds. Papert is more
concerned with how parents might exercise pressure to change the
'learning cultures' of schools; while Katz's model contract between
parents and children places the emphasis even more firmly on individualistic models of social change. Nevertheless, just as the 'death
of childhood' authors place the responsibility for change on parents,
all these writers appear to invest a kind of blind faith in the wisdom
of youth. In the process, children are effectively made to carry the
burden of all our hopes and aspirations. As Tapscott's book concludes, the best approach is simply to 'listen to the children' – as
though they will all be saying the same thing, and as though we
should place all our trust in simply following it.[33]

Towards alternatives

On one level, the arguments considered in this chapter are diametrically opposed to those discussed in chapter 2. Jon Katz's robust attack on the moral hypocrisy of America's 'mediaphobes', for example,

could easily be applied to the furious invective of Barry Sanders. Steinberg and Kincheloe, the editors of *Kinderculture*, clearly represent the 'boomers', whose tastes and values are so comprehensively dismissed by Douglas Rushkoff.[34] While Seymour Papert and Neil Postman might share some criticisms of contemporary schooling, their diagnoses of how it should change are poles apart. And more broadly, of course, the breathless optimism of these advocates of the 'electronic generation' stands in stark contrast to the pessimism of those who lament the 'death of childhood'.

Nevertheless, these apparently contrasting arguments also have a great deal in common. Of course, not all the accounts I have considered are equally determinist or one-dimensional. The analyses of Joshua Meyrowitz (on the one hand) or Jon Katz (on the other) are much more nuanced and equivocal than the more absolutist arguments with which I have grouped them here. Yet in their 'strongest' form – for example, in the works of Neil Postman and Don Tapscott – these arguments share several limitations. Both positions adopt an essentialist view of 'childhood' and 'youth', and an unduly determinist account of the role of media and technology. Both reflect a kind of sentimentality about children and young people which fails to acknowledge the diversity of the lived experience of childhood, and of children's relationships with the media. In this respect, the traditional view of children as essentially innocent and vulnerable to media influence is balanced by an equally romantic view of them as naturally 'media-wise'. Neither, I would argue, offers a realistic basis for cultural, social and educational policies that might enable *all* young people to cope with the changing cultural realities into which they are born.

To challenge these accounts is not, however, to deny that significant changes have indeed occurred in our conceptions of childhood, and in the realities of children's daily lives. Nor is it to imply that the media are somehow extraneous to these changes, or that they merely reflect them. In the second part of the book, I offer my own account of the changing nature of childhood and of the media, and of the relationships between them. As I shall argue, a positive and effective response to these changes will only be possible if we understand their complexity and their potential contradictions. Simply to blame the media, or indeed to celebrate them, is to overestimate their power, and to underestimate the diverse ways in which children create their own meanings and pleasures.

Part II

4

Changing Childhoods

The debates reviewed in the two preceding chapters invoke a whole range of empirical and theoretical claims about the changing nature of childhood. While some of the authors I have discussed take a much longer historical view, their central concern is with changes they perceive to have taken place in the past two or three decades – specifically as a result of the widespread availability of the electronic media.

As I have indicated, the arguments considered in these two chapters – and the evidence on which they are based – are in some respects diametrically opposed. Proponents of the 'death of childhood' thesis produce a very different account of the contemporary experience of children and young people as compared with the advocates of the 'electronic generation'. Barry Sanders's drug-crazed, violent youth, for example, inhabit a different universe from that of Don Tapscott's autonomous, socially responsible 'N-Geners'; while the apparent nihilism and irrationality of contemporary youth culture that so alarm Neil Postman and the contributors to *Kinderculture* are interpreted in a much more positive way by Douglas Rushkoff and Jon Katz. Yet, despite these differences, all seem convinced that we are living through a period of far-reaching and dramatic change, both in dominant definitions of childhood, and in children's own lived experiences.

In a sense, all the authors I have considered construct *stories* of childhood.[1] They invoke cultural representations of children, and build historical narratives around them. Children are represented here in diverse ways: as innocent and vulnerable, as sinful and in need of control, or as naturally wise and free-spirited. Similarly, there are diverse narratives of childhood here: stories of decline, of civilization, of liberation and of repression and control. As I have argued, representations and stories of these kinds characterize all our discourses about childhood, from the subjective and imaginative appeals of fiction and autobiography through to the authoritative claims to scientific objectivity embodied in academic writing. It is partly through such stories that the meanings and the lived experiences of childhood are typically regulated and defined.

In this chapter, I provide another such story, or set of stories. I argue that children's lives – and hence the meanings we attribute to 'childhood' – have indeed changed significantly in the past two or three decades. In some respects, my account confirms several of the key arguments on both sides of the debate; although it also suggests that childhood is changing in much less dramatic and much more ambivalent and contradictory ways than such commentators have tended to suggest. More fundamentally, I argue that understanding these changes requires us to move beyond essentialism, and to recognize the diverse and provisional nature of contemporary childhoods. In these respects, my story has a rather less satisfying narrative structure – and in particular, a lack of resolution in its ending – when compared with those I have considered thus far.

This chapter focuses on the changing nature of children's lives across the past two or three decades. My account is organized fairly conventionally, in terms of three principal domains. I consider, first, the place of children within the family; secondly, children's experiences of education and employment; and thirdly, their uses of leisure time. In doing so, I draw on several sources, ranging from historical and sociological studies to official reports and government statistics.[2]

Needless to say, this brief account is much less than a comprehensive survey. It relies primarily on material relating to the UK; and while some of these arguments can tentatively be generalized to other Western industrialized countries, some of them definitely cannot.[3] The situation of children in the United States – to which the arguments I have considered thus far primarily refer – is different in several significant respects, for complex historical and political reasons.[4] Furthermore, historical comparisons of this kind – and indeed the very gathering of data in the first place – are obviously fraught with difficulty. As I have noted, children have to some extent been 'hidden from history'; and official statistics still tend to use parents or families rather than children as their basic unit of accounting.[5] More fundamentally, the category of 'the child' remains an extremely slippery one. The question of where childhood ends and youth or adulthood begins is answered in very different ways at different times, and for different purposes. And of course we cannot talk about children as a homogeneous category: what childhood means, and how it is experienced, obviously depends on other social factors, such as gender, 'race' or ethnicity, social class, geographical location, and so on.

These kinds of qualifications would seem to make any attempt to generalize about 'children' effectively impossible. Yet the recognition that childhood is a social construction should not prevent us from talking about the material realities of children's lives – and hence about the systematic differences between children and other social groups.[6] Indeed, it is through the ongoing debate between competing constructions of childhood that social policies are formulated and the experiences of real, empirical children are thereby formed and defined. My aim, however, is not to call the preceding arguments to account in the light of objective facts. Rather, it is to provide the grounds for a rather different story of childhood – and particularly of children's relations with the electronic media – that will in turn suggest rather different material consequences for the individuals we now happen to call children. Some initial indications of this argument are contained in the concluding sections of this chapter.

Home and family

Perhaps the most unambiguous of these changes have occurred in children's experiences of family life. In the UK, and in most other industrialized countries, we have seen a steady decline in the traditional nuclear family. Of course, the nuclear family is itself a comparatively recent historical phenomenon; and in the UK at least, some working-class and ethnic minority families still conform to the 'older' model of the extended family, with three or more generations living in the same home, or in close proximity. In fact, it is doubtful whether there ever was a Golden Age of stable, supportive extended families;[7] although the fact remains that in recent decades 'non-traditional' family structures of various kinds have become increasingly common.

Thus, the proportion of 'traditional' households (comprising a couple with dependent children) has fallen over the last thirty-five years, from 38 per cent of the total in 1961 to 25 per cent in 1996–7. Although most British children under sixteen continue to live with two parents, the proportion living in single-parent families has more than doubled since 1972 to more than one in five. Such families are overwhelmingly headed by mothers: the proportion of lone fathers has changed little over the decades. The number of marriages has decreased, while the proportion of children born out of wedlock has increased dramatically, from 9 per cent in 1975 to 34 per cent in 1995. While the large majority of such births are registered by both parents, these children are less likely than those of married parents to remain living with both parents until they are sixteen. The divorce rate has also doubled over the past two decades, with two in five marriages now ending in divorce, and one child in every sixty-five affected in any given year. It is currently estimated that only half of all children in Britain can expect to spend their entire childhood living with their married natural parents.

Other changes have also significantly affected children's experience of family life. Families themselves are getting smaller: the proportion with three or more children declined from 41 per cent in 1972 to 26 per cent in 1996, although much of this decline took place in the 1970s. Fertility rates have declined, not so much because women are choosing to remain childless but because they are having fewer children. Meanwhile, the proportion of working mothers has increased significantly – rising from half to two-thirds of married women with children between 1979 and 1994 – while households in which the man is the only breadwinner are now just one-quarter of the total. Professional women with children are much more likely to be working than unskilled women with children, particularly on a full-time basis. In 1997, three-fifths of married couples with children were both working (either full- or part-time) as compared with one-half in the mid-1980s. While there is a growing expectation that fathers should become involved in child-care, evidence suggests that, at least in the UK, practice has largely failed to keep pace with a shift towards more egalitarian attitudes, not least because of the increase in working hours:[8] in 1996, full-time male employees worked an average of forty-six hours a week, more than in any other country in the European Union. At the same time, more than one-third of children are living in families with no full-time wage-earner; and the number of homeless families with dependent children has risen four-fold since the late 1970s. Estimates by the housing charity Shelter suggest that around 100,000 children are currently homeless in the UK.[9]

These changes are perhaps more gradual than some have argued, but they are none the less very significant. In sum, they suggest that for a high proportion of children the family is no longer the stable environment imagined by many conservative policy-makers.[10] Even for those who live in traditional nuclear families, children spend decreasing amounts of time with their parents,[11] and more in institutionalized child-care of some form; and they are also less likely to have siblings available for companionship. These changes are also contributing to a growing polarization between rich and poor. While there is certainly evidence (and some debate) about the psychological distress caused to children by family break-up, the *economic* consequences are clear-cut.[12] Single-parent families are much more likely to live below the poverty line, and to be dependent on state benefits; while lone mothers are less likely to be employed than those in two-parent families. Such families are also disproportionately represented among groups that already suffer from poverty, notably Afro-Caribbeans. Against a situation in which real household disposable income has almost doubled over the past twenty-five years, the proportion of people living on less than the average income has steadily risen.

At the same time, there is some evidence that children's place *within* the family has become more significant, at least symbolically. The statistics here are difficult to compare, but the proportion of household income devoted to children appears to have increased significantly over the past three decades. This is partly a result of the new emphasis on children as a potential market. If capitalism can be said to have created 'the teenager' in the 1950s, children are now increasingly addressed directly as consumers in their own right, rather than simply as a means of reaching parents.[13] The market in children's consumer goods in the UK is currently estimated at more than £10 billion a year, and is the focus of increasing commercial competition. The size of the children's toy market, for example, has grown dramatically; and children themselves also have more disposable income, both from pocket money and gifts and (among older children) from paid employment. Meanwhile, a whole range of consumer technologies – from video recorders and cable television to home computers – are much more likely to be found in families with children than in those without.[14]

In some respects, this new 'valorization' of childhood might be seen as a compensatory phenomenon. The economic value that children possessed in the nineteenth century has gradually been replaced by an emphasis on their psychological, and particularly *emotional* value for parents.[15] As parents in general spend less time with their children, they place a greater value on the time they do spend, and invest more heavily in it: 'quality time' becomes a kind of commodity.[16] In this situation, enjoying parenting, or being *seen* to enjoy it, has become almost mandatory.[17] As I shall indicate, the urgency –

and indeed the guilt – that surrounds this issue is intensified by the
growing emphasis on parental involvement in education, and increasing fears of risk in the outside world. The family is increasingly
being perceived both as a key site of children's education and as a
haven in a heartless world.

More qualitatively, it would be true to say that styles of child-care
– or at least *discourses about* child-care – have changed significantly
over the past four or five decades. Broadly speaking, there has been
a move away from behaviourist approaches, and towards those based
on developmental psychology.[18] The reliance on strict physical discipline and regulation has given way to an emphasis on guidance
and nurturing. Many historians and sociologists have perceived this
as a general 'mellowing' or 'democratization' of parental attitudes.
For example, one representative historical study concludes that 'most
children today have more friendly and intimate relationships with
their parents' than would have been the case in earlier decades.[19] On
the other hand, it has been argued that there are significant class
differences here: middle-class parents are generally more inclined to
use verbal reasoning as a means of control, while working-class parents continue to rely on more authoritarian, non-verbal approaches.[20]
Meanwhile, others have argued that the appearance of more egalitarian relationships between parents and children masks what is in
fact a more intrusive form of psychic regulation; and that increasing
pressure is now being placed on parents to ensure that their children
meet the appropriate developmental targets.[21]

At the same time, one can point to the growing prominence of
child abuse as an issue in social policy – although (as with all crime
figures) there is considerable debate about whether this reflects the
growing incidence of the phenomenon, or simply increased sensitivity towards it and hence increased reporting.[22] Child sexual abuse
has undoubtedly become one of the recurrent 'moral panics' of our
time, although the majority of reported cases of abuse are in fact
defined as neglect, which is itself strongly related to poverty. However, the range of behaviours which are popularly defined as 'child
abuse' has widened. In some circumstances, parents and teachers
can now be prosecuted not only for sexual abuse or overt cruelty,
but also for smacking children – which in previous years would have
been seen as quite acceptable, and even as positively good for children. And despite the widespread fear that children will be abducted
by marauding paedophiles, three-quarters of all violent offences
against school-age children are committed by their parents or other
relatives. Here again, the notion of the family home as a risk-free,
stable environment is one that is difficult to sustain.

Workplaces: education and employment

As I have noted, the introduction of compulsory education in the late nineteenth century was one of the principal means whereby children came to be segregated from adults; and in this respect, it was one of the major prerequisites of our modern conception of childhood. Across the twentieth century there has been a steady extension of the years of compulsory schooling, culminating in the raising of the school-leaving age to sixteen in 1972. Since that time there has been a continuing increase both in the proportion of children in preschool education of some kind, and in the proportion of young people staying on in post-compulsory education. The institutionalization of childhood appears to be starting earlier and ending later.

Thus, the proportion of three- and four-year-olds attending school (at least part-time) rose threefold between 1971 and 1996, to reach 58 per cent. The Labour government set a target in 1998 to provide free school places for all four-year-olds. Meanwhile, at the other end of the scale, the proportion of sixteen to eighteen-year-olds in some form of education or training has risen from one-third to three-quarters of the total age group. Enrolments in further education courses have increased by 50 per cent since 1971, while numbers in higher education have trebled over this period, with the most significant growth occuring in the 1990s. The proportion of female students has risen significantly, from one-third to slightly over half, although those from lower socioeconomic groups continue to be seriously underrepresented.

In recent years, education has become a much more prominent issue in public debate and in government policy. Between 1971 and 1996, total government expenditure on education increased in real terms by over 60 per cent (and by 86 per cent in nursery and primary education); although as a percentage of gross domestic product it remained comparatively stable, at around 5 per cent. The government's commitment to increase provision for younger children, and to reduce class sizes in primary schools, is likely to produce a small increase in this figure; although this will be offset by its decision to end free higher education and to move to a student loan scheme. Meanwhile, the government shows no inclination to reduce tax concessions for the growing proportion of wealthy parents whose children attend private schools (now attended by 8 per cent of secondary age children).

Concern about the 'erosion of standards' is of course perennial, but it has dramatically intensified in recent years. The Conservative government's introduction of a national curriculum in the late 1980s, backed up by an extensive apparatus of testing, marked a significant extension in the centralized control of education; yet it was also justified by appealing to notions of 'parental choice', whereby parents would be able to identify and select the 'best' schools for their children by means of published league tables.[23] Schooling has increasingly been subject to a form of marketization, and commercial corporations have been centrally involved in these initiatives at many levels, from providing tokens for shoppers to redeem in exchange for school equipment, through to involvement in school management via education action zones. Corporations are increasingly keen to be seen as 'sponsors' of schools, and to provide 'free' equipment, curriculum materials and e-mail accounts.[24] Yet, despite the rhetoric of consumer choice, children themselves still have comparatively little control over the day-to-day organization of schooling, let alone over the curriculum.

This new situation has led to an atmosphere of growing competition, not only between schools but also among children themselves. New Labour's much-vaunted emphasis on 'education, education and education' has intensified this pressure, with its insistence on national targets for schools, homework clubs and the need to call failing parents to account. Parents are also increasingly being urged to invest in their children's education by providing extra coaching at home. There is currently a massive boom in the publication of books and CD-Roms designed to 'help your child' with the tests at various Key Stages of the curriculum; and several commercial companies are franchising private supplementary classes in the arts and in computer literacy. Education, it would seem, is the *work* of childhood, and it cannot be allowed to stop once children walk out of the classroom door.[25]

The impact of these and earlier changes on the pattern of achievement in education has been complex. Results in public examinations have steadily improved, although this has only caused some to complain that the examinations have simply been made easier. The achievement of girls has also risen dramatically relative to boys, and has steadily reached into subject areas and sectors of the education system that were previously regarded as male preserves. At the same time, despite the partial elimination of a two-tier system of schools and of public examinations, social class continues to exercise a determining influence on educational achievement among older children.[26]

Developments in post-compulsory education also need to be seen against the background of rising youth unemployment. The decline of Britain's industrial base in the 1970s led to the steady reduction of conventional routes into employment: the proportion of young people in apprenticeships, for example, declined from 25 per cent in 1974 to 8 per cent in 1984. The threat of an unemployed, recalcitrant 'underclass' of young people became a major preoccupation for policy-makers, particularly following the inner-city disturbances of the early 1980s. In 1982, unemployment among young people aged sixteen to nineteen was 28 per cent, more than double that among the population as a whole. In the mid-1980s the Department of Employment (later significantly merged with the Department of Education) introduced a series of training schemes designed to address the problem; and this was subsequently reinforced in 1988 by the withdrawal of general state benefits for sixteen and seventeen-year-olds (which means that they are now no longer able to register as unemployed), and the subsequent reduction in benefits for those still entitled to claim them. In effect, young people have been conscripted into education or training. In 1974, 60 per cent of sixteen-year-olds went straight from school into employment, while only 3 per cent were unemployed; by 1990, under 25 per cent were employed, while 52 per cent were in full-time education and 23 per cent on training schemes.[27] While the boundary between 'education' and 'training' has become increasingly blurred in more recent years, the broad proportions have remained very similar.

Although youth unemployment has fallen in numerical terms in recent years, it has steadily risen relative to the national average over the past decade,[28] particularly among young men (over 20 per cent were unemployed in 1996) and among black young people, who are twice as likely to be unemployed as their white counterparts. Rates of pay for this age group have also declined relative to those for adults: 30 per cent of jobs offered to young people provide wages that are below the threshold for income support (state benefit).[29] Combined with 'qualifications inflation' and the changing nature of the employment market, these developments have inevitably affected children's expectations as regards their future careers. Fewer young people now expect to have a job for life, or to be employed anywhere other than in the marginal service areas of the economy. The government's introduction in 1999 of a lower minimum wage for young workers as compared with the rest of the population provides a clear indication of its priorities in this respect. With the abolition of student maintenance grants and the withdrawal of benefits for sixteen and seventeen-year-olds, young people are increasingly relying on their parents for accommodation and financial support: 64 per cent of young people aged sixteen to twenty-four now live with their parents.

Meanwhile the number of homeless young people – who have either rejected or been denied this possibility – rose dramatically during the 1980s and 1990s: the Children's Society estimates that 50,000 young people, most aged about fifteen, run away from home every year, the majority in order to escape abuse.[30]

While these developments strictly apply to 'youth' rather than 'children', they do effectively extend the period of young people's dependency and institutionalization. It should be noted, however, that paid employment is not confined to those above the minimum school-leaving age. Like the introduction of compulsory education, the child labour laws enacted in the late nineteenth and early twentieth centuries have been seen as a precondition of contemporary childhood. Yet evidence suggests that significant numbers of children – not just in the developing world, but also in industrialized Western countries – are involved in paid work, whether legally or not. Surveys over the past decade have suggested that more than one-third of children may engage in paid employment at any one time; and that as many as two-thirds may do so before they reach sixteen.[31] Such work is typically menial delivery or waiting work, and since much of it is illegal, it is often inadequately regulated (for example in terms of health and safety) and very badly paid. This phenomenon is not confined to children living in poorer families. On the contrary, it has been suggested that paid work among children is partly a response to the growth in teenage consumer markets, and that it is seen by children as a means of earning money for luxuries that parents are unwilling or unable to afford.[32]

Free time?

Historians have argued that children's leisure time has been increasingly privatized and subjected to adult supervision over the past fifty years.[33] Broadly speaking, the principal location of children's leisure has moved from public spaces (such as the street) to family spaces (the domestic living room) to private spaces (the bedroom). Anxiety about 'stranger danger', traffic and other threats to children has encouraged parents to furnish the home (and particularly the child's bedroom) as a diverting, technologically rich alternative to the perceived risks of the outside world.[34] This development has also been made possible by the overall increase in disposable income, and by specific innovations such as central heating; as well as by the decline in the average size of families, which means that children are now more likely to have their own bedrooms in the first place.

Thus, research in the UK suggests that children are now much more confined to their homes, and much less independently mobile, than they were twenty years ago.[35] Since the 1970s, 'playing out' has steadily been displaced by domestic entertainment (particularly via television and computers) and – especially among more affluent classes – by supervised leisure activities such as organized sports, music lessons and so forth. The availability of public play areas has been reduced, both in towns – where population density has increased – and in the countryside – where factory farming has rendered large areas inaccessible. Children are now twice as likely to be driven to school than they were in the 1970s (although, of course, car ownership has also more than doubled over the same period). Nevertheless, children from the most affluent families make nearly one-third more journeys than those from the least affluent.

As I have implied, these developments are partly a consequence of growing perceptions of risk.[36] Parents' fears of violence against children have risen to a much greater extent than the actual incidence of such crimes, not least as a result of the high-profile reporting of a small number of cases. While the incidence of child abductions has increased, for example, most of these are by family members (particularly estranged fathers); and the incidence of child murders has remained stable over several decades. Three-quarters of those convicted for violent offences against children are family members, although this proportion is significantly reduced where fifteen and sixteen-year-olds are concerned. It is the home rather than the street that is the main site for crimes against children.

Another key element here is the threat represented by motorized transport, which in many cities continues to increase exponentially. In fact, while road accidents are still the major cause of death among children (accounting for three-quarters of the deaths of ten to fourteen-year-olds), they have declined by two-thirds since the early 1970s. Statistics of this kind may obscure a complex process of cause and effect: high perceptions of risk may mean that parents are less willing to allow their children to go out of the house unaccompanied, which will in turn result in a lesser incidence of the dangers they fear. Yet the net result is that children's autonomy is further restricted.

Children's experience of the media will be dealt with in much more detail in the following chapter, but it is possible to trace a similar process here too. Broadly speaking, public entertainment (the cinema) has given way to domestic entertainment (family television) and thence to individualized entertainment (by way of a TV, computer or games console in the child's bedroom). Of course, this

picture is unduly schematic: among other things, it tends to underestimate the social dimensions of contemporary media use (computer
games, for instance, are a major focus of peer group interaction); and
it tends to neglect the changes in these media themselves – children's
admissions to the cinema have in fact increased in the 1990s, although
children are now much more likely to be accompanied by adults (and
to be attending 'family films') than they were in the early 1970s.[37]
Furthermore, it is important not to neglect the survival of more traditional cultural activities – and indeed, more traditional forms of play
and oral culture – among children. For example, children's reading
of books and use of public libraries have actually increased, albeit
not very significantly, in recent years; while more qualitative studies
suggest that children simply appropriate new media and technologies into traditional playground and outdoor games.[38]

If children's autonomy has in some respects been restricted as more
of their leisure time has come under the surveillance of parents, the
economic resources devoted to their leisure have also substantially
increased. Children's leisure has become inexorably tied up with the
'consumer revolution' of the postwar period; and in the process, many
leisure services that were previously provided by the state (libraries,
sports facilities, museums, youth clubs) have either fallen into decline or been required to reinvent themselves as commercial concerns – and have hence become less readily accessible to poorer
children. As I shall indicate in chapter 5, this is particularly the case
in relation to broadcasting.

On the other hand, the peer group culture of older children appears to be increasingly resistant to parental regulation; and in
several respects the onset of 'teenage rebellion' seems to have moved
steadily earlier. For example, young people are now having their
first sexual experiences at a much younger age than in previous decades; and they are maturing physically much sooner (across the century, the onset of menstruation has reduced by almost 2.5 years, and
increasing numbers of girls begin to menstruate at the age of ten).
The threat of AIDS may to some extent have changed sexual practices, although it has not resulted in widespread abstinence: 9 per
cent of people who are HIV-positive are teenagers. Rates of teenage
pregnancy increased significantly during the 1980s, although they
have since levelled off. Meanwhile, drugs are becoming an almost
taken-for-granted aspect of young people's recreational experiences:
despite the 'war on drugs', drug use among children is now at higher
levels than ever before. In 1996, approximately two-thirds of fourteen to fifteen-year-olds admitted that they had used illegal drugs,
while a similar proportion were drinking alcohol on a regular basis.

Numbers of registered drug addicts under the age of twenty-one more than doubled between 1990 and 1995.[39]

There is also increasing anxiety about the incidence of child crime, although statistics in this field are open to a range of interpretations.[40] The number of children found guilty of, or cautioned for, offences in the early 1990s was eight times the figure for the early 1980s; although the number of known child offences has fallen from its peak in the mid-1980s. Theft and burglary are the most common offences, and boys are much more likely to offend than girls by a ratio of more than three to one. Nevertheless, child crime remains confined to a minority: about 3 per cent of young offenders commit more than one-quarter of all such offences. And, of course, young people are much more at risk of victimization than other age groups: crime surveys suggest that a majority of children have been victimized in some way, although comparatively few (one-tenth) of such incidents are reported to the police.

Partly for these reasons, child crime has been one of the key social policy issues of the past decade. A small number of high-profile cases – notably the murder of two-year-old James Bulger by two ten-year-old boys in 1993 – have fuelled a drive towards much more punitive criminal justice policies. This culminated in the Crime and Disorder Act (1998), which (among other measures) lowered the age of criminal responsibility, making it possible for custodial sentences to be passed on children as young as ten, and enabled local authorities to impose curfews on children.[41] The late 1990s also saw the opening of the first of a number of privately run children's prisons. Meanwhile, there has been growing condemnation of the apparent lack of discipline in schools, again based on a small number of highly publicized cases: school exclusions are rising dramatically, 'truancy watch' schemes have been introduced in many areas, and the government has appointed 'hit squads' of school inspectors to sort out particularly troublesome schools.

Blurring boundaries?

Of course, there is a great deal more that could be added to this picture. My account undoubtedly oversimplifies some highly complex issues; and it does little justice to the inconsistencies and contradictions that characterize all forms of social change. Nevertheless, it does suggest that in several major respects the status and experience of children *as a distinct social group* have changed significantly over the past two or three decades. Whether this can be seen to amount to a 'crisis' in childhood – or indeed to its demise – is a more complex question.

In chapter 1, I argued that our contemporary conception of childhood – which goes on to determine the material realities of children's lives – is premised on various forms of *separation* or *exclusion*. As numerous historians have shown, the modern 'invention' of childhood depended on the separation between adults and children, and the exclusion of children from domains of life that were deemed to be exclusively 'adult'. This was achieved by, among other things, the partial removal of children from the workplace and the streets, and their containment within the institution of the school and the family home. Children were defined by their exclusion from the public worlds of commerce and politics, and by their subjection to regimes of moral and pedagogic guardianship expressly designed to police the boundaries between adults and children.

The arguments considered in the previous two chapters all suggest that these boundaries have become increasingly blurred in recent years – even if the consequences of this phenomenon are assessed in very different ways. In some respects my account confirms this view, although in others it clearly challenges it. The boundaries have indeed become blurred; yet in several respects, they have also been reinforced and extended.

Thus, on the one hand, children have increasingly gained access to aspects of 'adult' life, and particularly to those which are deemed *morally* inappropriate, or which they are seen as too psychologically 'immature' to handle. One could point, for example, to children's knowledge and experience of areas such as sex and drugs; their experience of divorce and family breakdown; their involvement in crime, both as perpetrators and as victims; and their increasing status as a consumer market. Although many of these phenomena apply particularly to older children, they do imply that children in general now know about – and in some cases actively seek out – many experiences that were hitherto denied to them. It would be an exaggeration to claim that these developments amount to the 'death of childhood', but they do suggest that the *end* of 'childhood' is arriving several years earlier than in the past.

On the other hand – and partly in response to this – children have been increasingly segregated and excluded. They now spend much more of their lives confined in institutions that are overtly intended to prepare them for, and yet to keep them safe from, the adult world. This is most obviously the case in relation to the extension of schooling, and children's confinement in the home; as well as in more punitive measures, for example in the area of child crime. Both in terms of work and play, children's lives have become increasingly institutionalized – and in the case of leisure, increasingly privatized or domesticated.[42] Particularly in the home, children have also become the focus for a great deal more investment, both of economic resources and of parental concern – if not so much of parental time. Children's leisure time has become more 'curricularized' and more consumer oriented, and the difference between the two is not always easy to identify. On this account, 'childhood' – or at least young people's period of dependency on adults – is being extended rather than curtailed. Children, it would seem, no longer want to be children; and hence we must try even harder to encourage them to remain so.

One fairly obvious way of interpreting these developments is through notions of risk and security, which have become prominent in the social sciences over the past decade.[43] Thus, it could be argued that children are increasingly under threat from dangers of various kinds: family breakdown, poverty, crime, economic exploitation and abuse. And it could be suggested that traditional sources of security for children – particularly that represented by the nuclear family – have been steadily undermined. In this context, contemporary social policies, not least those favoured by the current Labour government, could be seen as an attempt to legislate against the most obvious consequences of insecurity, by disciplining deviation and ensuring that children are kept more rigorously under adult supervision.

These developments are essentially political, in the sense that they are primarily to do with changing relations of power and authority between adults and children. Yet the contemporary politics of childhood can be interpreted in several ways. While there are some who wish to reassert traditional relationships, and to return to an era in which children were 'seen but not heard', there are others who welcome these changes as a much-needed increase in children's power and autonomy.

Thus, on the positive side, one can identify a process of *individuation*, a kind of extension of the rights of citizenship to children.[44] In this sense, children could be seen as one of a number of social groups (such as women, ethnic minorities, or the disabled) which were previously excluded from the exercise of social power, and are now being given access to it. Thus, children are now enjoying rights to education, legal representation and welfare provision which were previously denied to them. The issue of children's rights has also become much more significant in recent years. Following the UN Convention on the Rights of the Child, many countries have passed new legislation to protect children's civil rights, both in the family and in their dealings with state agencies. In the UK, for example, the Children Act (1989) represents an uneasy compromise between this new agenda of rights and participation and a more traditional emphasis on child protection; yet it requires that individual children's wishes should be taken into account much more explicitly by welfare agencies and government bodies, and in judicial proceedings (for example in divorce cases).[45] While there is often a significant gap between rhetoric and reality here, it would seem that children's voices are now beginning to be heard.

As I shall indicate in more detail in subsequent chapters, this broadly political empowerment of children has been accompanied (and to some extent driven) by a kind of economic empowerment, at least as defined by its advocates. Children have gained a new status, not merely as citizens but also as consumers: they are seen as an increasingly valuable market, but also as one that is extremely difficult to reach and control. They cannot simply be 'exploited', much less patronized by adults who claim to know what is good for them. Here, too, substantial energy is being expended on ensuring that children's voices will be heard. Yet, in the process, the distinction between the citizen and the consumer may have become increasingly difficult to sustain.[46]

Much more negatively, one can point to the ways in which the notion of childhood acts as a focus for broader concerns about social change, 'indiscipline' and moral collapse – and hence as a justification for more authoritarian social policies.[47] As I have argued, these concerns are decidedly double-edged: children are seen here as both threatened and threatening. In debates about child abuse, for example, children are increasingly constructed as helpless victims, in need of special protection by adults – even though it is adults (and indeed family members) who represent the primary cause of risk. At the same time, as in the debates around child crime, children are explicitly identified as a danger to the rest of us. Here the victimization of children by adults is largely ignored in favour of the need to discipline children ever more harshly and at an ever younger age. Children's apparently premature experience of aspects of 'adult' life is seen here not as a symptom of empowerment or as an extension of autonomy, but as an indication of wider failures in the social order; and it results in calls for children's freedom from adult control to be restricted rather than enhanced. Children's rights take second place here to the rights of parents – and if parents are seen to be 'failing', then they will in turn be subjected to the prerogatives of government.

However one interprets these developments, it is clear that the process of defining childhood has become increasingly problematic

– and increasingly urgent – in recent decades. As I have suggested, 'the child' only comes into existence in this way: it is defined primarily by distinguishing it from what it is not – that is, 'the adult'. The boundaries, in other words, have to be perpetually drawn and redrawn; and they are subject to a constant process of negotiation. Yet, over the past twenty or thirty years, the status of childhood and our assumptions about it have become more and more unstable. The distinctions between children and other categories – 'youth' or 'adults' – have become ever more difficult to sustain; but they are also increasingly significant, both in terms of social policy and in terms of the economy.

Unequal childhoods

If the status and experience of children as a distinct social group is certainly changing, we should also take note of significant developments *within* that group. At least some social differences appear to have been eroded over the past three decades. This is most clearly the case in relation to gender. While there are still significant disparities in the earning power of adult men and women, the inequalities between boys and girls have steadily reduced in all sorts of areas, from educational achievement through to pocket money allowances – not to mention crime figures.

At the same time, children have become more ethnically diverse: ethnic minorities constitute 9 per cent of children in the UK, as compared with 5.5 per cent of the population overall. Here, too, inequalities in educational achievement, youth unemployment and poverty have begun to reduce over the past decade, although young blacks and Asians are still more likely to be poorly paid, and Afro-Caribbean boys are significantly more likely to be excluded from school. However, it is among white working-class boys that the lowest levels of educational achievement are now being recorded; and 50 per cent of black eighteen-year-olds are in full-time education, as against 30 per cent of whites.[48]

However, the most striking development here (not only in the UK but in many other industrialized countries) has been the increasing polarization between rich and poor. Britain now possesses a growing underclass, in which families with children are disproportionately represented. For example, the proportion of dependent children living in households with less than half the average net income trebled from 1.4 million (one in ten) to 4.2 million (almost one in three) between 1979 and 1992. The percentage of children living in families without a full-time wage-earner rose from 20 per cent in 1979 to 36 per cent in 1993. One million children are now living in housing that is officially classified as unfit for human habitation.[49] Lone parents and families with disabled children are much more likely to be poor. While this development can partly be traced to broader economic changes, much of it follows directly from government policies during the 1980s and 1990s, for example in areas such as welfare provision and taxation. Despite an overall increase in disposable household income, income inequality grew faster in the UK during this period than in any other industrialized country (with the exception of New Zealand). For the poorest 10 per cent, average incomes are now no higher than they were ten years ago; while the richest 10 per cent now controls the same amount of income as the poorest 50 per cent.

This development has predictable implications in terms of the 'quality of life'. Here again, overall improvements tend to mask increasing inequalities. In the area of child health, for example, mortality rates for children have continued to fall, albeit not as quickly as in other countries (99.2 per cent of children now survive their first year, as against 97 per cent in 1950); while the average height of children (which is a good indicator of overall health) has risen by almost 1.4 centimetres since the early 1970s. Nevertheless, working-class children are more likely to suffer chronic sickness than middle-class children, and to have tooth decay; while doctors see a greater proportion of poorer children for almost all categories of consultation, especially for serious illnesses. And, of course, children from low-income families are much less likely to receive adequate daily nutrients, and more likely to go without meals when money is short.

As I have indicated, these widening inequalities have implications for almost every area of children's lives. Poorer children have fewer educational opportunities and achieve less well at school; they have fewer leisure-time options, and are less mobile; and they are obviously disadvantaged when it comes to purchasing the kinds of consumer goods and services that many critics have regarded as the defining symbols of contemporary childhood. Furthermore, poverty both compounds and is compounded by other forms of disadvantage, such as the effects of racism or family breakdown. Taken together, these factors suggest that rich and poor children are increasingly living different childhoods.

Childhood, then, certainly is changing. Children's lives are both more institutionalized and privatized, and less stable and secure, than they were thirty years ago. The boundaries between children and adults have been eroded in some areas, but strongly reinforced and extended in others. Children have been empowered, both politically and economically; but they have also been subjected to increasing adult surveillance and control. And the inequalities between rich and poor children have grown exponentially.

As we shall see in the following chapter, these changes have specific implications in terms of children's relationships with the electronic media, although it would be highly simplistic to regard the media as their primary cause. We cannot regard the media in isolation – as the agent of childhood's demise, or alternatively of its empowerment. On the contrary, it is essential to situate children's relationships with the media in the context of the broader social and historical changes I have outlined here.

5

Changing Media

Concerns about the changing nature of childhood have many echoes in contemporary debates about the electronic media. Here, too, traditional boundaries are seen to be breaking down and established certainties are being undermined. Even for those of us who have grown up in the age of television, the electronic media of the future will, it is argued, be more and more difficult to comprehend and control.

In this chapter, I review some of these changes in the media environment, placing particular emphasis on their implications for children and young people. As in the previous chapter, my aim here is to paint a broad picture rather than to provide a comprehensive account; and my examples are illustrative rather than necessarily definitive. My account is, again, fairly conventionally organized. I look in turn at *technologies*, *institutions*, *texts* and *audiences*.[1] In each of these areas, I will suggest, children and young people are in the 'avant-garde' of many contemporary developments in the electronic media.

Historically, different academic paradigms in Media Studies have tended to emphasize certain of these dimensions at the expense of others, and hence to arrive at very different estimations of the 'power' of the media. By contrast, my emphasis here is on the *interaction* between them, without conceding a necessary priority to any one. Implicitly, then, I am suggesting that the 'power' of the media is not merely a *possession* – or a function or consequence – of either technologies, institutions, texts or audiences. On the contrary, it is inherent in the *relationships* between them.[2]

Here again, my analysis is set against the contrasting accounts considered in chapters 2 and 3. As I shall indicate, it is possible to read these changes in very different ways. On the one hand, there is a

broadly pessimistic scenario, which echoes the concerns of Neil Postman and the authors of *Kinderculture*, discussed in chapter 2. This
account is informed by a kind of 'mass society' theory; and it is one
which has an appeal right across the political spectrum, from the
critique of capitalism developed by the Frankfurt School through to
the more overt elitism of some conservative cultural critics. From
this perspective, it is argued that we are moving into an era of increasing fragmentation and atomization, in which notions of common culture, the public sphere and participatory citizenship have
effectively been eroded. What appears to be increased choice is in
fact just more of the same – homogeneity masquerading as diversity. The public citizen has been reduced to the private consumer, at
the mercy of control by the consciousness industries.[3]

On the other hand, there is a much more optimistic scenario, which
is reflected in the enthusiasm of Douglas Rushkoff and others, discussed in chapter 3. This account is broadly 'populist'; and again it is
one that unites those of outwardly quite different political persuasions, from the commercial entrepreneurs who are leading the 'communications revolution' to the radical exponents of 'active audience'
theory in academic Cultural Studies.[4] Here, the emphasis is placed
on the liberating potential of new media technologies: they are seen
to increase the democratic control of communications, to transform
consumers into producers, and to enable new voices to be heard and
new forms of identity or subjectivity to be represented. Old constraints and hierarchies are being broken down as opportunities are
created for new, more challenging, more interactive cultural forms.

Of course, the debate is not always so starkly polarized – although
there is undoubtedly a good deal of mutual caricature on both sides,
not least within the academy. Here again, I want to acknowledge
some truth in both perspectives, although both appear to underestimate the resistances to change, and its ambivalent and contradictory nature. More significantly, however, I want to suggest that the
terms of this debate are themselves misleading. To regard children
as *either* passive victims of the media *or* as active consumers is effectively to view them in isolation from broader processes of cultural
and social change. This argument, and its implications in terms of
research, will be developed more fully in chapter 6.

Technologies

As we have seen, discussions of young people's relationships with
the media often attribute a determining power to technology. Such

arguments are problematic for several reasons. Technologies do not produce social change, irrespective of the contexts in which they are used; nor are the inherent differences between technologies as absolute as is often supposed. Nevertheless, in combination with other developments, new technologies – particularly digital technologies – have effectively revolutionized the process of production in almost every area of the media industries, and are now rapidly transforming distribution and reception.[5]

Recent changes in media technologies can be understood, first, as a simple matter of *proliferation*. Since the advent of television, for example, the domestic TV screen has become the delivery point for an ever broader range of media and means of distribution. The number of channels has grown, both on terrestrial television and (more spectacularly) with the advent of cable and satellite, while the screen is also being used for video in various forms, as well as for the multiplying forms of digital media, from computer games and CD-Roms to the internet.

Secondly, there has been a process of *convergence* between information and communications technologies. Like the other developments identified here, this has of course been commercially driven; but it has also been made possible by digitization. Over the coming decade, the advent of digital TV, internet set-top boxes, on line shopping, video-on-demand and other developments will increasingly blur the distinctions between linear broadcast media such as television and 'narrowcast', interactive media such as the internet.

These developments have implications, thirdly, in terms of *access*. Hitherto expensive and inaccessible aspects of media production, and a whole range of new media forms and options, have been brought within reach of the domestic consumer. The retail price of video camcorders, digital cameras and multimedia PCs has steadily fallen as their capabilities have increased; and, at least in principle, the internet represents a means of communication and distribution that is no longer exclusively controlled by a small elite. In the process, it is argued, the boundaries between production and consumption, and between mass communication and interpersonal communication, are beginning to break down.

To describe the process in this way is to suggest that absolute distinctions between technologies – between print and television, for example, or between television and the internet – can no longer be sustained, if indeed they ever could. At least in the case of the media, new technologies rarely replace old ones, even if they sometimes change the ways in which they are used. Attempting to separate 'traditional' and 'modern' technologies, and to isolate the social

or cognitive effects of either, is thus increasingly fraught with difficulty.

These changes have several specific implications for children.[6] As
I have noted, children and parents are among the most significant
markets for these new technologies. Cable and satellite television,
for example, have been strongly targeted towards the younger audience, while much of the advertising and promotion for home computers trades in a popular mystique about children's natural affinity
with technology.[7] In the UK, the take-up of satellite and cable television, video, camcorders and home computers is proportionately much
higher in households with children: 35 per cent of households with
children now subscribe to cable or satellite television, for example,
as compared with 25 per cent overall; while 90 per cent of households with children have access to a VCR as compared with 75 per
cent overall. Meanwhile, two-thirds of children live in homes with a
computer or games console, which is a significantly higher figure
than for any other age group. Sales of 'advanced' computer games
consoles and PCs with CD-Rom capability have grown exponentially:
families with young children recorded an increase in computer ownership between 1993 and 1996 of over 50 per cent, compared with
the overall increase of 23 per cent.[8]

This growing access to technology makes it possible for it to be
used in more individualized ways. Thus, children are also more likely
to live in households with two or more TV sets: half of seven to ten-
year-olds and three-quarters of eleven to fourteen-year-olds in the
UK now have televisions in their bedrooms, and a significant proportion have VCRs. These tendencies are encouraged by the general
democratization of relationships within the family, and the relax-
ation in parental authority, identified in chapter 4; although collective uses of media – 'family viewing' – are very far from disappearing.[9]

Similarly, many of the new cultural forms made possible by these
technologies are primarily identified with the young. Computer
games, for example, are predominantly addressed to the children's
and youth market; while popular music (particularly dance music)
is increasingly generated by digital technology, via sampling,[10] editing and other software. At the same time, the increasing accessibility
of this technology is enabling some young people to play a more
active role as cultural producers. More and more teenagers have home
computers in their bedrooms that can be used to create music, to
manipulate images or to edit video to a relatively professional standard. These technologies also permit a highly conscious, and potentially subversive, manipulation of commercially produced media
texts, for example through sampling and re-editing found material,

alongside 'original' creative production. In the process, they make a mockery of copyright and of notions of intellectual property.

Of course, it is important not to exaggerate the scale of these developments. At least in the UK, only a small minority of children are regular users of the internet, for example: most current estimates tend to be less than 6 per cent. Likewise, very few children are exploiting the creative potential of digital media: their home computers are primarily used for playing games and for word-processing homework.[11] Levels of access will certainly increase significantly in the coming years as prices fall; yet there is also a growing polarization here between the 'technology rich' and the 'technology poor'. In the UK, for example, fewer than half as many working-class children have access to a PC at home as compared with middle-class children; while the percentage with internet links is one-tenth of the figure for middle-class children.[12] As with other new technologies (not least television in the 1950s), those with greater disposable income are almost always the 'early adopters': they have newer and more powerful equipment, and more opportunities to develop the skills and competencies that are needed to use it. This applies not just to home computers but also to cable and satellite television, which (despite their rather 'downmarket' image) are significantly less likely to be found in the lowest income families. This polarization has been apparent for several years in the United States, where there is an enormous divergence between children who have access to cable television, whose parents can afford to buy or rent videos, and who live in areas where a broad range of material is available to them, and those who have none of these opportunities.[13]

As we shall see in more detail in subsequent chapters, children's growing access to media is generating increasing concern about their exposure to material hitherto largely confined to the domain of adults, most obviously to 'violence' and to pornography. In many instances, this has led to growing calls for stricter regulation and censorship; and to the search for a 'technological fix' in the form of the V-chip or so-called 'blocking software'.

This concern is partly a response to technological developments. When compared with older technologies such as the cinema or broadcast television, for example, media such as video and cable/satellite television significantly undermine the potential for centralized control of the media by national governments. Video, for example, makes it possible to copy and circulate material to a much greater extent than has ever been the case with moving images before. It also makes it possible to view the material, not in a public space to which access can be controlled, but in the private space of the home; and to do so at a time chosen by the viewer, not by a centralized scheduler working with ideas about what it is appropriate for children to watch. In this respect, video evades constraints of time and space; and it effectively shifts responsibility for control from the public sphere to the private sphere – from the state to the individual. As such, despite the best efforts of the industry, video is extremely difficult to police. The pirate video trade in the UK is currently estimated to be worth between one-third and one-half of the legal industry; and despite the very heavy penalties that can be imposed on those who supply it, a large majority of children have seen material on video which they should not legally have been able to obtain.[14]

This question of control is further accentuated by the advent of digital technology. It is now possible not only for material to be easily copied and circulated, but also for it to be sent across national boundaries on the telephone line. At present, the internet is the ultimate decentralized medium: anyone with access to the technology can 'publish' anything they like, and anyone else can get access to it – although in fact it is increasingly becoming a commercial medium, in which users are required to pay for information, either directly or indirectly through advertising (the costs of which are passed on to the consumer through the higher price of goods). The legal position here is even more confused: there is considerable uncertainty about whether the internet is a 'publishing' medium (in which case internet service providers might be liable to prosecution for carrying obscene material) or simply a 'communication' medium like the telephone.

Institutions

These technological developments have helped to reinforce – and have been reinforced by – fundamental institutional and economic changes in the media industries. Three broad tendencies can be identified here, each of which is symptomatic of much more widespread economic and political changes.[15]

First, we can point to the growing *privatization* of the media, and the relative decline in public sector provision. The large majority of new media outlets and forms identified above are commercially driven; and even those which initially were not – such as the internet – are increasingly subject to commercial imperatives, such as the need to carry advertising. Technological convergence has been mirrored by economic convergence, as tendencies towards monopolization have been fostered by the 'free market' ideologies of national governments. Meanwhile, public sector provision – for example in broadcasting – has gradually been commercialized from within; and regulation concerned with the social and cultural functions of the media is gradually being abandoned in favour of a narrower concern with morality.

One inevitable consequence of this development has been the *integration* of the media industries, both vertically and horizontally. The media market is now dominated by a small number of multinational conglomerates; and for nationally based companies, success in the international market is increasingly recognized as a necessity for survival.[16] In practice, globalization tends to mean US domination: most of the UK's cable and satellite industry, for example, is effectively owned by American companies. However, in this new world economy, even this is far from assured: companies like Sony, Matsushita and Bertelsmann, for instance, have major stakes in both US and world markets. Significantly, most of these corporations are cross-media empires: they integrate broadcasting, publishing, media and digital technology, and in many cases have interests in both hardware and software. *Vertical* integration has thus been accompanied by a form of *horizontal* integration. In this new environment, the media are no longer simply a means of delivering audiences to advertisers. They are also increasingly a means of delivering audiences to other media.

On the other hand, it is also possible to identify forms of *fragmentation*, at the level of both production and consumption. Thus, there has been a move towards casualized labour and 'outsourcing' over the past two decades, which has been particularly notable in the traditionally centralized industry of broadcasting. While some have argued that this has made for greater participation among hitherto underrepresented groups, small-scale 'independent' production is also highly precarious. Meanwhile, as we shall see below, audiences are also becoming much more specialized and fragmented, as increasing competition necessarily dictates a move towards 'niche marketing'.

To some extent, these developments reinforce particular tendencies that are implicit in technological change. Indeed, the pace of technological change is itself largely driven by capitalism's restless search for new markets. As the rate of obsolescence of 'old' technologies – and the software they use – accelerates, so too does the rate of profitability. Meanwhile, many of these new technologies, notably the internet and satellite television, cross national boundaries, effectively bypassing regulation at a national level. On the other hand, the increasing accessibility of digital technology reduces the costs of entry to many areas of media production (and, in some cases, of distribution) and thereby contributes to a blurring of the distinction between 'amateur' and 'professional' producers.

These developments affect children in quite ambiguous ways. As I have noted, children have been 'discovered' as a new target market in the past few decades. In the case of commercial television, for example, children were not initially seen as an especially valuable audience. In the early decades of the US commercial system, programmes would only be provided for children at minimum cost, and at times when other audiences were not available to view;[17] and even in the UK, where the public service tradition has been very strong, children's television has been comparatively underfunded. In the contemporary era of niche marketing, however, children have suddenly become much more valuable: they are seen to have significant influence on parents' purchasing decisions, as well as substantial disposable income of their own. Thus, the advent of cable television in the UK has led to a plethora of specialist channels competing to attract the child audience; and both on terrestrial and non-terrestrial channels there has been a significant increase in the *amount* of provision for children, if not necessarily in its quality or diversity.[18]

These developments have led to growing calls to defend the tradition of public service broadcasting against the invasion of commerce. Commercialization has been seen to result in the inexorable 'dumbing down' of children's television: domestic production of genres such as contemporary drama and factual programmes has, it is argued, steadily lost out to the global dominance of US cartoons. In fact, the evidence on these points is quite ambivalent,[19] and the debate itself clearly invokes much broader questions about national identity and cultural value, which (as we shall see) are often defined very conservatively when it comes to children. Nevertheless, these developments have led to a significant (and decidedly double-edged) shift in thinking about the child audience, at least within the media industries: as I shall indicate in more detail below, the vulnerable child in need of protection has increasingly given way to the child as 'sovereign consumer'.[20]

However, some notes of caution are in order here too. In economics as in technology, there is a risk of determinism, a tendency which has been characteristic of a good deal of media sociology. In this case, it is far too easy to fall back on traditional notions of children as vulnerable to commercial exploitation or to the seductions of media imperialism. At least in the UK, domestically produced media remain popular among children as well as adults; and particular British television programmes continue to serve as a form of

'common culture', both among children and between the generations. As I have indicated, the majority of children do not have access to cable or satellite television – let alone to the internet – in the
first place. Furthermore, a significant proportion of commercial
products aimed at children simply fail to generate a profit: the market is more competitive, but it is also much more uncertain. To this
extent, there is some justification in producers' recurrent claim that
children are a volatile, complex market which cannot easily be
known and controlled.[21]

Texts

Perhaps the most obvious manifestation of the developments I have
described is in the changing characteristics of media texts. Indeed,
postmodern critics suggest that the very *status* of texts may be changing: it may no longer be relevant to regard texts in a traditional liter-
ary manner, as discrete, finished objects that somehow contain a given
meaning.[22]

On one level, this can be seen as a further consequence of technological and economic *convergence*. Here, too, there has been a significant blurring of boundaries, both between texts themselves and
between media. Distinctions between videos, computer games, movies, TV shows, advertisements and print texts have become increasingly irrelevant; and the media have become much more firmly bound
up with the merchandising of a whole range of other products. More
and more media texts are somehow 'spin-offs' or advertisements for
other texts or commodities.

As a result, *intertextuality* has become a dominant characteristic of
contemporary media. Many of the texts that are perceived as dis-
tinctively postmodern are highly allusive, self-referential and ironic.
They self-consciously draw on other texts in the form of pastiche,
homage or parody; they juxtapose incongruous elements from different historical periods, genres or cultural contexts; and they play
with established conventions of form and representation. In the process, they implicitly address their readers or viewers as knowing,
'media literate' consumers.

Finally, many of these new media forms are characterized by types
of *interactivity*. As we have seen, some of the more utopian advocates of interactive multimedia have seen it as a means of liberation
from the constraints of more traditional 'linear' media such as film
and television. Hypertext, CD-Roms and computer games have been
seen to abolish the distinction between 'reader' and 'writer': the reader

(or player) is no longer a passive subject of the text – and indeed the only text is the one the reader chooses to 'write'.

These kinds of claims about the characteristic forms of postmodern culture need to be approached with considerable caution, however. Such arguments are often based on unrepresentative examples, and on relatively superficial characteristics of texts. Furthermore, many of these developments could be seen to be dictated by a primarily economic logic. Thus, intertextuality, pastiche and parody often serve as little more than a form of 'window-dressing' for texts that are in all other respects highly conventional. Indeed, it could be argued that 'irony' has become just another marketing device, enabling media corporations to secure additional profit by recycling existing properties. Likewise, intertextuality could be seen simply as a consequence of increasing commodification, and the need to exploit successes across a wider range of media within a shorter time-scale. And despite the potential for interactivity, there is an undeniable gap between rhetoric and reality in a great deal of commercial software: many so-called 'interactive' texts are far from interactive, offering a fixed and highly circumscribed repertoire of possibilities.

Nevertheless, many of these characteristics apply with particular force to media texts that are aimed at – or most popular with – children and young people.[23] Thus, many of the most innovative new cultural forms have begun by being targeted at this audience, and only later reach out to the adult market. One could point, for example, to the ironic, self-conscious intertextuality of contemporary comics; the use of sampling in rap and dance music; the allusive, montage-based style of music videos; the convergence of music, visual arts and electronic media in club culture; or the genuinely interactive – and highly complex – nature of some computer games. And for all the inflated rhetoric that surrounds 'cyberculture', there are some highly innovative uses of the internet among a small minority of young people that genuinely do point to its emergence as a distinctive cultural form.

However, these characteristics are not only to be found in the more arcane areas of youth culture: they can also be detected in many forms of mainstream popular culture aimed at younger children. Many of the most popular cartoons and TV magazine programmes for children, from *The Simpsons* to *Live and Kicking*, are permeated with references to other texts and genres, sometimes in the form of direct quotation or sampling. They raid existing cultural resources – both from high culture and from the popular culture of the past and present – in a fragmentary and often apparently parodic manner. Comparing current animation series with those of thirty years ago, one is struck not just by their rapid pace, but also by their irony and intertextuality, and their complex play with reality and fantasy. Meanwhile, one of the most striking developments in the UK over the past few years has been the growing popularity of 'retro-TV', particularly of the more knowing and camp 1960s series: programmes like *Thunderbirds*, *Batman*, *The Avengers* and *The Man From UNCLE* have all been rerun, not just as schedule fodder, but with promotion that marks them out as appropriate viewing for a self-consciously 'media-wise' young audience.

Yet TV programmes are not just TV programmes: they are also films, records, comics, computer games and toys – not to mention T-shirts, posters, lunchboxes, drinks, sticker albums, food, and a myriad of other products. Children's media culture increasingly crosses the boundaries between texts and between traditional media forms, most obviously in the case of phenomena such as *Teenage Mutant Ninja Turtles*, *Super Mario Brothers* or *Mighty Morphin' Power Rangers*. In this process, the identity of the 'original' text is far from clear: these commodities are packaged and marketed as integrated phenomena, rather than the text coming first and the merchandising following on. And this development is not confined to the work of exclusively 'commercial' corporations, as is illustrated by the success of public service productions such as *Sesame Street* and most recently the BBC's *Teletubbies*.

Disney is of course the classic example of this phenomenon.[24] Right from the early days of the Mickey Mouse clubs, merchandising and subsequently theme parks have been a key dimension of the enterprise, and in fact it is these aspects which have guaranteed its continuing profitability. However, this horizontal integration is now moving to a different scale. Once you have seen the latest Disney movie, you can catch the spin-off episodes on TV on the Disney Channel, or meet the characters at the theme park; you can visit the Disney store at your local mall and stock up on the video, the posters, the T-shirts, and other merchandise; you can collect the 'free gifts' of character toys in cereal packets and fast-food restaurants; and if you are being digital, you can buy the animated storybook on CD-Rom, play the computer game, visit the website, and so on. Children are very much in the vanguard of what the critic Marsha Kinder calls 'trans-media intertextuality' – and, as she argues, the logic of this development is primarily driven by profit.[25]

The same is true of popular music, as the success of performers like Madonna, Take That and the Spice Girls shows. Here again, perhaps the most obvious example is Michael Jackson. Michael Jackson as a musician or a singer is inseparable from Michael Jackson as a performer, as a video producer and film star, as an advertiser (at least until recently), as a charity worker, as an icon on T-shirts and posters, and – most spectacularly – as a public property, as someone who is the subject of a whole other set of texts, on TV, in the popular press, and in everyday conversation. Michael Jackson produces commodities, but he is also a commodity himself. And, of course, he is emblematic of many of the wider social changes that have been seen as characteristic of postmodernity, because of his fundamental ambiguity: he is simultaneously male and female, black and white (although of course it doesn't matter), and most problematically, an innocent child and a highly sexual adult.

Finally, it is important to recognize changes at the level of *content* – which (as we saw in chapter 2) are often those that cause most alarm among adult critics. At least in the UK, children's television has steadily changed over the past twenty years to incorporate topics such as sex, drugs and family breakdown that would previously have been considered taboo. Likewise, magazines and books aimed at the early teenage market have attracted widespread criticism for their frank and explicit treatment of such issues. The recent controversies surrounding London Weekend Television's sex education series *Love Bites*, for example, or award-winning 'realist' novels for teenagers like Robert Swindells' *Stone Cold* or Melvyn Burgess's *Junk* clearly illustrate the anxieties this can provoke.[26] Yet even cartoons aimed at very young children – from *Ninja Turtles* to *Biker Mice From Mars* – seem to play on 'adult' anxieties about environmental pollution, social decline and global destruction. And in mainstream popular culture for children there is a sensuality and a cynicism that would have been unthinkable even in the heady days of the 1960s.

Of course, it is vital not to ignore the significant continuities here. For all the differences between them, *The Simpsons* has a great deal in common with *The Flintstones*; *Teletubbies* with *Watch with Mother*; and Michael Jackson with Elvis Presley or Little Richard. Indeed, as popular texts from the past are increasingly recycled and appropriated in different ways by new generations, it is hard to make absolute distinctions on the basis of when they were originally produced.

Nevertheless, the media environment in which children are now participating is one which increasingly blurs the boundaries both between media and between texts themselves. As I have indicated, these developments are made possible by technological changes, but they are largely driven by commercial concerns. As such, this is an environment that assumes quite different kinds of competence and knowledge – and could be seen to encourage very different forms of 'activity' – on the part of audiences. Contemporary media are increasingly addressing children as highly 'media-literate' consumers. Whether they actually *are* more media literate, and indeed what we might mean by that, is a rather more complex question, however.

Audiences

In fact, the implications of these developments for audiences have been the subject of considerable debate. As we have seen, these arguments are often framed in terms of traditional concerns about the 'power' of the media. Thus, advocates of the 'communications revolution' have argued that audiences are increasingly 'empowered' by these new media, while critics have suggested that they are simply more open to manipulation and commercial exploitation. Yet in several areas, the implications of these changes are much less straightforward and much harder to predict.

Thus, it is frequently claimed that these developments will result in greater *choice* for consumers, while others argue that such choice is merely spurious. For example, the proliferation of television channels has led to a significant increase in the quantity of television available, even taking account of the fact that much of it is frequently repeated. Whether this increase will be sustained over the longer term is more debatable, however: the amount of new product cannot keep pace with the increase in outlets for it – not least because the audience for each channel is decreasing as more channels become available, and hence the funding for new productions will decline. In practice, therefore, what viewers are more likely to be offered is ever-increasing opportunities to watch the same things.[27]

Nevertheless, this in itself is a significant change: for those who have access to cable and satellite, the very act of 'watching television' is bound to be significantly different compared with the experience of those who only have access to terrestrial TV. On one level, these developments clearly do 'empower' viewers to schedule their own viewing, at least from the range of material that is available; yet they also raise more awkward questions about how viewers locate and select what they want to watch.

These issues are to some extent compounded by *interactivity*. Leaving aside for the moment the question of whether surfing the internet actually is more 'active' than surfing TV channels or browsing through a magazine (for example), there are significant questions about whether audiences actually *want* greater 'activity'. Research would suggest that a great deal of media use is far from committed or engaged: on the contrary, much of it is casual and distracted.[28]

Whether people will want to come home from school or work and navigate their way though interactive hypertext, or whether they would rather just relax in front of the telly, remains an open question – not least for producers and advertisers.

Even for those who are regular users, there is room for scepticism about the 'empowerment' that is apparently offered here. The internet clearly does allow users much greater control over the selection of content and the pace at which it is 'read'. Yet in the process it also permits much more detailed surveillance of consumer behaviour: it is now very easy to track users' movements between and within particular websites, and thereby to build up consumer profiles which can subsequently become the basis for targeted electronic advertising. Here again, there are new and problematic questions about the skills and competencies that are required to use these new media and (in particular) to *evaluate* what they make available.

Finally, as I have noted, these developments may result in a growing *fragmentation* of audiences, as texts are increasingly targeted at (and marketed to) specialized groups of consumers. Multi-channel television, for example, may bring about the decline of broadcasting (and the 'common culture' it makes possible) in favour of 'narrowcasting'; while the internet is the medium *par excellence* for those with specialist or minority interests. This development inevitably raises the question of whether we can continue to talk about a shared national culture, or indeed about culture that is shared between generations. As we move from a five-channel system to a thirty-channel system, and thence to a five hundred channel system, for example, television is inevitably becoming much less of a collective experience.

Nevertheless, announcements of the death of the 'mass audience' may be premature. Even in the US, where the majority of viewers have had a multichannel television system for many years, most viewing is still confined to a small number of network stations – although quite how long this situation will continue is open to question.[29] Again, industry researchers need to identify how far consumers actually *want* to pursue wholly individualized or 'customized' uses of media, or whether they want a more shared experience – at least to the extent of being able to talk about what they have seen the following day. Here again, there are questions about the *experience* of viewing or using new media that cannot simply be understood in terms of traditional notions of media 'power'.

While the eventual outcomes of these developments are difficult to predict, it is clear that children are regarded by many in the media industries as being in the 'avant-garde' of change – or at least that they are *positioned* in this way by the operations of the market. Children are encouraged to be the 'early adopters', and as such, they may serve as an indication of the future for all of us.

Thus, as I have noted, the take-up of new media in general is higher in households with children, and there is growing competition to attract the children's market. Children's television viewing in Britain has dropped by almost three hours a week since the mid-1980s; and the audience for terrestrial television is now significantly declining in cable and satellite households with children, while viewing of specialist children's channels is rising.[30] Children are also likely to have greater access to computers, games consoles, video and music technology, and so on. In several respects, children's uses of media do seem to be characterized by increasing choice, interactivity and diversity – although, as I have indicated, these opportunities are not equally available to all.

Nevertheless, the implications of these changes for children have been interpreted in highly contrasting ways. At least in the English-speaking world, sensational stories about the harm the media allegedly inflict on children have increasingly come to dominate the headlines. Journalists, of course, are primarily interested in such stories in so far as they are seen to provide 'good copy', and hence to sell newspapers, but they are assisted in this respect by those with other motivations. Thus, politicians routinely display the rigour of their educational policies by complaining about the anti-educational influence of 'trashy' soap operas or the 'dumbing down' of children at the hands of *Teletubbies*.[31] Religious groups build their evangelical crusades around condemnations of the materialistic influence and moral depravity of the contemporary media.[32] Meanwhile, academics seeking instant publicity only have to suggest that TV programmes like *The Big Breakfast* undermine children's attention span, or to condemn the 'ritualized humiliation' of *Gladiators* and *Blind Date*, to increase their column inches.[33] In recent years, the press has eagerly and uncritically published numerous examples of astonishingly weak 'academic research' purporting to show (for example) that up to one third of children were busily swapping computer pornography in the playground, or that young people were being encouraged to commit car crimes as a result of their exposure to video games.[34]

Significantly, much of this concern focuses on children's exposure to 'adult' media. What the *Daily Mail* in 1996 described as 'the scandal of the view-as-you-like generation'[35] reflects an acknowledgement that children are no longer restricted to material that is designed for them – although research suggests that in fact they have always preferred 'adult' media, at least in so far as they could gain access to them.[36] Thus, children are seen to be particularly at risk not just from screen violence but also from the negative images of family life in soap operas; and, of course, there is growing anxiety about the dangers of the internet, in the form of pornography and the seductions of paedophiles.[37] On the other hand, there is also concern about the introduction of what are seen as unsuitably 'adult' concerns in children's media – AIDS and homosexuality in children's drama programmes like *Grange Hill* and *Byker Grove*, or explicit advice on sexual positions in teenage magazines like *Bliss* and *More*.[38]

On one level, of course, these kinds of moral panics have always been with us: the fantasy of a Golden Age of childhood innocence and the view of media (of various kinds) as a corrupting influence have a very long history. And yet, as I shall argue in more detail in chapter 7, these concerns also take on different forms in different historical circumstances. Contemporary anxieties about the effects of the media on children are partly a displacement of much broader concerns about social change; but they are also a response to technological and cultural changes in the media themselves, changes which, as I have indicated, are inextricably tied up with the drive for new commercial markets. Of course, we should beware of the assumption that the headlines and editorials in the popular press are necessarily synonymous with public opinion. Yet the accelerating pace of change would suggest that these concerns are likely to intensify in the coming years.

If public debates about children and the media have become more and more preoccupied with defending children from harm – with a kind of moral protectionism – the discourses that circulate within the media industries seem to be moving in a rather different direction. Here, children are no longer predominantly seen as innocent and vulnerable to influence. On the contrary, they are increasingly regarded as sophisticated, demanding, 'media-wise' consumers. The attempt to protect and to educate children through media such as television has increasingly been condemned as paternalistic and patronizing. Adults, it is argued, have been talking down to children for far too long. It is none of their business – at least in the context of popular culture – to be telling children what to think and what not to think. This argument derives, on the one hand, from an explicitly liberationist emphasis on 'children's rights'; yet it has also been enthusiastically espoused by those who have championed children's role as *consumers*. For the latter, the commercialization of children's media culture is not a matter of exploitation, but on the contrary a means of liberation. In this new market-led environment, it is argued, children are at last being empowered to make their own

decisions about what they will experience and know about, without
the controlling hand of adults who purport to know what is good for
them.

This kind of shift is certainly apparent in the recent history of children's television.[39] The broadly 'child-centred' approach that flour-
ished in Britain under the regulated duopoly between the BBC and
the commercial companies in the 1960s and 1970s is increasingly losing ground to an essentially consumerist approach. The child viewer
is no longer seen as the developing consciousness of the psychological imagination, but as a sophisticated, discriminating, critical
consumer, an independent agent in the commercial marketplace.
Children have become 'kids'; and kids, we are told, are 'smart', 'savvy'
and 'street-wise'. Above all, they are 'media literate'. They are hard
to please; they see through attempts at deception and manipulation;
and they refuse to be patronized. Kids know what they want from
the media – and it is the job of adults to provide them with this,
rather than falling back on their own beliefs about what is good for
them.

This discourse is in turn often connected with arguments about
children's rights. Internationally, the most successful exponent of this
discourse has been the dedicated children's channel Nickelodeon.
What we find here is a rhetoric of empowerment, a notion of the
channel as a 'kids-only' zone, giving voice to kids, taking the kids'
point of view, as the friend of kids. This discourse is very explicit in
the statements of Nickelodeon executives,[40] but it is also reinforced
in the channel's publicity and on-screen continuity material. Significantly, children seem to be defined here primarily in terms of being
not adults. Adults are boring; kids are fun. Adults are conservative;
kids are fresh and innovative. Adults will never understand; kids
intuitively *know*.

These discursive changes clearly reflect broader changes in the status of children as a distinct social group, of the kind identified in the
preceding chapter. What remains most striking here is the way in
which economic and social changes are allied: there is a fundamental blurring or confusion between the notion of children as potential
or actual *citizens* and the notion of children as *consumers*. In the discourse of Nickelodeon, for example, the 'rights' that are being talked
about are essentially the rights of the consumer. Children have a right
to consume things that adults provide for them; and if children have
their own culture, it is a culture which adults have almost entirely
created for them – and indeed sold *to* them. Likewise, producers'
repeated assertions that children are 'demanding' or 'media-literate'
viewers often appear to mean simply that they are very quick to

change channels when they see something they don't like. In practice, therefore, this discourse does not define children as independent social or political actors, let alone offer them democratic control or accountability: it is a discourse of consumer sovereignty masquerading as a discourse of cultural rights.

Ultimately, however, the question of whether children can be seen as an 'active' audience or as 'passive' victims of the media – and whether these new developments encourage either tendency – cannot be answered in the abstract. Media power is not a 'zero-sum' game in which audiences are either powerful or powerless. Indeed, as I have suggested, the pattern of contemporary change raises new questions that go beyond the either/or choices that typically recur in this debate; and in investigating these questions, we need to take account of the diverse ways in which audiences use and interpret the media, and the social contexts in which they do so. As I shall indicate in chapter 6, the definitions of the child audience that circulate in academic research are also changing in this respect; yet it is certainly debatable whether these new ideas take adequate account of the broader changes in the media environment I have outlined here.

Back to the boundaries

Broadly speaking, it is possible to detect two sets of forces at play in the changes I have described. We might term these centrifugal and centripetal. On the one hand, there are forces pulling away from the centre, towards fragmentation, differentiation and individualization. On the other, there are forces reasserting centralized control, the power of the state or of capital – forces of homogeneity and uniformity. These forces operate at both the macro level of cultural policy and the micro level of everyday cultural experience: they characterize the global or the national and the local or the domestic. Many of these developments are driven by a complex combination of these tendencies; and it is for this reason that their political and cultural consequences are likely to prove quite contradictory.

Thus, new media technologies are bringing about a convergence of hitherto separate media and forms of communication that is largely subject to the operations of global capitalism. It could be argued that the media are merging into a form of endless intertextuality that is driven by commodification – a consumer culture that effectively swallows all in its path. Yet it could equally be argued that these same technologies undermine traditional forms of regulation and control. They make it possible for 'readers' to write their own texts, or to deconstruct and rewrite existing ones, in a great variety of ways. Constraints of geography and established social hierarchies no longer apply, as the media and channels of communication are becoming steadily more open to all – or at least to all who can afford them.

To return to our earlier metaphor, boundaries are being crossed and blurred in all sorts of ways here. Distinctions between production and consumption, between interpersonal and mass communication, between popular culture and high culture – all, it is argued, seem more and more irrelevant or redundant. Yet, on the other hand, boundaries are also being reasserted and redrawn. Media consumption and production are becoming increasingly individualized and privatized; while in relation to new technologies, the gaps between media 'haves' and 'have nots' are steadily widening.

The implications of these developments for children – and for the relations between adults and children – are equally double-edged. On the one hand, the boundaries appear to be blurring. To a much greater extent than broadcast television, new media technologies allow children access to material previously restricted to adults. Video, the internet and cable/satellite television make what Neil Postman terms 'adult secrets' available to children to a far greater extent than broadcast TV. Likewise, children can no longer be segregated from the world of consumption: while they may not have a disposable income, they are increasingly addressed as autonomous consumers, who are encouraged to make their own decisions about what they will buy, watch and read. Via the internet, they can communicate much more easily with each other and with adults, without even having to identify themselves as children. And even in the material that is produced explicitly for children, there are reflections of aspects of the world that were previously considered unsuitable for them to see or to know about.

Meanwhile, other boundaries are clearly being reasserted. As children's access to technology increases, they no longer have to watch or read what their parents choose. As the 'niche market' of children grows in importance, they are increasingly able to confine themselves to media that are produced specifically for them. Furthermore, the new 'postmodern' cultural forms that characterize children's and youth culture are in several respects highly exclusive of adults: they depend on particular cultural competencies and on a prior knowledge of specific media texts (in other words, on a form of 'media literacy') that are only available to the young. While children may increasingly be sharing a global media culture with children from other parts of the world, they may be sharing less and less with their own parents.

It is important to make some distinctions here, however. It is primarily older children who are gaining access to 'adult' media, while it is younger children who are being most aggressively targeted as a new niche market. While the boundaries between older children and 'youth' may be blurring, the gap between younger and older children may also be widening. At the same time, it is not merely the child audience that is being redefined, but the 'youth' or 'adult' audiences too. While many older children increasingly aspire to the freedom they imagine to lie in 'youth', many adults have conversely come to revel in the irresponsibility and subversion they identify with childhood.[41]

Thus, the age at which childhood *ends* – at least as far as the media industries are concerned – seems to be steadily reducing. Children's television producers, for example, now acknowledge that the bulk of older children's viewing is given over to 'adult' programmes, and the content and style of programmes aimed at them clearly reflect this. The social issues addressed in a children's soap like *Grange Hill* for example, have much in common with those in adult soaps like *EastEnders*; while the visual style and pace of kids' magazine shows like *Live and Kicking* have clearly influenced the approach of 'adult' programmes like *The Big Breakfast*. While some critics have always complained about the precocity of children's programmes, others are now beginning to bemoan what they see as the infantilization of 'adult' television.

On the other hand, 'youth' has become an extremely elastic category, that seems to extend ever further upwards.[42] In their shared enthusiasm for Britpop, Nike sportswear, Nintendo or *South Park*, for example, ten-year-olds and forty-year-olds can be seen as members of a 'youth' market that is quite self-consciously distinct from a 'family' market. In this environment, 'youth' has come to be perceived as a kind of lifestyle choice, defined by its relationship to specific brands and commodities, and also available to those who fall well outside its biological limits (which are fluid in any case). In 'youth television' and now in the marketing of popular music, 'youth' possesses a symbolic significance that can refer to fantasy identities as much as to material possibilities – a phenomenon which itself can only help to widen the audience, and hence to enhance its market value. Recent advertising campaigns for the computer game *Mortal Kombat* and the Sony Playstation, for example, have been explicitly addressed to young adults, suggesting that the games console is now being marketed as an acceptable adult toy. Here again, this has led some commentators to suggest that adults, and particularly adult *men*, are thereby being encouraged to retreat into 'immature', adolescent fantasies.[43]

Perhaps the most striking example of this confusion of age categories in recent years has been the cult success of the BBC's preschool series *Teletubbies*, launched in 1997. Far from appealing only to the under-fives, the series attracted a substantial following among much older children and among students, manifested in 'unofficial' websites and clothing, and even articles in style magazines. While some of this interest was perhaps merely nostalgic, some of it was undoubtedly ironic and subversively 'childish' – and although it has undoubtedly generated a great deal of money from the phenomenon, the BBC has done its best to discourage what it clearly sees as an 'inappropriate' enthusiasm.[44]

As Marsha Kinder has argued,[45] this reconfiguring of the relationships between generations is highly paradoxical. On the one hand, there is an 'exaggeration of generational conflict', even a form of generational warfare, that is apparent both in the media (for instance, in the promotional strategies of Nickelodeon, or in movies such as *Home Alone*) and in political campaigning. At the same time, there are new forms of 'transgenerational address' that permit the same products to be marketed to different generations. According to Kinder, this convergence between generations works in both directions:

> not only are adult spectators 'paedocratised' but also young spectators are encouraged to adopt adult tastes, creating subject positions for a dual audience of infantilised adults and precocious children. These subject positions seem to provide an illusory sense of empowerment both for kids who want to accelerate their growth by buying into consumerist culture and for adults who want to retain their youth by keeping up with pop culture's latest fads.[46]

As these examples suggest, therefore, the ways in which consumers are differentiated, at least in terms of age, are becoming more fluid, complex and uncertain. As I have noted, the official rhetoric of the media industries has increasingly represented children as an active and discriminating audience: far from being malleable and easily exploited, they are seen as extremely difficult to attract and to control. And yet, in the increasingly competitive environment of contemporary media, such distinctions have a growing commercial significance. How old you are – or how old you imagine yourself to be – is increasingly defined by what you consume. To this extent, 'childhood', like 'youth', has become a symbolic commodity in its own right.[47]

Changing media childhoods

In several respects, therefore, recent developments in the media could be seen to reinforce – and be reinforced by – changes in childhood of the kind identified in the previous chapter. In general terms, the changes in both domains seem to be characterized by a growing sense of instability and insecurity: established distinctions and hierarchies are breaking down as new cultural forms and new identities emerge. In both domains, children seem much more difficult to define and control. Yet there is a distinct danger here of lapsing into postmodernist rhetoric, as though all that is solid were finally melting into air. This kind of argument often seems to represent an abandonment of explanation, a dissolution into infinite difference and fluidity. It can lead us to neglect the continuities and contradictions that are at stake; and it may ultimately render any kind of intervention impossible or redundant.

In this chapter and the previous one, I have pointed to several tendencies that belie this view. Thus, as I have argued, the boundaries between children and adults are being reinforced as well as blurred, both in relation to the media and more broadly. The separation between children's and adults' social and media worlds is becoming more apparent, even if the terms of that separation are being reconfigured. On one level, older children can no longer be so easily 'protected' from experiences that are seen to be morally damaging or developmentally unsuitable. The walls that surround the sacred garden of childhood have become much easier to climb. And yet children, particularly younger children, are increasingly participating in cultural and social worlds that are inaccessible, even incomprehensible, to their parents.

Likewise, children are becoming 'empowered' both as citizens and as consumers; although in both cases the nature of that empowerment has distinct limitations. Children have increasingly been perceived as a distinctive market; and in the process, their characteristics and needs have been more fully investigated and recognized – and, to some extent, catered for. Yet children's own expressions of their needs are largely confined to adult terms: by and large, they can only assert their need for services or products that adults can provide. In debates about the changing nature of schooling, leisure provision or the media, their voices are still rarely heard. Education, for example, has been redefined as a consumer service – although here the consumers are seen to be parents rather than children themselves. Likewise, despite the enthusiastic pursuit of children as consumers, the extent of democratic accountability in the media remains negligible. Ultimately, children's autonomous *rights* – as consumers or as citizens – remain very dimly acknowledged.

Meanwhile, children's leisure activities are becoming steadily more privatized and commercialized. More of their time is spent in the home or in supervised activity of some kind; while the cultural goods and services they consume increasingly have to be paid for in hard cash. The public spaces of childhood – both the physical spaces of play and the virtual spaces of broadcasting – have increasingly fallen into decline or been overcome by the commercial market. One inevitable consequence of this is that children's social and media worlds are becoming increasingly unequal. The polarization between rich and poor is positively reinforced by the commercialization of the media and the decline in public sector provision. Poorer children simply have less access to cultural goods and services: they live, not just in different social worlds, but in different media worlds as well.

And yet it remains the case that there are significant creative and democratic opportunities in these developments, particularly in the potential they offer for children to become producers of media in their own right. New technologies bring hitherto inaccessible means of cultural expression and communication within children's reach; and they could enable their views and perspectives to be heard much more widely. Far from contributing to social polarization, the media could be a means of enabling children to communicate across their differences. However, these developments will not take place automatically, or simply as a result of the availability of equipment. As I shall argue, we will need much more concerted and creative interventions at the level of social and cultural policy if children's rights as producers and consumers of electronic media are to be more fully realized.

6

Changing Paradigms

In the introduction to this book, I argued that 'childhood' should be seen as a *social construction*. This is not to imply that real individuals called children somehow do not exist, or that they are just the products of collective imagination. It is simply to suggest that the idea of child*hood*, and the thoughts and emotions that attach to it, are not given or fixed: on the contrary, they are subject to an ongoing process of definition – a social struggle over meaning.

I suggested in my introduction that 'childhood' was defined through discourses of two kinds: those that are directed *to* children and those that are *about* them. My primary focus in the previous chapter was on discourses addressed *to* the child audience – that is, on the media texts that are aimed at them, and the conditions under which they are produced, circulated and consumed. In this chapter, I move on to consider discourses *about* the child audience – and in particular, the various ways in which children's relationships with the electronic media have been defined and debated within academic research.

Of course, such research cannot be seen in isolation, as a mere disinterested pursuit of scientific truth. Indeed, in this case, research has been very powerfully determined by the kinds of discourses that tend to dominate the wider public arena. To a large degree, it is the discourse of politicians and journalists to which researchers are called on to respond; and it is this discourse that implicitly sets parameters for the kinds of research which are likely to be funded in the first place. Academic discourse about the child audience has to compete for authority and credibility with these more popular discourses, as well as with those of the media industries themselves.

Nevertheless, such discourses often appear to assume that we are all talking about the same object – that is, the child audience. I want to suggest that, on the contrary, we are all engaged in *constructing* that object, in ways that serve our own intentions and purposes. Thus, we describe, measure and analyse the audience in various ways; we express our concerns and anxieties about it; we observe it, we count it, we experiment on it, we interrogate it; we seek to entertain, to inform, to manipulate, or to empower it; and some of us even fondly imagine that we are speaking on its behalf, or 'giving it a voice'. Yet however objective or open these activities may seem, they all inevitably define the audience in partial and particular ways.

From the scandalous press stories of children depraved by media violence right through to the technical complexities of market research and the sometimes arcane concerns of academic papers, this process of defining the child audience is itself a kind of industry. This is most obviously the case, perhaps, in the press: stories about 'children at risk' make for the kind of sensational copy which sells newspapers – a phenomenon that has become much more prominent as the boundaries between the 'popular' and the 'quality' press have become steadily more blurred.[1] Yet this is also the case in academic research. The relationship between children and the media has been the focus for a massive research enterprise, generating thousands upon thousands of studies, funded (for a variety of reasons) both by government agencies and by the media industries themselves. There has been more research and debate about this section of the media audience than any other, a phenomenon which in itself reflects complex emotional, political and economic investments in the idea of childhood.

Yet whatever the position from which we speak, we are engaging in a discourse that we as adults essentially control, if not completely monopolize. Both in the academy and in other arenas where children's relationships with the media are discussed and debated, the discourse about media audiences is unavoidably a discourse about *other* people. In the process, we are inevitably making assumptions about who these other people are – and, in this case, about what 'childhood' is, or should be. These assumptions may be unspoken, but they nevertheless infuse everything we do: they inform the questions we ask, the methods of investigation we adopt, and the criteria we use to define what counts as valid knowledge.

Some critics go further. The audience itself, they argue, is not merely a construction but a kind of 'invisible fiction'.[2] It is something we imagine or fantasize about, but can never ultimately know. This is seen to be increasingly the case in the media industries themselves.

Ien Ang, for example, suggests that the television industry is now engaged in a losing battle to control and define its audience.[3] In the era of multichannel TV, remote control 'zappers' and video, she argues, the behaviour of audiences has become steadily more difficult to predict. Ratings research is used as a kind of defence against the insecurity this situation generates, yet it is ultimately in pursuit of a chimera.[4] In its more extreme versions, this argument even appears to suggest that 'real audiences' are merely figments of the industry's – or indeed the researcher's – imagination. For academics, it leads to a position where we can remain in the comfort of our universities, debating the rhetorical validity of other people's discursive constructions of the audience, without ever having to sully our hands with empirical reality.[5]

My position here is less radically constructivist. I believe that there are real audiences out there in the real world, even if we can ultimately know them only through our own constructions or representations. While recognizing that there will never be final agreement, I would argue that these constructions can and should be judged in terms of the validity of their empirical evidence and the coherence and logic of their theoretical arguments. Furthermore, these constructions clearly *make a difference* to the lives of real children: they inform the making of cultural policy and the practice of media regulation and production, as well as the interventions of parents and teachers.

As I have argued, contemporary views of children's relationships with the media are characterized by two contrasting forms of sentimentality. On the one hand, there is an old, familiar sentimentality – a construction of children as innocent and vulnerable, and hence in need of adult protection. On the other, there is a more contemporary sentimentality – a construction of children as a 'media-wise', active audience, possessing a kind of natural wisdom that guides their dealings with new media and technologies. Broadly speaking, it is the former view that tends to dominate the public arena, while the latter is the one increasingly espoused by the media industries themselves. Yet even within the more specialized domain of academic research, debates about children's relationships with the media are often reduced to a simple choice between these two positions: if one is false, then the other must necessarily be true.

My primary aim in this chapter is to identify, and to point beyond, the limitations of these debates. As I have implied, both these conceptions derive from essentialist views of childhood and of the electronic media; and both seem to reflect a notion of the child as an isolated individual consciousness. By contrast, I want to argue for a more fully *social* account of the relationship between children and the media, which situates our analysis of the audience within a broader understanding of social, institutional and historical change.

It is not my intention here to provide a comprehensive review of academic research on the child audience: several such reviews can easily be found elsewhere.[6] My aim is merely to provide some indications of the changing ways in which the *object* of this research – the child audience – has been conceptualized and defined, particularly in more recent work. In doing so, I also intend to introduce some of the basic theoretical orientations and concerns of my own research, and hence to lay the foundations for the more specific investigations in the chapters that follow.

Action and reaction

It is possible to see the history of academic research about media audiences as an ongoing process of action and reaction, as a pendulum constantly swinging between 'powerful media' and 'powerful audiences'. Broadly speaking, the past two decades have seen a decisive swing towards the power of the audience in a whole range of disciplines and fields of research. Audiences, it is repeatedly asserted, are not witless dupes of media influence. On the contrary, they make complex, differentiated judgements about what they read and watch. They are active rather than passive; critical rather than credulous; discriminating rather than mindless; diverse rather than homogeneous. As this implies, there is often a remorseless either/or logic in such debates; and it is one that, in my view, urgently needs to be questioned.

Historically, the dominant tradition, particularly in the United States, has been that of 'effects' research. For reasons which reflect underlying assumptions about childhood, it is a tradition that continues to be more influential in relation to children than it is in relation to adults. The paradigm for this research was largely established through the early laboratory experiments on the effects of media violence. Based on a form of behaviourism or 'social learning theory', this research sought to demonstrate causal connections between violent stimuli and aggressive responses; and it was this model of 'effects' that subsequently came to inform research on areas such as sex role stereotyping and the influence of advertising.

As it has developed, however, effects research has increasingly emphasized the role of 'intervening variables' which mediate between the media and the audience. Far from seeing the audience as an undifferentiated mass, more recent psychological studies have tended to concentrate on the 'individual differences' which lead viewers to respond in different ways to the same messages. As a result, estimations of the power of the media have been significantly revised.

Thus, as we shall see in more detail in chapter 8, research on the effects of television advertising has increasingly challenged the view that children are simply passive victims of the seductive wiles of the 'hidden persuaders'.[7] Likewise, research on the influence of sex role stereotyping has questioned the idea that sexist portrayals necessarily result in sexist attitudes, and that 'heavy viewers' are therefore likely to adopt more traditional roles.[8] Meanwhile, the notion that television viewing inevitably displaces more 'constructive' activities such as reading books, or that it leads to a decline in print literacy, has been systematically undermined.[9] In each of these areas, the potential influence of the media has increasingly been studied in relation to other social forces and influences in children's lives. As we shall see in chapter 7, it is only in the area of media violence that the notion of 'direct effects' has continued to dominate the field, a phenomenon which is itself symptomatic of the broader political investments that are at stake.

Towards the active audience

Over the past two decades, psychological researchers have increasingly moved away from a behaviourist to a constructivist (or cognitive) perspective – from the study of stimulus and response to the study of how children understand, interpret and evaluate what they watch and read. Children are seen here not as passive recipients of media messages, but as active processors of meaning. In making sense of the media, they are seen to use 'schemas' or 'scripts', sets of plans and expectations which they have built up from their previous experience both of media and of the world in general. The meaning of media texts, from this perspective, is not simply delivered *to* the audience, but constructed *by* it.[10]

In studying children's understanding of the media, cognitive psychologists have tended to concentrate on the 'micro' rather than the 'macro' aspects – on specific forms of mental processing, rather than on questions about the media's role in forming attitudes or beliefs. Thus, for example, there have been detailed studies of children's attention to television; of their developing understanding of media narratives; of the relationships between 'symbol systems' and styles of cognitive processing; and of children's ability to interpret the formal features of television. Much of this research has used a Piagetian approach, in an attempt to identify 'ages and stages' in children's developing understanding of the media.[11]

A good example of this approach can be found in research into children's judgements about the relationship between television and reality. From a constructivist perspective, these judgements are seen to depend both on their general cognitive development and on their experience both of the medium itself and of the real world.[12] Thus, in terms of development, children gradually acquire the ability to 'decentre', and thus to hypothesize about the intentions of media producers. At the same time, they also learn to use formal or generic 'cues', and build up a growing body of knowledge about the processes of television production – for example about special effects, or about the working practices of actors – which enables them to discriminate between messages they are prepared to trust and those they are not. Finally, children are increasingly able to draw on their own knowledge or beliefs about the real world in order to assess the plausibility or authenticity of what they watch.

Research in this field suggests that even comparatively young children (aged six or seven) are capable of making quite complex judgements about the reality status of television: far from regarding the medium as a 'window on the world', they employ diverse and potentially contradictory sets of criteria in evaluating its claims to represent reality. By the time they reach early adolescence, children have an emerging awareness of *realism* as an aesthetic category: they come to appreciate the care that has been taken to construct the illusion of realism, while simultaneously acknowledging that it remains an illusion. This research thus provides an important corrective to the traditional view of children as somehow incapable of distinguishing between television and reality, a view which is frequently expressed in public debate, and still seems to be implicitly shared by some researchers, not least in relation to the issue of screen violence.

As this example suggests, the constructivist approach provides a valuable alternative to the behaviourism of 'effects' research. Yet it also has significant limitations. 'Activity' (a problematic term, in any case) is still largely perceived here in asocial, individualized terms: it is something that happens in the isolated encounter between mind and medium, rather than in the social processes of everyday interaction. Furthermore, 'activity' often seems to be conceptualized as an *intervening variable* in a process which is still essentially seen as one of cause and effect. Thus, the cognitive processes by which children make sense of advertising, for example, are seen to mediate between stimulus and response – they represent what are significantly often defined as '*individual* differences'.

These theoretical limitations are also manifested in the methodological problems of much of this research. Many of the basic methodological procedures – notably the laboratory experiment – seem to have been taken over wholesale from effects research. Like effects research, much of this work seems to assume that an activity like television viewing can be conceptualized in terms of a series of variables, whose nature and meaning can be assessed in advance through the use of objective scales and instruments. These variables can then be systematically controlled in the experimental setting, for example by 'matching' groups of subjects. To say the least, the extent to which the findings of such work can be extrapolated to real-life situations is very limited.

Meanwhile, psychological research on children and the media has remained largely untouched by some of the more dramatic changes that have taken place within the broader field of psychology over the past twenty years – for example, the development of work on socially situated cognition, the influence of psychoanalytic theory, and the rise of 'discursive psychology' and 'critical psychology'.[13] In this context, developmental psychology has increasingly been criticized for its oversimplification of the social contexts of children's lives, for its neglect of emotion and for its reliance on evolutionary ideas. Developmental psychologists are frequently accused of presenting socially and culturally specific models of 'healthy' development as though they were universal norms, and of being implicated in the oppressive control and regulation of mothers and children through various forms of measurement and testing. Developmentalism is thus increasingly seen as asocial, ahistorical and individualistic.

From these more critical perspectives, there are significant problems with the 'map' of the human mind that is offered in this research. Cognitive psychologists who have studied children's relationships with the media continue to believe that they can make straightforward distinctions, for example between cognition and affect (or emotion), or between attitudes and behaviour, and that these can easily be assessed via mechanical ratings scales and psychometric tests. Yet the idea that such mental phenomena exist, and can be studied, in isolation from broader social and interpersonal processes has been widely challenged.

Likewise, much of this research implicitly adopts a rationalistic notion of child development as a steady progression towards adult maturity and rationality. In the case of work on children and the media, this developmentalist approach inevitably privileges certain kinds of judgements (particularly rational, 'critical' judgements) at

the expense of others. By contrast, there has been very little engagement with questions about pleasure (or displeasure) and fantasy. From
this perspective, the ideal 'critical viewer' is seen to be surrounded
by a kind of rationalistic character armour which provides a form of
protection against the pleasurable delusions promoted by the media.

Social audiences

While they do have a certain amount in common, it is important to
distinguish between the *psychological* emphasis of this research and
the more *sociological* analysis of the child audience that has recently
begun to emerge in Media and Cultural Studies. Here too, there has
been a general shift away from questions about *effects* to questions
about the *meanings* and *uses* of media; but there has also been a much
stronger emphasis on locating media use within the broader context
of social and interpersonal relationships.

Bob Hodge and David Tripp's *Children and Television* was one of
the first attempts to develop this perspective on the child audience.[14]
Hodge and Tripp apply a 'social semiotic' approach both to the analysis of children's programming and to audience data. In common with
constructivists, they regard children as 'active' producers of meaning, rather than passive consumers; although (unlike the majority of
psychologists) they are also concerned with the ideological and formal constraints exerted by the text. While the combination of theoretical perspectives is somewhat uneasy at times,[15] the central focus
of their work is on the *social* and *discursive* processes through which
meaning is constructed, and the power relationships which inevitably characterize them. How children interpret a cartoon, for example, and what they choose to say about it in the company of other
children and an adult interviewer, depend on their perceptions of
their own social position and their relations with others.

More recently, I have developed and extended this approach in a
series of studies that investigate how children define and construct
their social identities through talk about television.[16] Children's judgements about genre and representation, and their retellings of television narrative, for example, are analysed here as inherently social
processes; and the development of knowledge about television ('television literacy') and of a 'critical' perspective on the medium are
seen in terms of their social motivations and purposes. These studies
use a form of discourse analysis which emphasizes the functions of
talk as a form of 'social action'.[17] Thus, for example, I have analysed
how boys' talk about soap operas – and their judgements about what

is or is not realistic or plausible – is inextricably related to their ongoing construction of their own masculinity; or, to choose another example, how black children's and white children's discussions of 'positive images' in a programme like *The Cosby Show* are bound up with the dynamics of interracial friendships.[18]

In parallel with this work, it is possible to identify a more strictly 'ethnographic' or observational approach to studying children's uses of media, both in the context of the home[19] and in the peer group.[20] Marie Gillespie's study of the use of television among a South Asian community in London, for example, integrates an analysis of the role of television within the dynamics of the family and the peer group with an account of children's responses to specific genres such as news and soap opera.[21] The media are used here partly as a heuristic means of gaining insight into 'other' cultures, although (as with the work discussed above) there is a self-reflexive emphasis on the role of the researcher, and on the power relationships between researchers and their child subjects, which is typically absent from psychological research. Finally, there is now a growing body of action research in media education which focuses on the interaction between students' 'everyday' knowledge about the media and the more 'academic' knowledge they encounter in the context of formal schooling. The school is seen here, not as necessarily inimical to youth culture (as it is by some Cultural Studies researchers), but on the contrary as one of the key social arenas in which that culture is constructed and played out.[22]

Broadly speaking, then, this research views children as active agents, rather than as passive recipients of adult culture. It sets out to investigate children's experiences in their own terms, rather than judging them in terms of their inability to use or understand the media in appropriately 'adult' ways. In principle, it also offers a perspective on the child audience which is significantly more 'social' than that of the psychological research discussed above. In making sense of the media, children are seen to employ a range of discourses and strategies, deriving from different social locations and experiences (for example, in terms of social class, gender and ethnicity). The production of meaning from the media is therefore seen here as a complex process of *social negotiation*.[23]

Reality revisited

In the following chapters, I will incorporate findings from this kind of research in my discussion of a range of specific aspects of children's relations with the media. At this stage, a more extended discussion of my earlier example of children's judgements about the realism of television should provide an indication of the differences and similarities between this approach and that of cognitive psychology.

Rather than such judgements being seen as simply cognitive phenomena, my research suggests that they can serve a variety of social functions.[24] In the context of group discussion, condemning programmes as 'unrealistic' provides a powerful means of defining one's own tastes, and thus of claiming a particular social identity. For example, girls' frequent complaints about the 'unrealistic' storylines or events in action-adventure cartoons often reflect a desire to distance themselves from what are seen as boys' 'childish' tastes, and thereby to proclaim their own (gendered) maturity. On the other hand, boys' rejection of the 'unrealistic' muscle-bound men in a programme like *Baywatch* may reflect anxieties about the fragility of their own masculine identity. Boys' rejection of melodrama or girls' rejection of violent action movies can thus be seen as rather more than the mechanical application of fixed judgements of taste: on the contrary, they represent an active *claim* to a particular social position – a claim which is sometimes tentative and uncertain, and in many cases open to challenge.

Furthermore, such judgements may also play a role in enabling viewers retrospectively to regulate or indeed disclaim their own *affective* responses – for example, of fear or sorrow. Speculating about the special effects in horror films, or condemning them as 'unrealistic', for instance, may serve to preclude the accusation that one might be 'soft' enough to find them frightening, and appears to be a particular preoccupation for some boys. While the pleasure of such films clearly must depend to some extent on the willing 'suspension of disbelief' – in effect, on consenting to let yourself be frightened – this kind of subsequent discussion can serve as a means of learning how to 'handle' potentially unwelcome emotional reactions.

However, it would be false to present this in terms of a simple *opposition* between reason and pleasure, or cognition and affect. There is undoubtedly a considerable pleasure in this kind of critical talk: mocking the 'unrealistic' nature of television, speculating about 'how it's done' and playing with the relationship between television and reality would seem to be important aspects of most viewers' everyday interaction with the medium. This kind of talk clearly does rely to some extent on disavowing one's own pleasure – or indeed displeasure – at the moment of viewing. Yet it also seems to offer a sense of power and control over that experience, and thus a pleasurable sense of security.

Above all, it is important to stress that this is not merely a psychological phenomenon, which happens 'inside children's heads'. On the contrary, this kind of critical talk serves particular social or interpersonal functions in the context of *dialogue* with others. The context of the research itself is clearly crucial here. Any adult asking children questions about television – particularly in a school context, as has generally been the case in my research – is likely to invite these critical discourses. Most children know that many adults disapprove of them watching 'too much' television, and they are familiar with at least some of the arguments about its negative effects on them. In some instances, these arguments are addressed directly, although children are generally keen to exempt themselves from such charges: while their younger siblings might copy what they watch, such accusations certainly do not apply to *them*. Just as adults appear to displace the 'effects' of television on to children – thereby implying that they themselves are not at risk – so children tend to suggest that these arguments only apply to those much younger than themselves.

In a sense, judgements about the 'unreality' of television could be seen to serve a similar function, albeit in a more indirect way. They enable the speaker to present himself or herself as a sophisticated viewer, able to 'see through' the illusions television provides. In effect, they represent a claim for social status – and, particularly in this context, a claim to be 'adult'. While these claims may be at least partly directed towards the interviewer and towards other children in the group, they often seem to rely on distinguishing the speaker from an invisible 'other' – from those viewers who are immature or stupid enough to believe that what they watch is real.

Significantly, there are often clear distinctions here in terms of social class. Broadly speaking, the middle-class children in my studies are more likely to perceive the interview context in 'educational' terms, and to adjust their responses accordingly. By contrast, many of the working-class children tend to use the invitation to talk about television as an opportunity to stake out their own tastes and to celebrate their own pleasures for the benefit of the peer group. While the middle-class children direct much of their talk towards the interviewer, and tend to defer to the interviewer's power, this is much less true of the working-class children, for whom the interviewer occasionally appears to be little more than an irrelevance.

Thus, judgements about the reality of television are much more of a preoccupation for middle-class children. Both quantitatively and qualitatively, their judgements are more complex and sophisticated than those of the majority of their working-class counterparts. Yet these arguments should not be seen to support any simplistic conclusions about the levels of 'media literacy' in different social classes. It is not that middle-class children are somehow 'more critical' or indeed 'more media literate' than working-class children. Rather, it would seem that these critical discourses serve particular social functions which are more salient for them in this context, and which are at least partly to do with defining their own class position. They provide a powerful means of demonstrating their own critical authority, and thereby of distinguishing themselves from those invisible 'others' – the 'mass' audience – who are, by implication, more at risk of suffering the harmful effects of television.

In my research, this has been particularly the case for some of the older middle-class boys (aged eleven to twelve), for whom sneering at the shortcomings of popular television appears to confer considerable peer group status. There is often a great degree of competition here, as the children vie to deliver the wittiest put-down of the most awful game shows, or to perform the most damning imitation of bad acting in the soaps. Admitting to enjoying anything, with the possible exception of documentaries and 'adult' films, is much more difficult. In many cases, these boys would only admit to watching programmes 'to see how stupid they are' – although their knowledge of them is at least equal to that of their self-confessed fans. By contrast, the middle-class girls appear to be much more comfortable in acknowledging and celebrating their own pleasure, particularly in the context of a single-sex group. Yet in mixed groups, with competition from the boys, it is often the most damning critics of television who win out.

While this critical discourse is not explicitly phrased in class terms, there is clearly a thin line between contempt for popular television and contempt for its audience. As Pierre Bourdieu suggests, critical discourse represents a valuable form of cultural capital, and a tangible demonstration of social distinction.[25] The process of 'becoming critical' is part of the way in which middle-class children come to distinguish themselves from the 'others', and thereby actively socialize themselves into class membership. Yet a great deal may be lost – or at least disavowed – in this process. Critical discourses about the media often embody a form of intellectual cynicism and a sense of superiority to 'other people'. They may result in a superficial irony or indeed a contempt for popular pleasures which is merely complacent. Perhaps particularly for boys, for whom the expression of pleasure appears much more risky and problematic, the discourse of critical judgement seems to offer the security of appearing to exercise absolute rational control.

As this example suggests, children's judgements about the reality of what they watch on television cannot be seen as a purely cognitive or intellectual process. On the contrary, it is through making 'critical' judgements of this kind that children seek to define their social identities, both in relation to their peers and in relation to adults. Making sense of the media is thus not simply a matter of what goes on inside children's heads: it is a fundamentally *social* phenomenon.

The limits of the active audience

In summary, then, three central emphases can be identified in this research. Broadly speaking, it defines children as an 'active' audience; it seeks to understand the child's point of view in its own terms; and it attempts to situate children's uses of media within the broader context of social and interpersonal relationships. While all of these characteristics are important and valuable, there are problems and limitations with each; and in identifying these, I shall aim to indicate areas for future development.

The view of children as 'active' participants in the process of making meaning is one that Cultural Studies researchers share with the constructivist approaches outlined above. Meaning is seen here, not as inherent in the text, but as the product of a 'negotiation' between text and reader. Children are seen as a competent, sophisticated audience rather than simply as passive victims of media manipulation. In these respects, this kind of research offers an important challenge to many of the assumptions that typically circulate in public debate.

Nevertheless, this research has also been rather overdetermined by its reaction against these kinds of anxieties about the negative effects of the media. As a result, it runs the risk of adopting a rather simplistic 'child-centred' approach, seeking to celebrate the sophistication of the 'media-wise' child and to prove (endlessly) that children are not as gullible or as passive as they are often made out to be. There is a sense in which the term 'active' (and the opposition between active and passive) has become a kind of empty slogan.[26]

There are several obvious problems here. For instance, there is often an implicit assumption that if children are 'active', then they are somehow not going to be influenced by what they watch or read. Yet this does not necessarily follow. Indeed, one could argue that in some instances to be 'active' is to be more open to influence. Contemporary advertising, for example, increasingly appears to address a sophisticated, 'critical' viewer, and to positively *require* an 'active' response; and by effectively flattering the viewer in this way, it may well prove to be more powerful than the more old-fashioned approach of the 'hard sell'.[27]

Furthermore, this kind of celebration of children's sophistication as users of media can lead us to neglect the fact that there are areas they need to know more about. There are bound to be gaps in children's knowledge, although those gaps may not necessarily be where they are often assumed to be. Likewise, children's knowledge of the media obviously develops as they grow older, and this clearly depends on the critical perspectives that are available to them, both within and beyond the media. Simply to celebrate the 'power' of audiences is effectively to ignore the fact that audiences' relationships with the media develop and change – and indeed, the possibility that they can *be changed*.

Ultimately, therefore, there is a danger that the argument about children's 'active' relationship with the media – and indeed their high levels of 'media literacy' – will become a kind of rhetorical platitude. For many researchers (myself included), there is an uneasy coincidence here between the constructions of the child audience that circulate within the industry and those that have increasingly been voiced in the academy. In both contexts, the romantic figure of the 'media-wise' child is coming to dominate the debate. As I have implied, such assertions can easily become confused with arguments about consumer sovereignty; and in the process, researchers who take this point of view may end up becoming mere apologists for commercial corporations. Rather than simply exploring the *nature* of children's 'activity' as an audience, we need to say more about its *consequences* and *implications*, not least in terms of cultural and educational policy.

The second key emphasis in this research is the claim that it takes the child's point of view. Unlike a good deal of psychological research, this work does not set out to judge children primarily in terms of what they *cannot* do – that is, in terms of their inability to make rational, 'adult' judgements, for example about the differences between media texts and the real world. On the contrary, the aim here is to make sense of children's experience of the media in their own terms, rather than in adults' terms. Against the broader context of public debates about children and the media, this emphasis is also vitally important. As I have noted, such debates are almost exclusively conducted among adults; and there are many who do not even see it as necessary to find out what children have to say. Yet even for those who purport to represent children's interests, there is a real danger of assuming that adults can easily speak or act *on behalf of* children.

As I have implied, there are significant difficulties in establishing *evidence* about children's experiences and views. Social statistics carry

an undeniable authority, but they often depend on aggregating children together in ways which are designed to minimize their differences. By contrast, presenting and analysing verbatim reports of
children's talk – as I have done at some length in my own research –
has obvious limitations in terms of its representativeness; yet it often
possesses an air of directness and authenticity that is largely absent
from the results of quantitative surveys or accounts of laboratory
experiments.

Nevertheless, there is a danger of romanticism here too. It is clearly
naive to believe that we can *ever* take the child's perspective – or that
this perspective is something which will simply be revealed to us if
we ask the right kinds of questions. This kind of research sometimes
implicitly assumes that the data speaks for itself, and that research
merely provides a forum in which children's voices can be directly
heard.[28] The idea that we can simply 'listen to children' in this way
is, to say the least, somewhat disingenuous.

At least in principle, discourse analysis offers a way of moving
beyond this view of talk as a transparent means of access to what
goes on in people's heads.[29] From this perspective, talk is seen as a
form of *social action*: it is used to stake out and construct identities, to
establish and negotiate interpersonal relationships, and to claim and
enact social power. Far from taking what children say at face value,
therefore, this approach sees talk as an arena – albeit often a very
fraught and contested one – in which children define what it means
to be a child, or a child of a particular social group. This is the kind of
analysis I have developed in my own research; and it informs my
account of children's judgements about the reality of television, outlined above.

The evident limitation of this approach, however, is its refusal to
look beyond the level of linguistic behaviour and address the psychic or emotional dynamics of children's relations with the media.
Moreover, in rejecting the 'realist' use of talk as data, it may ultimately make it impossible to assess its truthfulness (or lack of it),
and hence to make any judgements about its reliability or accuracy.[30]
Paradoxically, returning talk to its social context in this way can reduce it to the level of mere performance.

The third significant emphasis in this research is its attempt to
analyse children's uses and interpretations of the media as part of
the wider pattern of *social* relationships and processes. The media
are seen here not as 'outside influences' but as inextricably inter-
woven in the dynamics of family and peer group relationships –
relationships that are necessarily characterized by social inequalities and by the exercise of social power. This is a key point which

differentiates Cultural Studies from mainstream psychology, even where they appear to share the emphasis on 'active' audiences. Children are seen here not merely as cognitively active, but also as socially active – as social agents in their own right.

Ultimately, however, much of this research has been quite superficial in this respect. Despite occasional claims to 'ethnography', very little media research entails the long-term immersion that characterizes ethnography in the field of anthropology.[31] Much of it is based on a very limited acquaintance with the subjects themselves: all sorts of assumptions are typically made about children, and about how representative they are of particular social categories, on the basis of what is often little more than a couple of interviews.

In this respect, there is still a long way to go in developing a broader social analysis of the child audience. Here there are some important connections to be forged between research on children and media and the growing body of research on the sociology and history of childhood that I have drawn on at various points in this book. The focus in much of this work is on children's everyday social experiences and relationships, and researchers are typically using ethnographic or qualitative methods in order to investigate this. As I have implied, the sociology of childhood offers a broader theoretical challenge to the universalizing tendencies of psychology – to the view of childhood as a decontextualized sequence of ages and stages, and to the notion that we can understand psychological processes (such as cognition and affect) in isolation from the social contexts in which they occur. Furthermore, the sociologists of childhood have argued against what they have seen as a deficit model of childhood – a view of childhood as a kind of rehearsal of adult life – that is implicit not just in cognitive notions of child development, but also in social psychological theories of socialization.[32]

As yet, however, this work has been dominated by a comparatively conventional sociological agenda: it has paid very little attention to culture, to the media, or even to children's use of commercially produced artefacts more generally, such as toys.[33] In the process, it has effectively neglected the mediated nature of contemporary childhood. As Sonia Livingstone has recently argued, the new sociological child appears to live a *non-mediated* childhood: this is 'a carefree child playing hopscotch with friends in a nearby park, not a child with music on the headphones watching television in her bedroom'.[34]

Furthermore, the sociology of childhood has been characterized by some of the same problems I have identified in relation to media research. Broadly speaking, the sociologists have attempted to replace what they regard as the 'incompetent' child constructed by psychologists with the 'competent' child, understanding the world on its own terms, and capable of making decisions about its own life. Yet, as I have implied, one might well question the value of simply replacing notions of childhood incompetence – a view of children as merely incomplete adults – with an opposite view of them as somehow naturally competent and sophisticated. Here, too, there is a danger of overreacting against the marginalization and implicit denigration of children by attributing to them an overwhelming degree of self-knowledge and autonomy.

Reconstructing the child audience

Contemporary debates about the power of the media in Media and Cultural Studies have become increasingly polarized. On the one hand, there is a form of populism, in which popular culture has been seen to represent a means of 'resistance' to dominant ideologies, and hence a form of 'empowerment'. On the other hand, there is now a growing reaction against what is seen to be the celebration of audiences, and a tendency to lapse into an all-embracing cultural pessimism. When it comes to young people as an audience, the debate often seems to be conducted in terms of equally polarized choices. On the one hand, there is the traditional notion of children as innocent and vulnerable to influence; while on the other there is the equally sentimental notion of children as sophisticated, street-wise, somehow naturally competent and critical. Both are *constructions* of childhood, and both have a genuine emotional appeal, albeit of different kinds; but ultimately both appear to oversimplify the complexity and diversity of children's relationships with the media.

In terms of future developments, then, there may be two possible directions for research on the child audience. Both, in a sense, are the project of this book. On the one hand, we need to relocate our analysis of children's relationships with the media in the context of a broader understanding of their social lives, and indeed of the recent history of childhood, of the kind outlined in chapter 4. As I hope to indicate in the following chapters, this might give us a rather different perspective on contemporary public debates about these issues – debates which, particularly in the case of discussions of violence and commercialism, seem to have become increasingly simplistic and repetitive.

On the other hand, we also need to take a broader view of the media. The analysis of audiences in Media and Cultural Studies has increasingly become divorced from questions about media texts and institutions; and there has been a good deal of mutual caricature on all sides. As Graham Murdock has argued, the analysis of audiences needs to 'move beyond immediate acts of consumption and response to analyse the underlying structures that provide the contexts and resources for audience activity'.[35] While not denying the creative, interpretive activity of audiences, therefore, we also need to look at the broader material and symbolic conditions in which this occurs – for example, at the constraints and possibilities embodied in media texts, and the economic, institutional and social dynamics that determine specific forms of media consumption. As I suggested in chapter 5, we need to understand the *relationships between* technologies, institutions, texts and audiences, without conceding a necessary priority to any one of them.

On the face of it, these two prescriptions seem to point in opposite directions. Nevertheless, they are far from incompatible. In different ways, both suggest that we need to move beyond the individualistic construction of childhood, and to work towards a broader social analysis. In this context, the child audience is no longer seen in essentialist terms – as *either* active *or* passive, competent *or* incompetent. On the contrary, our aim is to identify a range of different *forms* of activity and competence which are more or less likely under particular social and cultural conditions.

In this chapter and the two that preceded it, I have attempted to lay out the broad parameters of this approach. It is an approach which offers a more complex – but also, I hope, more productive – way of understanding contemporary developments in children's relationships with the media than either of those identified in chapters 2 and 3. In the three chapters that follow, I seek to apply this approach in more detail. Chapter 7 looks at the perennial issue of media violence; chapter 8 at commercialism and advertising; and chapter 9 at the issue of politics and citizenship. Each of these chapters draws on my own empirical studies, which are set in the context of broader research and debate in the field. In each case, I focus on the implications of children's increasing access to social and cultural worlds that have until recently been largely confined to adults. In discussing children's experiences of those worlds, and the debates that have surrounded them, I seek to provide a more constructive basis both for future research and for cultural and educational policy.

Loan Receipt
Liverpool John Moores University
Learning and Information Services

Borrower ID: 21111133657114
Loan Date: 21/01/2009
Loan Time: 11:59 am

After the death of childhood :
111010145843

Due Date: 11/02/2009 23:59

Please keep your receipt
in case of dispute

Part III

7

Children Viewing Violence

ALL RELEVANT

To discuss the issue of violence in this context is perhaps to surrender to a kind of tedious inevitability. In the large majority of public debates about children's relationships with the media, violence has become a growing obsession, often seeming to exclude any other aspect of interest or concern. Among the enormous range of experiences that the media offer children, violence seems to be regarded as the defining instance – the phenomenon that somehow encapsulates everything we really need to know about the place of the media in their lives.

Over the past two decades, media violence has become implicated in a series of much broader 'moral panics' about childhood.[1] In the process, questions about the impact of the media have frequently been caught up with debates about the impact of real-life events. Indeed, media violence is often seen as itself a form of violence *against* children, committed by adults whose only motivation is that of financial greed. According to many campaigners, it represents a form of electronic child abuse, all but indistinguishable from physical abuse and cruelty.[2]

At the same time, of course, media violence is routinely identified as the primary cause of what is seen as a rising tide of youth crime. It is rare to read reports of violent crime that do not at some point attempt to attribute responsibility to the media. Coverage of the murder of London head-teacher Philip Lawrence, for example, and the spate of random killings in US high schools – not to mention the random mass murders at Dunblane and Port Arthur in Australia – dwelt at length on the question of media influence, despite its complete irrelevance to the circumstances of all these crimes.

The furore around the impact of violent videos which followed the murder of two-year-old James Bulger by two ten-year-old boys in 1993 is probably the most spectacular recent example of this kind of 'media panic' in Britain, and certainly the most widely discussed.[3] In this instance, as in many others, the media were clearly used as a convenient scapegoat for events which were too complicated, or simply too horrible, to explain. Yet there was no evidence that the killers of James Bulger had even seen the film that was said to have provoked them, let alone that the murder was in any sense a 'copy-cat' crime.[4]

Nevertheless, this kind of connection between 'bad' media and violent crime has become part of a commonsense demonology which can easily be invoked by politicians and others seeking to demonstrate their moral authority and responsibility – and in the process, to distract attention from more deep-seated causes of violence in society. Proposals to regulate media violence are less likely to encounter opposition than attempts to address what are by any measurement more significant contributory causes of violent crime, such as poverty and family breakdown – or, in the United States, the ready availability of lethal weapons. What is perhaps most striking here is how, in many apparently secular societies, forms of evangelical Christianity have been so successful in defining the terms of public debate on this issue.[5]

As I have noted, these anxieties typically lead to calls for stricter control – for increasing censorship and other forms of centralized regulation. Here, the addition of children to the equation provides a crucial element of rhetorical strength that might otherwise be lacking. While censorship directed at adults could be rejected as authoritarian or as an infringement of individual liberty, the call to protect children is much harder to resist. Particularly in the United States, the notion of childhood has increasingly come to replace the notion of 'national security' as a justification for censorship, not least because of its ability to command political assent. Children, apparently depraved by a 'diet' of media sex and violence, have implicitly come to be seen as an *internal* threat to the continuation of the social order.

Media panics?

As numerous critics have shown, these kinds of 'media panics' have a very long history, stretching back at least as far as the Greek philosopher Plato, who proposed to ban the works of the dramatic poets from his ideal Republic on the grounds of their corrupting influence on impressionable young minds.[6] In modern times, anxieties have been caught up with broader concerns about the pending collapse of the social order at the hands of the undiscip. 'masses' – and in particular, about the criminal proclivities of w ing-class, urban, male youth.[7] Such arguments, like more generalized laments for the 'death of childhood', are often motivated by a nostalgia for an imaginary Golden Age that always seems to lie at least two generations in the past.

On one level, such concerns can be seen as a manifestation of a kind of elitist disdain for 'mass culture', and of a contempt for the 'common herd' with which it is identified. Yet they also reflect a fear of the 'irrational' forces that would apparently be unleashed by these new media. Right from the earliest criticisms of popular journalism and the dangerous habit of novel-reading, through to contemporary fears about computer games, there has been a continuing concern about the dangers of overstimulation, sensuality and sensationalism. Both in social and psychological terms, the anxieties provoked by the media can be seen to reflect a broader fear of losing control.[8]

Nevertheless, these concerns cannot be seen as merely timeless. On the contrary, they take quite particular forms in particular historical circumstances. As I have implied, the growing intensity of these debates needs to be seen in the light of the increasingly contested, problematic status of childhood itself. In the 1980s, Britain saw the emergence of a series of interdependent moral panics about perceived threats to children: serial murder, child pornography, abductions by paedophiles and satanic ritual abuse were frequently claimed to be reaching epidemic proportions.[9] These issues provided a powerful focus for the activities of quite diverse interest groups, and indeed for alliances between them. The issue of children's access to media violence has served as a vehicle for similar campaigns, and the same 'moral entrepreneurs' have repeatedly featured in them. Here, too, the specific emphasis on children has served as a powerful means of commanding support for much broader campaigns: the intrusion of the state into the private sphere becomes significantly more palatable when proposed in the name of children.[10]

It is possible to detect some quite contradictory constructions of childhood in these debates. On the one hand, most obviously, there is a post-Romantic notion of the child as innocent and vulnerable, as requiring protection from the unnatural influences of the adult world. Underlying this, however, is a much older view of the child as the bearer of original sin. From this perspective, children are 'natural' not in a positive sense, but in a negative one: they possess drives towards violence, sexuality and anti-social behaviour which are only

barely kept under control – and which 'irrational' influences like the
media are seen to have the power to release. Here again, the Bulger
case is a very interesting example, not least because the film that
allegedly caused the killers to commit the murder – *Child's Play 3* –
keys into some very real anxieties around the question of childhood,
and displays a considerable hostility towards adult authority.[11]

However, the notion of 'moral panic' can be used in rather misleading ways. In fact, the debate that surrounds the question of
media violence only rarely rises to the level of 'panic' – if 'panic' is
seen to mean something irrational and uncontrollable. Indeed, the
use of this term sometimes appears to imply that the general public
is suffering from a kind of false consciousness, artificially created by
irresponsible, sensationalist journalism.

To be sure, there have been instances where concerns about media
violence have been provoked and used for much broader political
purposes.[12] Yet this would not have been possible or meaningful if
they did not in some way connect with anxieties that already existed. The concern about media violence is so powerful partly because it draws on genuine hopes and fears that have always been
invested in parents' care for their own children. Of course, we should
beware of the assumption that the headlines and editorials in the
popular press are necessarily synonymous with public opinion: we
need to know much more about how these arguments are interpreted
by parents and children themselves.[13] Yet to imply that parents who
attempt to protect their children from what they perceive as harmful
are merely suffering from an irrational 'panic' is, to say the least,
somewhat arrogant.

Moreover, contemporary concerns about the impact of media violence on children need to be recognized as a genuine response to
changes in the media themselves. As I have indicated, new media
technologies – video and the internet in particular – are less amenable to centralized control than those that preceded them, such as
the cinema or broadcasting. This is not to suggest that young people
did not gain access to violent (or indeed sexually explicit) material in
the past, although it would be hard to deny that such material is
now much more easily available to children of all social classes, and
at an ever younger age. Crucially, these technologies take control
away from the state and place it in the hands of parents – many of
whom, it is alleged, are unable or insufficiently responsible to exercise it. This debate thus connects with a broader attempt to blame
the apparent crisis of discipline among the young on what is seen as
'permissive' parenting.

In fact, statistical evidence about any alleged increase in the *amount* of media violence is fairly inconclusive.[14] Nevertheless, the nature of these representations themselves has undeniably changed. Comparing modern horror films with their classic counterparts, or contemporary gangster movies with the originals of the 1930s, it is clear that screen violence has become much more graphic and spectacular. In fact, these changes date back several decades, with films like *The Wild Bunch* (1969) and *The Exorcist* (1973) often being seen as 'watersheds' in their respective genres. These developments can be traced to the revision of the Hays Production Code in Hollywood, and to innovations in special effects technology; and (more contentiously, perhaps) to the emergence of film as a 'director's medium'.[15] Gunfire sequences, for example, have become much more realistic, particularly in displaying the *consequences* of injury – although whether or not this has resulted in a 'glorification' of violence (let alone in particular behavioural effects) is of course much more debatable.

The popularity of such characteristics is by no means confined to 'adult' material. Horror, for example, has increasingly become the genre of choice for many children, girls as well as boys; and this is equally apparent in their preferences for 'old' media as well as new, as the extraordinary commercial success of children's book series such as Goosebumps and Point Horror indicates.[16] In the marketing of such series, the boundaries between 'children's books' and the more 'adult' works of authors like Stephen King are becoming increasingly blurred.

For all these reasons, therefore, it is important to engage with the issue of children's relationship with media violence, rather than simply dismissing it as yet another irrational moral panic. Yet even if media violence – or at least children's access to it – is increasing, how might this be explained? Why do children actively choose to expose themselves to such material, and what do they make of it?

In fact, some critics suggest that audiences in general actually prefer to watch films and television programmes *without* violence. Audience figures consistently point to the dominance of what the critic Michael Medved approvingly terms 'family-friendly entertainment'.[17] Yet, it is argued, the apparent rise in media violence is driven by global marketing: violence serves as a dramatic ingredient that requires no translation and is instantly comprehensible in most cultures.[18]

Meanwhile, others have regarded the popularity of media violence as symptomatic of broader changes in the *Zeitgeist*. Thus, it is seen to reflect the anxieties produced by changing male and female roles, or more general feelings of insecurity induced by the accelerating pace of social and technological change. Still others perceive it as the return of a form of repressed paganism, an attempt to reconnect with nature and with the lost sensual truths of the body.[19]

The fundamental problem with such arguments, as with much of the research and debate more broadly, is the implicit assumption that 'violence' is a singular phenomenon. As the common ingredient that apparently unites such disparate genres as horror, science fiction, action movies, computer games, police series and cartoons, 'violence' is seen to provide the explanation for the popularity of all of them. Yet even if we confine ourselves to the kinds of films that recur most frequently in these debates, it is clear that the functions, consequences and representations of violence – and hence any possible 'effects' it may have – are very diverse. To equate the violence in *Die Hard* with that in *Henry, Portrait of a Serial Killer* or *Pulp Fiction* or *Evil Dead* is effectively to neglect its meaning and purpose. As Martin Barker argues, this conflation ignores differences of form, context and narrative. As a result, he suggests, 'whenever the phrase "media violence" is used it conjures up one image above all else: an image of motiveless mayhem, to which words like "gratuitous" easily attach themselves'.[20] And in the process, the question of how audiences interpret violence – or indeed, whether 'violence' is the reason why they choose to watch such material in the first place – is effectively ignored.

If screen violence itself has changed, we also need to ask whether audiences' perceptions of it have changed as well. Accounts of early cinema describe how audiences would scream and rush from the movie theatre when confronted with sequences of train crashes or falling buildings; and even further back, spectators would faint in the more melodramatic moments of Jacobean tragedies.[21] As the conventions of realism change, so too do audience expectations; and it would also be reasonable to expect that, over time, the age at which viewers become able to 'handle' such potentially disturbing material is likely to decrease. The elements of excess, humour and 'camp' that characterize many contemporary representations of violent behaviour need to be understood in this light: they enable films to provide thrills and excitement while simultaneously allowing audiences to laugh at the exaggerated and implausible events they portray.[22] Rather than being taken as evidence of 'desensitization', this apparently distanced attitude to violence could well be seen as a reflection of the sophistication of contemporary audiences.

And yet, as with the arguments reviewed in chapters 2 and 3, the issue of children's relationship with media violence has come to stand for something much larger and more difficult to define. The spectre of the child depraved and brutalized by media violence has come to represent an all-embracing social malaise, a terminal decline in our civilization. As a result, it has become much harder to understand this relationship in its own terms. Yet if we are to respond effectively to children's apparent enthusiasm for media violence, we need to look more closely at how they experience and interpret it; and in the process, we need to detach the issue from the wider sets of concerns it has come to embody and represent.

The limits of 'effects'

It is here, of course, that audience research should have a significant role to play. Yet research on children's relationships with media violence remains dominated by a particularly reductive understanding of its effects. While media violence could conceivably be seen to produce many different kinds of effects – to generate fear, for example, or to encourage particular beliefs about the nature of crime and authority – the central preoccupation has been with its ability to produce aggressive behaviour, particularly among children.

Here again, children are largely defined in terms of what they *lack* – that is, in terms of their inability to conform to adult norms. Imitative violence is implicitly seen to arise from their inability to distinguish between fiction and reality. Children copy what they see on television, it is argued, because they lack the experience and the intellectual capacities that might enable them to see through the illusion of reality which the medium provides. They take what they watch as an accurate reflection of the world, and as a trustworthy guide to behaviour, because they are simply too immature to know any better.

'Violence' is typically seen here as a quantifiable property of the 'message' or 'stimulus', while controlled experimentation in the artificial context of the laboratory is regarded as the only truly scientific means of demonstrating how viewers respond. Even where researchers have used surveys or more naturalistic methods, violence – both in the media and in everyday life – has generally been abstracted from the contexts in which it occurs and from the motivations of those who perpetrate it.[23] And in much of the research, *correlations* between viewing and behaviour continue to be seen as evidence of *causality*.

There is now a growing body of criticism directed at the methodological and theoretical shortcomings of this research, and several reviews have demonstrated the weak and often contradictory nature of its findings.[24] Meanwhile, as I have indicated, research into other aspects of children's relationships with the media – even within mainstream psychology – has largely moved beyond the behaviourist assumptions that continue to inform the large majority of the violence research.[25]

In the estimation of many other researchers, this research in fact fails to prove its central hypothesis: that media violence makes people more aggressive *than they would otherwise have been*, or that it causes them to commit violent acts *they would not otherwise have committed*. It may influence the form or style of those acts, but it is not in itself sufficient cause to provoke them. Sociological research on real-life violence consistently suggests that its causes are multifactorial; and it rarely gives much credence to exaggerated claims about the impact of the media.[26] In this context, to seek for evidence of 'the effects of media violence' is to persist in asking simplistic questions about complicated social issues.

Nevertheless, for a variety of reasons, 'effects' research of this kind remains especially popular in the United States. This is partly a result of the continuing dominance in that country of relatively conservative, empiricist academic traditions, which were themselves partly legitimated through the early experimental studies on television violence; and it also reflects a particular set of institutional relationships between academic researchers, government and the media industries.[27] Yet the continuing prominence of such research must also be symptomatic of the deep-seated political paralysis that surrounds the issue of gun control, in a nation where there are more handguns than there are people. Researchers in other countries can justifiably feel exasperated by the way in which US research is routinely cited by campaigners against media violence as though it were universally applicable, a process which ironically echoes what George Gerbner and others see as the market-driven imperialism of media violence itself.[28]

As this implies, much of the motivation for challenging effects research has been *political* rather than purely methodological or theoretical. The challenge has arisen not so much from narrowly 'academic' concerns, but in response to the ways in which research has been used in the context of public debate and policy-making, both as a justification for stricter censorship and as a means of deflecting attention away from more deep-seated causes of phenomena such as violent crime.[29]

Of course, challenging the assumptions of effects research does not thereby mean denying the fact that the media have a degree of power to influence audiences. It is simply to suggest that the nature of that power and influence cannot be seen as a one-dimensional process of cause and effect. Nevertheless, most researchers who have questioned this approach have strategically avoided the issue of violence in their own work, and to that extent, they may have contributed to the polarization that currently characterizes the debate. Simply challenging the methodological limitations of effects research and insisting on the theoretical complexities of the issue is an essentially negative strategy. In the heated debates that surround events like the murder of James Bulger, such arguments are quickly incorporated into an either/or logic. Are we really saying that the media have *no* effects? Can we prove it? And since we can't, then surely it is better to err on the side of safety. The logic, it would seem, is inescapable – and to challenge it is simply academic obfuscation.

This situation is complicated further by the fact that many who seek to challenge simplistic assertions about imitative effects also wish to sustain arguments about the influence of media violence in other areas. There are many who would dispute the charge that violent television leads directly to acts of physical aggression, while simultaneously arguing that it encourages an ideology of militarism or traditional forms of masculinity.[30] While these are clearly different *kinds* of 'effects', such tensions and apparent contradictions cannot easily be resolved.

When confronted with the urgency and passion of the pro-censorship lobby, it is thus extremely difficult to articulate a positive alternative, particularly one which will have any kind of purchase in popular debate. To defend media violence on the grounds of 'freedom of expression' or to base one's argument on claims about 'artistic quality' is almost guaranteed to produce incredulity. And to challenge censorship, as some have attempted to do, on the grounds that it is inevitably 'political' – and that the censorship of violent pornography is somehow to be equated with the censorship of news reporting from Northern Ireland – is to take far too much for granted. So what grounds might there be for an alternative approach?

Talking 'violence'

Rather than assuming that 'violence' is an objective category – which can then be measured by simply counting how frequently it occurs – we might begin by investigating what *audiences themselves* define as violent. Research suggests that there is significant variation here. Studies have found, for example, that certain actions on television are perceived as 'violent' by girls but not by boys;[31] that British viewers perceive violence as more 'serious' in British programmes as compared with American ones;[32] and that the same action can be perceived to be violent in one context (a realistic drama, for example) but not to be violent in another (such as a situation comedy).[33] One might also expect to find differences here between children and adults – or at least adult researchers. Thus, studies have found that children do not generally perceive cartoons as violent, even though they regularly top researchers' lists of the most violent programmes.[34] Likewise, the 'violence' that so preoccupies adult critics of computer games is often so ritualized and dream-like that players themselves do not perceive it to have any significant analogy with real-life behaviour.[35] Indeed, it has been argued that the term 'violent' is itself one that is predominantly used by outsiders wishing to pass negative judgements on particular genres: it is not generally used by experienced fans of those genres, except for the purposes of irony.[36]

To be sure, surveys frequently indicate that audiences do express concern about the incidence and the effects of 'violence in the media'; but what they might actually mean by this is a more complex question. In my own research into children's and parents' views on such issues, I have frequently encountered such arguments.[37] Both groups will regularly define television violence as a 'bad influence' – albeit, of course, on those other than themselves. Yet it is important to acknowledge the social functions and the motivations of such arguments, rather than simply taking them at face value.

For parents, assertions about the negative effects of television appear to confer a considerable degree of social status on those who make them. To lament the harmful effects of television violence and to proclaim the need for strict control represents a very effective way of staking out a position as a 'concerned parent'. Such responses are, of course, more likely to be produced in situations where people are addressed and defined as 'parents', not least in response to the earnest investigations of academic researchers. As numerous studies have shown, there is a 'social desirability bias' written into such encounters, leading parents to take up such apparently 'principled' positions, and to overestimate the degree of control they exert over their children.[38]

However, these kinds of generalized assertions about media effects often prove difficult to sustain in the face of the evidence, particularly about one's own children. Idealized accounts of parental control frequently begin to crack when one is asked to describe the realities and compromises of family life. Parents will often acknowledge that their children imitate what they watch on television; although they will go on to imply that their children see such behaviour as a form of 'play', and that it is unlikely to be carried through into real life. Of course, *other people's* children might be led to commit acts of copycat violence, but the primary blame for this is seen to lie, not with the media, but with what is seen as inadequate parenting.

When talking to children, a similar kind of displacement often occurs. Of course, ten-year-olds will say, television violence can cause violence in real life. But *we* aren't influenced by what we watch: it's only little kids who copy what they see. We might have done this when we were much younger, but we certainly don't do it now. And yet, when you talk to these 'little kids', the story is the same: 'other people', it would seem, are always elsewhere. There is a kind of infinite regression here, as children in each age group claim to have already attained the age of reason several years previously. Such anecdotes about media effects are often part of a broader 'narrative of the self', in which children construct a positive identity through disavowing the immaturity of their younger selves.

In my research, both children and parents have regularly cited cases such as the murder of James Bulger or the Hungerford massacre[39] as evidence of the negative influence of media violence – despite the lack of evidence which characterizes such stories. Yet such arguments are often surrounded by a considerable degree of ambivalence, qualification and inconsistency. In the case of the Bulger killing, for example, most of the individuals in my research challenged the notion that the film *Child's Play 3* alone had been to blame; and many of the children mocked such arguments, implying that they were symptomatic of the hypocrisy and hysteria of the popular press.[40] Unlike a great deal of the press coverage, they insisted on the need to explain such actions in the light of a broader range of social and psychological influences.

Ultimately, however, the concerns of parents and of children were rather different from those of politicians and other social commentators, and indeed from those of most researchers in this field. The central concern among the parents in my research, at least in relation to their *own* children, was not that they would become aggressive as a result of what they had seen, but that they would be emotionally disturbed or upset. Likewise, older children agreed that younger ones should not be exposed to such material, on the grounds that they might find it too hard to handle. In this respect, a 'video nasty' was defined not as a film which would make children do nasty things, but as one which might give them nasty dreams.

As these observations suggest, discourses about media effects carry a considerable social charge: they provide a powerful means of defining oneself in relation to others, not least in terms of maturity and emotional 'health'. Yet, at the same time, we should beware of assuming that people simply swallow such arguments whole – and hence that campaigns to increase the censorship of media violence necessarily represent the views of the population at large, however much appeal they may have for their elected representatives. Most importantly, perhaps, we need to understand more clearly what people mean by the complaint that 'there is too much violence on television', rather than assuming that it necessarily reflects a belief in the widespread existence of 'copycat' crimes.

Reading 'effects'

As I have implied, therefore, we need to be much more precise about the *kinds* of effects which are at stake here. Violence on television, for example, may have *behavioural* effects – for example, in leading to aggression, or in encouraging people to take steps to protect themselves. It may have *emotional* effects – for example, producing shock, disgust or excitement. And it may have *ideological* or *attitudinal* effects – for example, by encouraging viewers to believe that they are more likely to be victimized by particular kinds of people, or in particular kinds of situations, and hence that specific forms of legislation or social policy are necessary to prevent this. These different levels of 'effect' might be related – emotional responses might lead to certain kinds of behaviour, for example – but the connections between them are likely to be complex and diverse. And the question of whether any of these effects might ultimately be seen as harmful or beneficial is equally complex, depending on the criteria one uses in making the judgement.

In my research in this field, I have concentrated specifically on the emotional 'effects' of television and video on children.[41] In this area at least, it is clear that television frequently has very powerful effects, and indeed that children often choose to watch it precisely in order to experience such effects. Television can provoke 'negative' responses such as worry, fear and sadness, just as it can generate 'positive' responses such as amusement, excitement and pleasure – and indeed, it often generates 'positive' and 'negative' responses at one and the same time.

Nevertheless, the question of whether these responses are to be seen as harmful or as beneficial is far from straightforward. Emotional responses which are perceived as 'negative' may have 'positive' consequences, for example in terms of children's learning or their future behaviour. Thus, children (and adults) may be extremely distressed by images of violent crime or social conflict shown on the news; but many people would argue that such experiences are a necessary part of becoming an informed citizen – and indeed, this is an argument that children frequently make on their own behalf. A fear of crime, for example, of the kind that is sometimes seen to be induced by television reporting, can lead to an illogical desire to retreat from the outside world; but it may also be a necessary prerequisite for crime prevention. Likewise, children's fiction has always played on 'negative' responses such as fear and sadness, on the grounds that experiencing such emotions in a fictional context can enable children to conquer the fears they experience in real life. Experiences that are perceived as negative in the short term may have positive benefits over the longer term. In this respect, therefore, the *consequences* of such emotional responses cannot easily be categorized as either 'positive' or 'negative'.

One fundamental distinction that needs to be made here – and it is one that is often ignored in public debates on the issue – is that between fact and fiction. Many children are certainly frightened by horror movies, and by some explicit representations of crime, particularly where they involve threats to the person. But they can also be very upset and even frightened by what they watch on the news or in documentary programmes.

My research suggested that children develop a range of strategies for coping with the unwelcome feelings induced by fictional material. These range from straightforward avoidance (simply refusing to watch, or – more ambivalently – hiding behind the sofa) to forms of psychological monitoring (self-consciously preparing oneself, or attempting to 'think happy thoughts'). While these strategies are clearly carried over from responses to stressful situations in real life, children also develop forms of generic knowledge – or 'media literacy' – which enable them to cope specifically with media experiences. For example, they will attempt to predict the outcome of a narrative on the basis of their previous experience of the genre; they will use information from beyond the text, both from conversations with others and from publicity material of various kinds; and they will use their understanding of how the illusion of realism is created, for example through editing and special effects. In all these ways, they seek reassurance from the knowledge that what they are watching is, precisely, fictional. Of course, this is not to suggest that any of these strategies is necessarily always effective, or that 'mistakes' of various kinds cannot be made: indeed, it would be impossible to learn such strategies without at some point having such negative experiences.

These strategies are simultaneously 'cognitive' and 'social': they involve forms of internal self-awareness and self-control, but they are also manifested in social performances of various kinds, both in the immediate context of viewing and subsequently in talk. To a large extent, they depend on prior knowledge or experience; and there is some evidence that they can be explicitly taught, for example by parents or older siblings.[42] Nevertheless, there will clearly be differences in this respect between experienced and less experienced viewers, a point that applies to both adults and children. 'Fans', having committed themselves to a particular genre, are likely to be much better at predicting what will happen – and hence at monitoring or controlling their responses – than casual or infrequent viewers. Indeed, a crucial aspect of the appeal of genres such as horror and 'action' movies is the way in which they play to and feed on the knowledgeability of their fans – their familiarity with the established conventions of narrative, characterization and dialogue.[43] A great deal of the irony and sardonic humour that infuses the use of 'violence' in such genres will simply be lost on the less experienced viewer, who will be inclined to take it literally – except perhaps where the humour is at its most overt, for example in movies such as *Demolition Man* or *Scream*.

By contrast, children often find it much harder to cope with the negative feelings induced by *non-fictional* material. They may learn to control their fear of a monstrous villain like Freddy Kruger by reassuring themselves that he is merely fictional; yet such reassurances are simply not available when one is confronted with news reports about grisly serial killings or images of suffering and war in Bosnia or Rwanda. As they gain experience of watching fictional violence, children may indeed become 'desensitized' to fictional violence, or at least develop strategies for coping with it; although the notion that they are thereby 'desensitized' to *real-life* violence has yet to be substantiated.[44] By contrast, however, there may be very little that children can *do* in order to come to terms with their 'negative' responses to non-fictional material, precisely because they are so powerless to intervene in issues that concern them. In my research, for example, children frequently described the disturbing effects of news reports about violent crime, and they reported experiencing much greater anxiety about the media reporting of the Bulger case than they did about the film that had allegedly provoked it.

Nevertheless, this distinction between fact and fiction is not always clear-cut. Within these different forms, children are also learning to make fine distinctions as to what they perceive to be more or less realistic or plausible.[45] As I have implied, these distinctions depend on the nature and context of the violence, and on children's existing expectations and knowledge of the genre and the medium. *Child's Play 3*, for example, was described by many of the children in my research as a comedy (in my view quite accurately); yet other horror movies, such as *Pet Sematery* and even *The Omen* appeared to be seen as more plausible, and hence more likely to prove upsetting. Fictional programmes that were judged to be more realistic (such as the TV hospital drama *Casualty*) were granted considerable credibility and power to disturb, while factual programmes that used 'fictional' devices, such as crime reconstructions, were sometimes treated in a more irreverent way.

Significantly, however, the programme that was often described as the most frightening was one that deliberately set out to violate these distinctions: it was not a 'video nasty' but a television play called *Ghostwatch*, transmitted by the BBC at Hallowe'en in 1992. This programme apparently featured a real-life ghost hunt being conducted at a house on the outskirts of London; and by using all the conventions of a 'live' outside broadcast report, including well-known presenters playing themselves, it appears to have succeeded in fooling many viewers. Yet while several children found the programme very disturbing, a number of the older ones expressed considerable interest in seeing it again; and video copies are still in circulation, testifying to its continuing cult status. As this implies, the distinction between fact and fiction is not a fixed or straightforward one; yet playing on the boundaries between them provides a distinctly risky kind of pleasure.

So why do children watch?

Rather than simply condemning screen violence, therefore, it makes sense to begin by asking *why* people – and children in particular – actively choose to watch it. Research on such issues typically seeks to answer this question by recourse to a pathological conception of the viewer. A taste for violence is seen to be a symptom of sexual immaturity, lack of intelligence, or more fundamental personality defects. Ultimately, it would seem that people only watch this stuff because there is something fundamentally *wrong* with them.

The potential appeal of screen violence is, on one level, fairly easy to understand. For many viewers, there is a visceral thrill in watching graphic representations of violence – a thrill that has of course been recognized since the tragedies of the Ancient Greeks. Critics will occasionally enthuse about the 'poetry' or 'beauty' of set piece instances of screen violence, while others acknowledge its vaguely 'countercultural', subversive appeal.[46] As I have implied, many films encourage a self-conscious irony, a 'sick' humour, in responses to screen violence which suggests that it is not to be taken literally. The publicity come-ons for violent movies – 'can you take it?' – also attest to the pleasure that can be gained from self-consciously 'testing' one's own psychological responses.[47] Extreme instances of graphic violence can raise challenging moral and philosophical questions about our own complicity in it, not just in 'art movies' such as *Man Bites Dog* or *Broken Mirrors* but also in more mainstream entertainment such as *Reservoir Dogs* or *Natural Born Killers*.[48]

All these are potentially significant aspects of the experience and the pleasure of screen violence *per se* – and few of them have been acknowledged, let alone systematically investigated, by mainstream research. Yet the presence or absence of 'violence' may not in itself be a sufficient, or even a particularly meaningful, explanation of why people choose to expose themselves to such material. Here again, we need to look *beyond* 'violence' to the generic and dramatic contexts in which it occurs.

Let us consider the example of horror. In so far as they do generate negative emotions, apparently violent genres such as horror may be popular because they enable us to understand and deal with real-life anxieties and concerns in the comparatively 'safe' arena of fiction. Indeed, many horror films would seem to be implicitly addressed to children, or at least to 'the child in us all'. It is no surprise that so many of the apparently horrific books, films and television programmes children prefer are those which play on their fear of the large and incomprehensible 'monsters' that surround them. Alternatively, they are about child-like figures, or repressed dimensions of childhood, taking revenge on the adult world. This may well be why the figure of Chucky from *Child's Play 3* proved to be so offensive to many adults: he represents a direct and highly self-conscious affront to cherished notions of childhood innocence.

In my research on children's responses to horror, I found a considerable degree of ambivalence. On the one hand, the children's accounts of horror films were frequently accompanied by a good deal of disclaiming. Many vehemently denied that they were scared by horror films, and occasionally mocked those who said they were. Many were keen to assert that they were no longer scared by such material, even if they had been when they were younger. Some of the children retold extremely gory scenes of torture and dismembering, yet in a studied deadpan tone, as if to guarantee their fearlessness.

Many of the children attempted to use their limited knowledge of the genre, and their understandings about the production process, to distance themselves from the fears such films had evidently invoked – although for the younger or less experienced viewers, this knowledge was uncertain, and its effects could not always be guaranteed. Films like *Child's Play* and *Nightmare on Elm Street* were often described as 'unrealistic' and even as laughable, particularly by the older children. Many were keen to draw attention to the liberal use of 'tomato ketchup' and make-up; although they also expressed a kind of aesthetic appreciation of special effects that were done well.

On the other hand, there was plenty of evidence that horror films do frighten children, and that such responses are occasionally quite lasting. Such experiences often seemed to crystallize around a single decontextualized image or scene which the children would 'rewind' in their heads. In many instances, the children described how the experience of fear intensified after viewing. Some spoke of the fear of going into a dark bedroom or out to the kitchen to get a drink after they had seen a horror film. Others described how clothes hanging on a door or a shadow on the curtain could temporarily appear like a shape from *Alien* – although, of course, such fears are commonplace and do not solely result from viewing.

One possible reason why such fears might intensify in this way is because many of the coping strategies that are available at the point of viewing no longer apply in the darkness and isolation of one's bedroom, where the only option is to hide under the bedcovers. Yet this also raises interesting questions about the notion of 'suspension of disbelief', which is sometimes seen to be a prerequisite of the experience of horror. Noel Carroll argues that horror does *not* in fact depend on such a suspension of disbelief – at least in the sense of a conscious act that happens once and for all.[49] We do not, he suggests, ever give up our belief that the monster is fictional: rather, our fear is in response to the *thought* or the imagination that the monster *might* be real. Thus, the fear evoked by horror often depends on a more general *doubt* about the supernatural – and a willingness at least to entertain the possibility of its existence – that is very widely shared, even in apparently secular societies.

What it is perhaps most crucial to emphasize here, however, is that in almost all the children's accounts they took on the position of the victim rather than the 'monster'. As Carol Clover has convincingly argued in her study of the dynamics of 'rape revenge' and 'slasher' movies,[50] contemporary horror is often 'victim-identified': what is perceived as 'good horror', she suggests, may be that which is most successful in 'hurting' its viewers, and playing on fears and desires that are often perceived as 'feminine'. Far from glorying in a sadistic and misogynistic identification with the (male) killer, viewers may in fact be adopting the masochistic position of the (female) victim. The notion that here, as in cinematic spectatorship in general, viewers are necessarily led to adopt the masterful, sadistic 'male gaze' is one that is certainly open to question.

To some extent, of course, this ambivalence could be seen as a function of the interview situation. To claim that you were scared is, in some respects, an admission of weakness; yet to argue that the film is not scary is to undermine its 'adult' or 'countercultural' status, and hence your own status as a viewer. Nevertheless, this ambivalence can also been seen as an indication of the tensions involved in the experience of viewing itself.

Thus, while many of the children described how they had been scared and given nightmares as a result of watching horror, their prime motivation for doing so was clearly to do with pleasure. Even where it was acknowledged that films were scary, this was often seen to be synonymous with the enjoyment they offered. Many of the children expressed the wish to watch 'scary' things again, even where their first experiences of them appeared to have been quite traumatic. The wish to 'see it again' – and the practice of repeat viewing – are, on one level, simply about reliving the pleasure. Many children claimed to have seen favourite horror films 'over and over again', while others described how they would use the video to fast-forward to the 'best bits' – that is, the scariest or most 'violent' moments – or to watch those parts again.[51] At the same time, repeat viewing of this kind also helps children to cope with negative feelings: rewinding the tape enables you to 'see how it's done' and hence to conquer your fear.

This suggests a rather different view of the impact of technology than is often promoted in public debate. As I have noted, the 'problem' of video in this context is that it is seen to undermine centralized regulation; and it is also sometimes seen to encourage an obsessive and unhealthy preoccupation with decontextualized moments of violence. Yet, as I have implied, it may also afford much more positive control for viewers themselves, and play a part in developing their competencies as viewers.

Even for the more enthusiastic horror viewers, therefore, pleasure was seen to be inextricably tied up with the possibility of pain – although the balance between the two was sometimes difficult to achieve. This ambivalence is perhaps most clearly manifested in the characteristic pose of the horror viewer, described by several children: peering over the top of the cushion, or peeking through half-closed fingers, this pose allows you to feel 'safe' and yet also to fulfil the desire to know the outcome of the narrative.

Nevertheless, transgression and disruption were the major focus of the children's pleasure in the genre. They did not, by and large, choose to focus on the restoration of order or the demise of the monster, but on the films' violations of social, sexual and physical taboos. It is an enormous leap to suggest, as some critics have done, that these transgressions are somehow politically 'progressive', or indeed psychically therapeutic – that the monster somehow stands in for all the underprivileged social groups, or for the repressed sexual energies, whose inherent threat must be contained by bourgeois society.[52] Nevertheless, much of the appeal of horror must surely lie not only in the pleasure of watching evil destroyed or controlled, but also in watching it triumph, however temporarily. This is not to suggest that viewers simply 'identify' with the monster – if anything, the opposite is the case. Nevertheless, it is to imply that the 'pain' of viewing should not be seen simply as the polar opposite of the pleasure, as though the presence of one implied the absence or removal of the other.

The ambivalence and complexity of children's experiences of horror should lead us to question many of the assumptions that are frequently made about it – assumptions that are often based on ignorance, not merely of children, but also of the genre itself. To be sure, children do often get frightened or disgusted by horror films, but then so do adults. The notion that the experience is therefore necessarily negative and traumatic, or indeed that it inevitably 'depraves and corrupts', is no more valid than the idea that it is somehow automatically therapeutic. It may be the case that, as adults, it is our responsibility to help children learn to cope with such experiences; but it is important that we do so in a way that respects the complexity of the process, and empowers children to make decisions on their own behalf.

Changing sites of regulation

The technological changes of the past two decades have dramatically undermined the ability of the state to control the traffic in moving images. Substantial and growing numbers of 'under age' children have seen the kind of material which it is officially illegal for them to obtain – and which some would like to ban outright. While they may be exceptional, I have interviewed children as young as six who have seen films from the *Nightmare on Elm Street* series; and I would guess that a majority of boys and girls in their early teens have seen at least one film from this or the *Child's Play* series – nearly all of which have an '18' certificate in Britain. Likewise, films like *Pulp Fiction* and *Goodfellas* and series like the *Terminator*, *Die Hard* and *Lethal Weapon* movies have a substantial following among early adolescent boys, aged well below their official rating of fifteen or eighteen. If the aim of media regulation is to prevent children gaining access to such material, then it is clearly failing.

In this situation, much of the responsibility for regulation has inevitably shifted to parents. Yet this in itself has generated considerable cause for concern. As I have noted, the debate about media effects has become increasingly caught up with the debate about parenting – a debate which, in the wake of the child abuse scares of recent decades, has taken on an increasingly urgent tone. Perhaps the most offensive aspect of this debate has been the way in which so much of the blame has been allocated to working-class parents. It is these supposedly inadequate parents, living chaotic and aimless lives on council estates up and down the country, who are alleged to have absolved themselves of all responsibility for their children, not caring less if they are depraved and traumatized by images of senseless violence.[53]

Of course, it is difficult to know whether such parents actually exist. Throughout several years of research in this field with children and parents from a wide range of social backgrounds – including some that were distinctly deprived – I have yet to meet or be told about parents who do not attempt to control the kind of material their children watch, at least until their early teens. Yet, as I have noted, parents' central concern in relation to so-called 'violent' material is not that they fear their children will become criminals or child-killers. On the contrary, they are seeking to protect them from material they might find frightening or upsetting. And at the same time, children are also learning to protect *themselves* from such experiences, in a variety of ways.

Nevertheless, the problem for parents (and indeed for media producers) is that it is very hard to predict what children will find disturbing or upsetting. Many of the children I have interviewed have described quite unlikely experiences from their early childhood, such as being frightened by apparently innocuous films like *Mary Poppins* or *Chitty Chitty Bang Bang*. Nor is this simply a matter of psychological development: I have interviewed six-year-olds who blithely profess that they were not frightened by *Nightmare on Elm Street* and fifteen-year-olds who say precisely the opposite. For parents, this makes it hard to know when or how to intervene. Simply banning material gives it the attraction of forbidden fruit, and means that children will try that much harder to see it elsewhere. Instinctive responses – turning the thing off when it gets too much, or sending the kids out of the room – may deprive them of the reassurance that is provided at the end of the narrative.

At least in principle, children generally accept that parents are correct to try to protect them from such experiences. In practice, however, there is a great deal of negotiation over what is seen as 'appropriate' for children to watch; and many children appear to be extremely successful in evading their parents' attempts at regulation. Here again, such debates within the family necessarily invoke much broader assumptions about the proper characteristics of childhood and of adulthood, although several of the parents in my research acknowledged that they had learnt a great deal from their own children in this respect, and that their views had changed over time.[54] Yet while parents and children may well come into conflict, both will typically claim the right to make their own decisions about what should be seen. While both groups are generally aware of forms of media regulation – such as the video classification system and the 'family viewing policy' on terrestrial television – they often question and dispute them. In broad terms, they agree that the responsibility for regulation should be shared between them, and not be in the hands of others.

Technological, economic and cultural changes – as well as the increasing diversity of opinion on issues of taste and morality – have thus significantly undermined the status of centralized regulation. So does that mean it should simply be abandoned? Ultimately, I do not believe it is realistic to espouse a wholesale libertarianism, at least in relation to children. For a variety of quite genuine reasons, adults will always want to 'censor' or control the images and texts that are made available to young people. The question is not *whether* but *how* and *where* this takes place.

For better or worse, the inexorable tendency here is towards 'privatized' forms of regulation, which place greater responsibility in the hands of the individual consumer.[55] To be sure, politicians and campaigners will continue to fulminate about the need for stricter censorship. In the wake of the Bulger case, for example, the film classification authorities were given greater powers to censor violence on video; while penalties for supplying 'under age' young people with '18'-rated videotapes in some cases now exceed those for supplying hard drugs. Nevertheless, the regulatory bodies themselves are beginning to accept the logic of this situation.[56] At least in Europe, there seems to be little support for the introduction of the V-chip;[57] and there have been positive moves towards providing more detailed 'consumer advice' about the content of films and programmes, particularly where this relates to areas of general concern. Nevertheless, a great deal more could be done to make the system more informative and publicly accountable, and to ensure that ordinary citizens are involved in the decision-making process. More fundamentally, we need to move towards a situation in which media regulation on the grounds of taste or morality is advisory rather than legally enforced, as it is in Britain at present.[58] The continuing refusal to allow teenagers the right to make informed choices about their own viewing is, to say the least, an anachronism: it is out of step with most parents' views, and seems almost designed to stimulate the behaviour it purports to prevent.

To suggest that we should pass responsibility to parents and children in this way is not, however, to imply that we should place all our faith in 'consumer power'. At its worst, this argument would seem to collude with the privatization of childhood – and indeed of the media – identified in previous chapters. As Patricia Holland has argued, we need a 'wider vision' that will 'allow children to grow beyond the narrow and over-heated family environment into a diverse public sphere'.[59] While I would broadly support a more privatized system of regulation, at least in relation to issues of taste and morality, any such system will need substantial support from within the public domain. In this respect, mere 'consumer advice' is not enough. We need much more coherent and consistent initiatives at the level of educational and cultural policy that will enable children and parents to become informed, critical participants in media culture. As I shall argue, this will require some fresh thinking about the relationships between the public and the private, and about the role of public institutions such as schools.

These points, and the 'wider vision' of which they might form a part, will be developed more fully in my concluding chapter. By moral campaigners, however, I suspect they will still be seen to avoid what is really at stake in the debate about children and media violence. As I have implied, this debate is really a debate about other things, many of which have very little to do with the media or with children. The issue of media violence has come to serve as a cipher for some very diverse, but fundamental, anxieties – about the decline of the family and of organized religion, about the changing nature of literacy and contemporary culture, and about the pace of technological change. These are feelings that are difficult to engage with, let alone to displace; and their sources lie more in the broader social upheavals of the past three decades than in the more 'local' changes in the media themselves. While there may be some benefit in attempting to address children's relationship with media violence on its own terms, these broader anxieties will ultimately prove impossible to ignore.

8

Children as Consumers

If public debates about the impact of media violence have largely been dominated by those on the political right, the issue of consumerism and advertising occupies a similar status for many on the left. In both instances, children have been identified as a particular focus of concern, on the grounds of their apparent vulnerability to media influence. In both instances, the media have been seen to possess an overweening power to govern behaviour, to mould attitudes and to construct and define children's identities. And in both instances, these concerns have led to calls for increased child protection, in the form of stricter censorship or media regulation.

As I have argued, this emphasis on children could be seen as part of a broader 'politics of substitution'.[1] Here again, expressions of anxiety and concern about children provide a means of commanding assent to positions that are not in fact specifically or uniquely concerned with children at all. Introducing children into the equation undoubtedly dramatizes the issues; but in the process, it can represent children themselves as effectively powerless.

Books like the collection *Kinderculture*, discussed in chapter 2, embody these concerns at their most rhetorical.[2] Children are seen here as helpless victims of a kind of brainwashing at the hands of capitalist media conglomerates. Commercial corporations are accused of 'colonizing children's consciousness', imposing false ideologies and inculcating materialistic values that children in particular are seen to be unable to resist. Of course, concerns about children's relationship with consumer culture are not always motivated by such explicitly anti-capitalist arguments. Yet, as with the debate about violence, there is a general assumption here that children are a 'special audience', a group whose innate needs and characteristics render them uniquely at risk.

Here again, it is not my intention to suggest that such concerns are simply misguided, or indeed to dismiss them as a kind of 'political panic'. There are genuine reasons why such concerns have intensified in recent years; and there is a need for more thoughtful responses, both in media policy and in education. Nevertheless, as with the debate about screen violence, concerns about children's relationship with consumer culture have been invested with much broader symbolic significance. The popular image of children as merely innocent victims of the seductive wiles of evil capitalists is one that invokes much more fundamental ideologies of childhood.

In this respect, the anxiety that surrounds children's relationship with consumer culture could be related to much earlier concerns about children's involvement in the workforce. As the historian Ludmilla Jordanova has shown, criticisms of child labour in the late nineteenth century reflected much wider beliefs about the essential nature of childhood:

> Children were [seen as] tender, impressionable, vulnerable, pure, deserving of parental protection, and hence all too easily corrupted by the market-place. Two main justifications existed for this characterisation of children: a Christian one, which portrayed children as in a 'sacred state of life'; and an ideological one, according to which they were somehow 'naturally' incompatible with the world of commodities.[3]

As Jordanova argues, children's relationship with the economy is a key site of tension in their apparent transition from the status of child (in the domain of 'nature') to that of adult (in the domain of 'culture'). As such, it is a crucial arena in which the meaning of childhood is negotiated and defined.

Here again, therefore, the central issue is to do with how we interpret and respond to children's growing involvement in areas of 'adult' life from which they have traditionally been excluded. In attempting to develop a more constructive response to the issue, we will again need to disentangle it from the broader concerns that it has come to symbolize and represent.

The rise of the child consumer

The past fifty years have seen a remarkable increase in the scope and scale of consumer activity.[4] The range of consumer goods on the market has significantly increased; shopping has become a popular leisure-time pursuit, second only to watching television; and the range and availability of opportunities to buy has steadily grown. Meanwhile, more and more activities and aspects of human inter-action – particularly those relating to leisure – are now being made available through the commercial market.

However, it is only in the last couple of decades that capitalism's restless search for new markets has come to focus so intensely on children. Just as teenagers were apparently 'discovered' as a distinct consumer group in the postwar economic boom, so children are now becoming one of the most sought-after targets for 'niche marketing'. Reduced family size, the increase in divorce and in single-parent families and the general (albeit unevenly distributed) increase in dis-posable income, combined with the new symbolic 'valorization' of childhood, have all given children greater say in household purchas-ing decisions. As advertisers have recognized, children may not have much disposable income of their own, but they possess a form of 'pester power' that exerts a significant influence on the purchasing decisions of others in the household. In the US, for example, the chil-dren's market is estimated to be worth around 10 billion dollars each year; while children have been estimated to influence more than 130 billion dollars worth of household purchases annually.[5] Retailers have accordingly become more 'child oriented' in their sales techniques; spending on advertising directed at children has grown exponen-tially, and there has been a marked increase in more general promo-tional activities aimed at children, not least in schools.[6]

Meanwhile, the gradual deregulation of the media industries and the shift towards global, multichannel media systems have led to a new ascendancy of commercial interests, and a corresponding de-cline in public sector provision. The question of whether children will be adequately served in this new media environment has been particularly acute in relation to television. As I have noted, the *quan-tity* of television available to children has significantly increased, both on terrestrial and (most spectacularly) on non-terrestrial channels; although this has not necessarily been accompanied by an increase in its diversity or quality (however these might be defined). Yet in many countries, advocates of children's television have perceived themselves to be engaged in an ongoing struggle, not so much to extend and improve provision for children, but simply to *preserve* it. While apparent victories have been won – for example, around the 1990 Broadcasting Act in the UK, and the 1990 Children's Television Act in the US – the *enforcement* of broadcasters' statutory respon-sibilities to children is nevertheless a continuing concern.

Such debates are now increasingly focusing on the internet, where there has been a similar proliferation of commercially based sites aimed at children. Such sites often combine superficially 'educational' activities with advertising messages and attempts to gather market research data.[7] Here too, children are beginning to emerge as a significant new target market; and in the process, the boundaries between 'education' and 'entertainment', and between content and advertising, have become increasingly blurred. The convergence of media and the rise of integrated marketing have led to a situation in which all media texts could effectively be seen as advertisements for other media texts. And yet, as I have noted, the steady commercialization of media aimed at children is also contributing to a widening gap between the 'information rich' and the 'information poor', in which viewers who are restricted to free-to-air broadcast channels and who do not have access to new technologies are significantly disadvantaged.

Responses to these developments have been starkly polarized. On the one hand, there are many critics who perceive the market as inherently inimical to the true interests and needs of children. Commercial media, they argue, are little more than an incitement to consumerism, and an exploitation of children's vulnerability. Stephen Kline, for example, states this position in bleak terms:

> The marketplace will never inspire children with high ideals or positive images of the personality, provide stories which help them to adjust to life's tribulations or promote play activities that are most help to their maturation. Business interests trying to maximise profits cannot be expected to worry about cultural values or social objectives beyond the consumerist cultural vector that underwrites commercial media.[8]

By contrast, there are those who argue that the market is in fact a more effective means of meeting children's needs than the old-fashioned, paternalistic system of public service broadcasting. In the words of Geraldine Laybourne, one of the founders of the children's channel Nickelodeon, 'what's good for business is good for kids.'[9] As we have seen, the new commercial providers typically claim not just to be serving children (or, as they are more often termed, 'kids') but also to be 'empowering' them. Children are characterized here as a sophisticated and demanding audience, who are difficult to reach and to satisfy. Far from being passive victims of commercial culture, children are seen as all-powerful, sovereign consumers.

These debates thus inevitably invoke all sorts of assumptions about the needs of children, and how they are to be met. Stephen Kline, for example, asserts that children require 'high ideals' and 'positive images of the personality', and that they need help to 'adjust' and 'mature' – and he implies that such things can only be provided for them by well-meaning adults, who are free from commercial motivations. Geraldine Laybourne and others would probably share this general view of children's needs – although they would also argue that children themselves are the best placed to identify and articulate those needs, and that the market provides the most effective means of enabling them to do so.

Critiques of advertising

Nevertheless, these kinds of assumptions about children's relations with the marketplace are not always coherently defined, or justified by the empirical evidence. These limitations are particularly apparent in debates about the effects of *advertising*.

Almost since its inception, mass market advertising has been seen as the pre-eminent symbol of the failings of capitalism, for left-wing and conservative cultural critics alike. It is typically condemned not simply for making us buy things that we do not want or need, but also for inculcating consumerism and materialistic values. Advertising is accused of creating 'false needs' that replace authentic human values and relationships, and of promoting the belief that our identities are fundamentally derived from what we own and consume.[10] And it is seen to exercise this power by using deceptive techniques that bypass rational control – and in some cases even escape our conscious awareness.[11]

Such critiques of advertising are often informed by a more general suspicion of the symbolic functions of material objects. Raymond Williams's famous condemnation of the 'magic system' of advertising,[12] for example, seems to reflect a much broader distrust of what he terms 'fantasy'. Like many on the left, Williams sees the power of advertising and the consumerist values it promotes as a consequence of alienation: people need this false 'consumption ideal' to overcome the dissatisfaction and sense of powerlessness that characterize their everyday lives. From this perspective, the values and desires people invest in material goods are seen as merely irrational. If people were only *more* 'materialist', Williams argues, they would see possessions merely in utilitarian terms, and would have no need for such spurious fantasies.

The problems with this position are fairly self-evident. The notion of 'false needs' inevitably implies that there are *true* needs which can be identified and agreed on; while the rejection of 'fantasy' and 'magic' implies a wholly rationalistic model of human behaviour. The critics' apparent nostalgia for more authentic or 'human' forms of social relationship seems to hark back to an imaginary Golden Age in which culture was somehow uncontaminated by commerce.

Furthermore, these rhetorical arguments about the effects of advertising are typically based merely on critiques of advertisements themselves. As in the case of debates about violence, 'effects' are presumed to flow automatically from particular characteristics of texts. Such arguments implicitly position the audience – the consumers of advertising and the products it promotes – as powerless victims of manipulation. While such critics will occasionally acknowledge that audiences may be sceptical about advertising, they nevertheless suggest that such scepticism is positively *used* – and hence easily incorporated – by the cunning wiles of the advertisers.

This view of audiences as merely 'malleable consumers' is increasingly difficult to sustain when applied to adults. Yet even critics who reject this view tend to draw the line when it comes to children. Children, it is typically argued, are much more amenable to persuasion, simply by virtue of their immaturity. For example, in one of the leading textbooks on advertising, Leiss, Kline and Jhally argue as follows: 'children as viewers have neither the ability to understand the persuasive intent of advertising nor the level of conceptual and experiential maturity needed to evaluate commercial messages rationally.'[13] Here again, broader arguments about the negative influence of the media have come to rely on a particular construction of the *child* as more or less 'incompetent' or 'irrational', and hence as uniquely vulnerable to persuasion.

Evidence from research

To what extent are such arguments about the effects of advertising on children substantiated by empirical research? As with the work on screen violence, much of the evidence here is actually quite weak and inconclusive.[14] Here again, it is important to distinguish between different types of 'effects'. When it comes to *consumer behaviour*, it seems that advertising can influence consumers' choice of brands, but that it rarely encourages them to purchase more of any given type of product. Younger children, who might be presumed to be more at risk from advertising, are generally least able to remember and to understand advertisements. For children in general, advertising is less significant as a source of information than other sources such as peers and parents, or visits to the shops. Likewise, advertising appears to make a fairly limited contribution to children's *beliefs* about the qualities of products. For example, researchers have tended to conclude that advertising has a relatively weak influence on children's nutritional knowledge (for instance, the belief that sugary foods are healthy), and that parents and socioeconomic status are more significant. And, perhaps predictably, the claim that advertising contributes to broader *ideologies and values* of the kind identified above – that it makes children more 'consumerist' or 'materialistic' than they would otherwise be – is far from adequately substantiated by the available research. In so far as they can be meaningfully measured, 'materialistic' orientations also appear to derive primarily from family and peers rather than from any direct influence of advertising.

As with the violence research, there are distinct dangers here in attempting to isolate a single variable from among a range of potential influences. Yet perhaps the more fundamental problem is with the essentially behaviourist perspective that seems to inform the debate. As Brian Young argues,[15] the dominant approach regards the child as innocent and the advertiser as a seducer. Children are defined here as inadequate rather than competent, trusting rather than sceptical, pure rather than corrupted. It is a view that, as Young implies, carries a considerable emotional charge, not least because it invokes much broader assumptions about childhood; and, like most such arguments, it serves to justify forms of adult protection that are designed to keep children in their place.

By contrast, research within the constructivist paradigm has placed much greater emphasis on children's cognitive processing of advertising, rather than on assessing effects.[16] These researchers have argued that far from children being passive consumers of advertising messages, their attention to advertising is highly selective and their interpretations of it quite diverse. As in the case of 'perceived reality' (see chapter 6), cognitive processing is typically seen here as a variable that intervenes between stimulus and response. The central question is whether children possess 'cognitive defences' that will enable them to protect themselves against the persuasive influence of advertising. Thus, there have been attempts to identify the age at which children become aware of the differences between advertisements and programmes, and of the persuasive intentions of advertising – and, predictably, estimates vary significantly depending on the methods used. Broadly speaking, however, this research suggests that children are able to distinguish between programmes and advertisements from a very early age; and that by the age of about seven or eight they are well aware of the motivations of advertisers, and in many instances extremely cynical about them. In general, it would seem, children are regarded here as discriminating viewers of advertising: they do not necessarily trust it or believe that it tells the truth, they are aware of the persuasive devices that it employs, and they consistently attempt to compare it with real-life experience.

These findings significantly challenge generalized assertions about children's lack of 'conceptual and experiential maturity' of the kind quoted above. Nevertheless, they leave several significant issues unresolved. Like constructivist research in general, these studies tend to rely on a normative, rationalistic developmental model, in which adults are implicitly defined as logical, 'wise consumers', and children are assessed in terms of their (in)ability to achieve this state. Meanwhile, what might loosely be called the expressive, emotional or symbolic aspects of consumer behaviour tend to be ignored. In this respect, localized studies of the cognitive processing of advertisements seem bound to neglect broader aspects of consumer culture, of the kind that will be addressed in due course.

Wise consumers?

My own research, with children aged between eight and twelve, largely confirms this picture, although it also begins to suggest other questions.[17] In our interviews, we encountered a considerable degree of scepticism – and indeed cynicism – about television advertising. The children were clearly aware of the persuasive functions of advertising, and of the potential for deception. Many described how advertisers would attempt to 'make things look better than they are'; and many reported instances in which their experiences of products fell far short of the claims made in the advertisements. Advertising in general was rejected by many as merely a 'con' – a confidence trick.

The children were also very ready to parody or mock particular advertisements, often with great hilarity. Far from admiring the glamorous role models that allegedly populate the world of advertising, the children seemed to reject the large majority of the people featured in them as hopeless 'wallies' and 'has-beens'. The children claimed to know a great deal about the process of production, speculating about how the actors were recruited and auditioned, and how much they were paid. They questioned the way in which allegedly 'real' people were used in ads; they complained about bad acting and poor dubbing; they asserted that surveys and 'before-and-after' tests were merely faked; and they drew attention to 'camera tricks' achieved via editing or special effects. Ads were frequently rejected as 'phoney', 'unrealistic' and exaggerated, while some were directly challenged for making misleading claims.

Several of the children also displayed more sophisticated 'metalinguistic' skills. They were able to hypothesize about the motivations of the advertisers, and about their assumptions about the likely responses of audiences. For example, they were aware of the kinds of strategies that advertisers use to counteract the scepticism of viewers, or to command their attention; and of the uses of irony and deliberate ambiguity. There was considerable criticism of advertisements that were perceived to be stereotyped or patronizing, or to be making illegitimate connections between particular values and products.

On the face of it, then, these children were more than adequately equipped with 'cognitive defences' against the influence of advertising. Yet the fact that such defences may be available does not automatically guarantee that they will be used – or indeed that they will necessarily enable children to resist the appeals of particular advertisements. Knowing that advertisements have designs on you does not necessarily mean that you will always reject them; and a generalized cynicism about advertising clearly does not preclude the enjoyment of particular ads.

Here again, it is important to consider the social and interpersonal functions of this 'critical' discourse about advertising, and the positions it allows children to take up. Many of the children here were keen to be seen as 'wise consumers' who were capable of making rational decisions about product quality and value for money. They reported how they would 'test' products before they bought them; how they would compare prices; and how they would refuse to be deceived by attractive packaging, brand names or premium offers. They also described how they would read food packets for information about sugar content and additives. Yet this display of 'wise consumerism' – and of cynicism about the claims of advertisers – also had a distinctly competitive edge. In general, the children were inclined to reject the claim that they themselves had been influenced by advertising. Here again, the gullible audience always appeared to consist of *other* people – not just younger children, but also (in some cases) ignorant adults. As in other aspects of this research (see chapter 6), there were distinct differences here in terms of social class. In general, the middle-class children were much more fluent in this 'critical' discourse about advertising, and much more likely to engage in such competitive displays of cynicism. By contrast, the working-class children appeared to have much less invested in demonstrating their ability to 'see through' advertising.

As this implies, these responses need to be seen in terms of the social context in which they were produced. They arose in response to our relatively 'teacherly' questions – and the middle-class children in general were more inclined to perceive our interviews as an 'educational' encounter. In presenting themselves as 'critical readers' of advertising, or as 'wise consumers', these children were implicitly laying claim to a more powerful (more 'adult' or 'sophisticated') identity.

To this extent, the use of interviews is bound to invite these kinds of 'knowing' responses; and as such, it may inevitably reproduce the 'cognitive bias' that I have argued is characteristic of research into children and television advertising more broadly. Nevertheless, there was also a considerable amount of pleasure expressed in these discussions. Several of the children displayed a generalized enthusiasm for advertising that was rather at odds with the cynicism identified above; while some even claimed to be 'fans' of television advertisements, seeking them out in preference to the programmes. Many of the children sang or 'acted out' adverts, a practice that several claimed was an everyday activity. While some of these were ones they had enjoyed, others were mercilessly parodied and satirized. There was great competition to offer the most hilarious renditions of jingles, catchphrases, comic moments and strange accents.

In many instances, however, these pleasurable elements appeared to be unconnected to the products themselves, and in some instances the children were unable to identify or recall the products concerned. 'Good adverts' were far from guaranteed to relate to 'good products'. As Mica and Orson Nava have suggested, young people may increasingly relate to advertising on an aesthetic level that is independent of the products being marketed.[18] Even the self-declared 'fans' of advertising in my research appeared to enjoy a comparatively distanced relationship with it, in which pleasure and appreciation were tinged with mockery and parody.

Ultimately, to define the issues here solely in terms of children's resistance or susceptibility to persuasion, or indeed in terms of the extent of their 'cognitive defences', is to underestimate the complexity of what is taking place. The danger is that, like the critics of advertising discussed above, we set up an opposition between 'rational' and 'emotional' responses, and assume that the 'problem' of advertising can be solved by providing children with a kind of rationalistic character armour. I would argue that such attempts to convert children into 'rational consumers' are bound to fail, not least because they aspire to a norm that even adults are incapable of sustaining. People are not always rational consumers, not only because they do not have time to plough through consumer magazines and evaluate all the alternatives before deciding what to buy, but also because material objects are inevitably invested with symbolic values, and cannot be separated from them. To imply, as the critics of advertising tend to do, that the 'fantasy' and 'magic' that infuse our relationships with material objects derive wholly from advertising, and that they can simply be displaced by a good dose of rationality, is merely wishful thinking.

At the same time, there are significant limitations in focusing solely on *advertising* in isolation from consumer culture more broadly. As I have noted, the boundaries between advertising messages and 'content' in the media have become more and more blurred, and promotional activities in general have become increasingly significant. Where marketing to children is concerned, statistics from the US suggest that spending on promotion and public relations – not least in previously 'sacred' venues such as schools – now exceeds spending on advertising. Much of this is additional expenditure rather than simply a reallocation of spending on advertising – a fact which itself reflects the growing significance of the child market.[19] Strategies such as sponsorship and event marketing have increasingly been recognized as valuable means of achieving brand awareness, and of overcoming consumers' scepticism about advertising *per se*. Meanwhile, of course, the media themselves have become steadily privatized: media texts are now commodities in their own right, rather than inducements to watch or read advertisements for other commodities.

As yet, however, little is known about children's understandings of these processes, or their grasp of the operations of the economy more broadly.[20] In the case of my own research, for example, children rarely volunteered information about the economic functions of advertising for the television companies themselves. By and large, they understood what advertisements were attempting to do, but they knew much less about why they appeared on television in the first place.[21] Yet in the context of this more general 'promotional culture', it may make little sense to ask whether children understand the differences between television programmes and advertisements, or whether they are able to identify the persuasive intentions of advertising in isolation. We need to consider much broader questions about their experience of consumer culture, and their place within it.

Animating consumers

A good example of the characteristics – and indeed the limitations – of debates in this field can be found in discussions of children's television, and particularly of its relationship with merchandising.[22] The deregulation of US television in the 1980s led to the advent of a new wave of toy-related animation series. *He-Man, She-Ra, Thundercats, The Smurfs, My Little Pony, The Real Ghostbusters, Transformers* and *Teenage Mutant Ninja Turtles* were among the best known of these titles, which have been screened in scores of countries around the world, accompanied by an extensive range of licensed merchandising.[23] In the case of the *Turtles*, for example, it was almost impossible to avoid the plethora of toys, clothes, playsuits, lunchboxes, foodstuffs, sweets and drinks that bore the ubiquitous amphibian imagery. As I have noted, such programmes have also formed part of the 'trans-media intertextuality' that increasingly connects television, films, comics, books, records and computer games.[24]

The global dominance of US animation can, of course, be partly explained in economic terms. The size of the US domestic market permits major economies of scale, which means that material can be offered to overseas programmers at a fraction of the cost of home-grown product. While the costs of live-action drama have spiralled, animation has become cheaper to produce, particularly since the advent of digitization; and while critics have bemoaned the decline of artistic quality in recent animation, the use of simplified backgrounds and 'shorthand' styles of drawing (which make the process significantly faster) can in fact be dated back to the early days of Hanna-Barbera in the 1960s. Animation is also much easier to dub into other languages,[25] while the frequent reliance on non-human characters means that the series do not come laden with overt cultural baggage. Such series are, of course, very popular with children, a fact which often proves inexplicable or inconvenient for their critics, but which represents a significant temptation for broadcasters. On the face of it, filling the schedules with US animation would seem to be an inexpensive and lucrative way of discharging one's statutory obligations to provide a minimum amount of programming designed for the child audience.

Rather like screen violence or pornography, these series serve as a convenient 'bad object' which critics of widely divergent persuasions can agree to abhor.[26] They are routinely condemned as 'formula' productions which deal in one-dimensional characters and predictable narratives, and which are lacking in emotional or psychological 'depth'. They are accused of encouraging sexism, racism, militarism and violence; and of confining children's play to a limited rehearsal of unimaginative, set routines. In many respects, of course, such concerns – and the criticisms that one might make of them – are not particularly novel. Yet it is in relation to the issue of merchandising and 'consumerism' more broadly that these cartoons have been seen to represent something fundamentally new.

In fact, the relationship between merchandising and children's media is not a recent phenomenon. In the early 1930s, for example, Disney established 'Mickey Mouse clubs' for children, both with the intention of building brand identity and brand loyalty, but also with the explicit aim of selling merchandise relating to the films. The foyers of the film theatres were effectively transformed into extensions of the department store.[27] Indeed, for several decades the financial success of the Disney empire was crucially dependent on the 'secondary' activities of merchandising and, later, theme parks, and could not have been sustained on the basis of the films alone.[28]

For critics of the more recent animation series, however, the crucial concern would seem to be that merchandising is no longer a 'secondary' activity, but the primary one. Toy manufacturers, for example, are no longer involved as secondary licensees 'exploiting' the success of an established programme. On the contrary, they are now involved in producing (or at least commissioning) the programmes; and, it is argued, crucial decisions about form and content, about the characters and narrative situations, are now being made primarily with a view to their potential for launching new products.[29] Thus, for example, superhero teams (as in the case of *Transformers*, *Turtles* and *Captain Planet*) offer much greater potential for creating a range of toys and individualized accessories than lone crusaders such as the classic Marvel characters. Series based on communities (*My Little Pony*, *Sylvanian Families*, *Smurfs*) provide similar opportunities for children to *collect* toys, and then to invest in houses or castles in which they can 'live'. It is largely for this reason that academic critics and campaigners in the US have labelled the cartoons as 'program-length commercials'. The implicit point here is precisely that the series are not *recognized* as commercials – that they are not seen as such by the regulatory authorities who have been accused of 'turning their back' on such shady practices,[30] or by children themselves. There is, in other words, an accusation of deliberate deception.

In fact, the empirical evidence in support of such arguments is somewhat limited. To be sure, lists of top-selling toys are routinely – though by no means exclusively – dominated by TV tie-ins. But this does not in itself imply that children are unaware of what is going on, or that they have somehow been deceived into wanting things they would not otherwise want. As I have noted, children recognize the persuasive intent of television advertising from a comparatively young age, and quickly become quite cynical about it. Admittedly, the primary target audience of these shows is very young, and there is a significant difference between the explicit sales pitch of spot advertising and the less overt approach of the 'program-length commercials'. Yet children must consciously recognize that there is a *connection* between the programmes and the merchandise, even if we still know very little about how they interpret and respond to it. Several questions remain to be answered here. Why is it, for example, that some such media-related products succeed in reaching a large audience, while others fail?[31] Is there any basis for assuming that children are more vulnerable to such influences than adults – who may, for example, remain equally unaware of the extensive use of product placement in feature films? And even if children were to recognize the fact that these shows have persuasive intentions, would this necessarily make them less likely to want the products that are displayed?

As I have indicated, the fundamental concern for critics of these series would seem to be that the merchandising comes *first*, rather than following the programmes and 'exploiting' their success. In fact, however, such distinctions are fairly spurious. In the case of the early days of Disney, for example, the relationship between the movies and the merchandise was always a dialectical one: the movies 'sold' the merchandise, but the merchandise also attracted children to watch the movies. Indeed, it was the success of the merchandise that ultimately made the movies possible in the first place. Yet, even in the case of public service television, marketing to children has always played an important role. The BBC's major successes in the 1950s and 1960s – like the puppet shows *Muffin the Mule* and *Sooty* or the science fiction drama *Doctor Who* – were surrounded by quite extensive licensed marketing of toys, books and clothes; while the educational series *Sesame Street* (broadcast on public television in the US since the late 1960s) has been a worldwide marketing phenomenon.

In the current climate, the production of children's programmes is increasingly tied in with the need to generate revenue. The most successful children's programmes in the UK, particularly those for preschoolers such as *Thomas the Tank Engine*, *Playdays* and now *Teletubbies*, have generated a plethora of licensed merchandise. The BBC publishes a number of books and magazines that tie in to its most successful children's programmes; increasing numbers of children's programmes are sponsored by the manufacturers of 'educational' toys; and the content of children's entertainment magazine programmes is permeated by barely concealed forms of product promotion, such as music videos, give-away merchandise and 'reviews' of new products.[32]

This pattern of commercial involvement is replicated on a global scale: even the most highly regarded examples of 'quality' children's production, such as the work of the Australian Children's Television Foundation, or of the Children's Television Workshop in the US, are ultimately dependent on the generation of revenue through merchandising. Indeed, it is debatable whether children's television would exist *at all* without this kind of commercial involvement. Broadcasters have argued that the removal of commercials from children's television, or the banning of toy-related series – called for in some countries – could well result in the demise of children's programming as a whole.[33]

Ultimately, to pose the issue in terms of a binary opposition between public service and commercial concerns is not only to neglect these fundamental economic realities. It is also to ignore the genuine possibilities for public service that can and do exist within a commercial framework; and it is to proclaim an illusory purity for public service television, as though programmes which were somehow free of any connection with the dirty world of marketing would thereby automatically be 'good for children'. The *scale* of commercial involvement in children's culture has undoubtedly increased, but it is false to suggest that this necessarily implies a form of 'exploitation'. The evidence that children are any more vulnerable to commercial influence than adults – or that they are merely victims of processes from which they do not stand to benefit – is highly questionable. Here again, the construction of children as the pre-eminent focus of concern would seem to underestimate their capacities, and to preclude more realistic strategies for dealing with change.

Culture, commerce and childhood

As I have implied, these debates raise some fundamental questions, both about the changing relationships between 'culture' and 'commerce', and about the place of children within them. Culture – like childhood – is typically defined here as a pure, Eden-like space, a source of positive moral and aesthetic values, of 'imagination' and 'innocence', which is progressively invaded and corrupted by the dread hand of commerce.

Stephen Kline's book *Out of the Garden* (1993) is the most comprehensive recent example of this approach. Kline argues that the commercialization of children's culture has fundamentally destroyed the traditional activities and experiences of childhood. 'The rise of the electronic media', he argues, 'seems to have undermined the traditional healthy preoccupations of street play, peer conversations and just wandering in the garden long associated with a happy childhood.'[34] Parents, it would seem, no longer talk to their children, and 'family viewing' is little more than a 'passive ritual':

> Something is missing from childhood . . . when we give a child a musical tape of children's songs because we don't have time to sing to or with them; when we give them a My Little Pony colouring book as a substitute for drawing; when we let them watch fantasies on TV, without reading to them or exposing them to the intimacy of personal story-telling; when we give them Nintendo, but fail to teach them the finger games or craft skills (knitting, carpentry, gardening) that have been traditions within our families.[35]

Like similar assertions about the 'death of childhood', Kline's arguments could be challenged on the grounds of evidence. The assertion that these media-related activities have *replaced* more traditional activities, and that the latter are fundamentally more 'healthy', is not substantiated here – nor indeed in the research literature more broadly.[36] These changes in children's leisure pursuits (if indeed they can be proven to have occurred) are seen in isolation from other social developments, and the media are identified as the single cause. Kline's 'garden' would appear to be a literal as well as a figurative one; although quite where it leaves the millions of children who have never had access to a garden is an interesting question.

Yet aside from these more empirical issues, Kline's account raises two fundamental questions. The first is that of *cultural value*. As in a great deal of Marxist cultural critique, Kline paradoxically takes the position of the 'old' bourgeoisie in his attack on the new ruling ethos. His contrast between the 'Golden Age' of children's literature and the limitations of contemporary children's television is suffused with value judgements which are neither explained nor justified. While the Victorians are unstintingly praised for their 'rich emotional texture' and their 'unfettered imagination', contemporary television is condemned for lacking their 'psychological depth', 'exuberance' and 'innocence'. The 'quality, higher values, noble inspiration and broader vision' of children's literature are simply lacking in the 'stilted', 'repetitive' and 'predictable' output of television, with its 'mindless simplicity', its 'tedious violence' and, above all, its 'consumerism'. Cartoons in particular are condemned as universally 'formulaic', 'inane' and 'mind-numbingly banal': by virtue of their 'truncated characterisation', their 'stylised narratives' and their 'stultified animation', they are deemed to be unable 'to deal adequately with feelings and experience'.[37]

The problem with these judgements is not just that the criteria themselves remain undefined, but that the *evidence* that might exemplify and support them is simply taken for granted. It is easy to condemn *The Care Bears* and *My Little Pony* for lacking 'the wit, individuality and subtle humour of A. A. Milne's eternal characters',[38] not least when very few of one's readers will ever have seen such programmes. If there is any doubt, a few silly quotations taken out of context will easily do the trick. Such assertions are seen as self-evidently true, and as somehow neutral. In the process, the *social* basis for such judgements of taste is simply evacuated. In particular, the question of what it might mean for *adults* to pass judgements on *children's* media culture is never raised. *The Care Bears* is implicitly judged by the criteria one might use to evaluate the relative claims of George Eliot's *Middlemarch* and her *The Mill on the Floss*: depth of character, complexity and moral seriousness are seen as 'eternal' values whose meaning is self-evident. The possibility that children might positively *prefer* the 'simple' to the 'complex', that they might actively seek out 'one-dimensional' characters and 'predictable' narratives, and that there might be very good reasons for this, is one that cannot be entertained.

The second issue, perhaps predictably, concerns the *audience*. Kline's account of the role of contemporary media is primarily based on the analysis of texts and of broad economic trends. His evidence about children themselves is extremely limited. Yet assumptions about the nature of the audience and about the 'effects' of the media are central to the argument. Like the authors of *Kinderculture*, Kline repeatedly asserts that the cultural industries exert a powerful 'hold' over children's imaginations; that they undermine their capacities for critical thought; and that they routinely manipulate, deceive and intimidate children into submission. Their mesmeric control would appear to be absolute. Kline occasionally pays lip-service to the idea that children are not 'passive' viewers, and that the child audience is not homogeneous, yet he frequently falls back on a much more traditionally behaviourist view of the effects of television violence, of stereotyping and of advertising. Nevertheless, the audience seems to represent a repressed worry which occasionally returns to disruptive effect. In the end, the problem is that children actually seem to *like* this mindless nonsense.

Ellen Seiter's *Sold Separately* (1993) provides an important critique of this approach to 'consumerism' in children's culture – an approach which, as she argues, appears to unite broadly Marxist critics such as Kline with the work of more conservative campaigners. She accuses such critics of an implicit snobbery, based on unarticulated middle-class (and, to a lesser extent, male) cultural values. For example, she argues that distinctions between 'educational' and 'non-educational' toys, or between 'quality' television and 'trash', are little more than a reflection of the 'smug self-satisfaction of educated middle-class people'.[39] Seiter argues that 'consumerism' is far from confined to the working classes, or indeed to children: the market for middle-class toys, for example, is based on different aesthetic values, but it is just as 'commercial' and 'manipulative' as the mass marketing of companies like Toys 'R' Us.

More broadly, Seiter challenges what she sees as the relentless didacticism of middle-class child-rearing, which is particularly embodied in the marketing of so-called 'educational' toys. Through a historical analysis of toy advertising, she suggests that the notion of toys as simply a source of pleasure has gradually given way to an emphasis on play as a form of *work*, which will ensure the child's subsequent social and academic achievement – an approach which has been encouraged by the popular dissemination of a particular form of developmental psychology.[40] Seiter suggests that the critics of commercial media culture have implicitly enforced middle-class norms of 'proper parenting', and thereby encouraged a sense of guilt in those who fail or refuse to conform to them. She sees this as part of a wider process whereby male critics have condemned women for their interest in consumer goods, while assuming that they themselves are somehow not implicated in consumer culture. Finally, Seiter argues (as I have done above) that this approach neglects the active and diverse ways in which children make sense of the media, and in particular their considerable cynicism about commercial messages.

Seiter's argument poses a significant challenge to the position of the critic. As I have argued, critical discourse about popular culture is almost always a discourse about *other people*. These 'others' have been defined in various ways, but they are almost invariably the less powerful groups in society, or those whose voices are somehow excluded from the debate – the working class, women, and above all children. As Seiter argues, this process also characterizes the critical account of 'consumerism'. In this debate, hedonism is a quality that always seems to be attributed to *other people's* consumer behaviour. If critics acknowledge their own consumption practices, they do so by erecting a distinction between 'good' consumption, which reflects refinement and restraint, and 'bad' consumption, which does not. By virtue of their condemnation of the hedonism of 'bad' consumption, they affirm their ability to stand outside the sphere of commerce, and to transcend the 'false needs' it is seen to promote. Seiter suggests that this view is little more than a 'middle-class delusion' which ignores the 'consumerist' character of middle-class behaviour. Children, she argues, cannot be 'shielded from consumption' in this way.

Seiter is undoubtedly correct to draw attention to the class and gender bias which characterizes the discourse about 'quality' in children's media culture. Yet children's tastes are also – perhaps by definition – bound to be different from those of adults, irrespective of other social forces. This may be partly a matter of moral or intellectual development: for example, children of a certain age may actively *need* stories that represent the world in terms of binary oppositions between good and bad – or male and female, for that matter – in ways that adults might deem to be impossibly crude or stereotypical. Yet these differences may also possess a dimension which we might call 'aesthetic'. There clearly is something about the *look* and the *sound* of these cartoons – their relentless energy, their visual boldness, their lack of restraint – that adults (and not just middle-class adults) find aesthetically repellent. On the other hand, of course, we should avoid the temptation to romanticize children's tastes as a form of 'resistance' or 'subversion'. Seiter, for example, occasionally comes close to an essentialist view of children's culture as a form of 'rebellion' against that of adults, a view which at least neglects children's persistent desire to gain access to what they take to be adult pleasures.[41]

Ultimately, these debates about taste and cultural value cannot be resolved by appeals to an easy relativism. Yet one of the most significant problems with the debate about 'quality' in children's television in the UK is the implicit assumption that it can only possibly be located in certain genres or types of programming. This discourse rests on a series of binary oppositions that are routinely taken for granted: British is good, American is bad; public service is good, commercial is bad; live action is good, animation is bad; education is good, entertainment is bad; and so on. In the process, certain genres – game shows, action-adventure, teenage romance – are deemed to be simply incompatible with quality. Meanwhile, historical costume dramas about white middle-class children having exciting adventures in their private schools are seen as the epitome of quality, particularly if they are adapted from the 'classics' of children's literature. Of course, this is not to imply that children would be much better served by wall-to-wall imported cartoons. It is simply to suggest that any such judgements are bound to reflect the social positions and investments of those who make them; and that if we are to develop meaningful policies in this field, we need to look much more closely and sympathetically at what *children themselves* define as 'quality'.

Children and consumer culture

In recent years, Cultural Studies has begun to move away from judgemental critiques of 'consumerism', towards a more anthropological analysis of what is now termed 'material culture'.[42] According to this approach, the process of investing symbolic values in material objects is not just a characteristic of modern capitalism, and hence something that can be dismissed as false or inauthentic. On the contrary, the acquisition and use of material goods is seen as one of the primary means whereby people construct and define their social identities and relationships. From this perspective, 'consumer culture' in some form can be seen as an abiding characteristic of all societies.

To date, the most sustained attention in this field has been paid to *youth* rather than to children – a phenomenon which may itself reflect the sociological status that seems to come with age. Here, as in many other areas of Media and Cultural Studies, there has been a significant shift over the past two decades, from approaches that emphasize the power of the producer to those that privilege the audience or consumer.[43] Mainstream commercial culture is no longer perceived simply as a site of ideological reproduction – that is, as a means whereby dominant relations of power between social classes, or between men and women, are sustained and reinforced. On the contrary, there is now a central emphasis on young people's autonomy and freedom. Far from imposing false needs and values, the market comes to be seen here as an infinitely flexible terrain, on which consumers create their own identities, often in diverse and innovative ways.[44]

While such arguments present an important challenge to the puritanism that often informs analyses of consumer culture, they can be accused of neglecting the material and institutional constraints on consumption. As I have noted, the gap between rich and poor has steadily widened over the past two decades. Growing proportions of children and young people live below the official poverty line – which is itself well below the level of prosperity that would allow them to participate in anything but the most basic forms of consumer culture. In this respect, theories of consumer culture have tended to generalize about the nature of 'postmodern consumption' on the basis of the activities of a small fraction of the so-called 'new middle classes'.[45]

More fundamentally, this inversion of the argument can leave unquestioned the basic distinction between 'culture' and 'commerce'. Both the critics and the enthusiasts for consumer culture seem to assume that there is some kind of essential, pre-existing human need ('culture') which is either corrupted or alternatively expressed through the consumption of commodities ('commerce'). Yet, at least in the case of 'youth', it could be argued that there is no essential or inherent identity that pre-exists consumption. As I have noted, the modern category of 'youth' emerged in the postwar period, not only as a result of broader social changes – in which the period of young people's dependency on adults has been steadily extended – but also as a direct consequence of capitalism's search for new markets. Yet this should not be taken to imply that young people are merely victims of a process that lies outside their control or that inevitably works against their authentic interests. Consumer culture is not simply a means of manipulating people's authentic needs, or indeed of creating false ones; but neither is it necessarily one of 'subversion' or autonomous creativity, in which such needs are unproblematically expressed. The social and cultural needs that are manifested in our uses of material objects do not exist in some supposedly pure, non-commercial sphere. On the contrary, consumer culture is now the arena in which those very needs are defined, articulated and experienced.

There are some obvious difficulties in extending these arguments about consumption from the context of youth culture to that of 'children's culture'. To what extent is it meaningful to conceive of children as 'consumers', particularly when it comes to purchasing actual commodities? Children do clearly consume goods and services, but the economic means which enable them to do so are not (by and large) under their control. There is at least a degree of irony in adults accusing children of 'consumerism' when their power to consume at all is almost entirely in the hands of adults themselves. Nevertheless, there are striking differences between these debates about youth and consumer culture and the kinds of arguments that typically apply to children. If a high degree of autonomy is increasingly attributed to youth as consumers, children are yet again perceived as the vulnerable audience *par excellence*.

As I have indicated, these debates have invoked two fundamental questions. First, there is the question of how children understand and respond to advertising, and to other forms of promotional culture such as merchandising. And secondly, there is the question of whether the commercialization of the media has resulted in a decline in the quality or cultural value of the material that is produced specifically for them.

In both cases, the responses of critics have reflected an implicit distrust of children. On the one hand, there is a view of children as particularly vulnerable to persuasion and exploitation by commercial interests; while on the other, there is a suspicion of children's 'natural' tastes – a fear that if left to their own devices, they would wallow in material that adults judge to be positively unhealthy, or dismiss as merely 'trash'. The commercial emphasis on satisfying children's *wants* is thus rejected in favour of a renewed insistence on their *needs*; and the market is seen to be fundamentally incapable of meeting those needs – as defined, of course, by well-meaning adults. Ideally, therefore, children must be kept pure from contamination by commercial interests, and, at the very least, their relationship with the market must be strictly regulated and controlled.

Ultimately, such arguments are based on a conservative, paternalistic notion of childhood. The claim that children are simply 'exploited' by commercial interests is one that neglects the diverse and complex ways in which they use and relate to cultural commodities. There is little reason to believe that children in general are significantly more vulnerable to commercial persuasion than adults. Yet in seeking to challenge these arguments, we need to be wary of the dangers of simply inverting them. If children are not simply passive victims of commercial manipulation, neither are they 'creative consumers', using the market freely for their own self-realization. In a situation where millions of children live in conditions of poverty, the marketplace clearly does not provide the same opportunities for all. And however 'active' they may be, there is also a great deal that children (and indeed many adults) do *not* know about the activities of the market and its operations in many spheres of social life, not just the media. Here again, both 'positive' and 'negative' views of children's relationships with the market reflect a kind of sentimentality that is symptomatic of so many contemporary discussions of childhood.

By contrast, I have argued that contemporary childhoods – and adulthoods – are inextricably entwined with consumer culture. Children's social and cultural needs are unavoidably expressed and defined through their relationships with material commodities, and through the commercially produced media texts that permeate their lives. Like 'youth', the meaning of childhood is socially and historically constructed; and this is a process in which the commercial market plays an increasingly central role. Children are *always already* consumers, even if much of the actual purchasing that takes place on their behalf is done by parents.

Towards new policies

To begin from this recognition of children's status as consumers is to imply a rather different basis for social policy. Attempting to create a 'safe space' for children, in which they will remain uncontaminated by commercial influences – as is the case in current moves to ban advertising from children's television – is to retreat into an unreal fantasy world. Rather than seeking to *protect* children from the marketplace, we need to find ways of *preparing* them to deal with it.

This will involve *education* – albeit a form of education that is designed, not to wean children away from their unhealthy preoccupation with material goods, but to encourage them to reflect on their relationships with consumer culture and to understand the economic principles on which it operates. Despite growing commercial involvement in education, this is an area that schools generally neglect; yet there is evidence to suggest that children can develop 'economic literacy' at a much earlier age than is typically assumed.[46]

Secondly, it will involve a stronger legal recognition of children's *rights* as consumers: rights to accurate information and advice, to fair treatment and to public accountability on the part of corporations. This should not be seen in negative terms, merely as the right 'not to be exploited'.[47] On the contrary, it should be regarded as a form of 'consumer empowerment' for children, enabling them to assume greater authority and control in their dealings with commercial companies.

Finally, it will also require a much more rigorous examination of what is assumed about children's cultural *needs*, and of the ways in which the media might be said to fulfil them. This will involve distinguishing between *wants* and *needs*, and recognizing that the latter are not necessarily so immediate or self-evident to the individuals concerned. Identifying children's needs is therefore bound to be a problematic process; yet it must surely be accomplished through a process of dialogue with children themselves, rather than simply being left to adults.

As with the debate about screen violence, criticisms of the effects of consumer culture on children tend to serve as a vehicle for much broader concerns. Yet there is, to say the least, a certain irony in left-wing critics choosing to focus on the apparent shortcomings of popular taste while simultaneously ignoring the widening inequalities of access to consumer culture. Condemning 'consumerism' may prove therapeutic, but it can deflect attention from the complexity of the issues at stake, and result in unduly optimistic prescriptions for social change. Like my brief suggestions on the issue of screen violence, my proposals here are pragmatic rather than utopian. Nevertheless, they are based on a set of more general principles; and it is these principles – and their more detailed implications for policy – that will be developed in my concluding chapter.

9

Children as Citizens

In many areas of social life, debates about childhood have increasingly been characterized by calls for *empowerment*. As we have seen, this is particularly true in discussions of children's relationships with the commercial market. While some critics have regarded the apparent 'commercialization of childhood' as little more than a form of exploitation, others have argued that it has liberated children from paternalistic, class-bound assumptions about what is good for them. Either way, it is clear that children now enjoy a new status and authority as consumers: more money is being spent on them, and they are more highly valued and keenly pursued by commercial providers of many kinds.

There is undeniably a form of 'empowerment' here, but it has distinct limitations. Children may indeed have acquired a new status within the private sphere of consumption, but how far has this extended to the public sphere of social institutions and of politics? Children may have become 'sovereign consumers', but to what extent have they also been recognized as *citizens* in their own right? And what role might the media play in extending and developing young people's sense of their own political agency?

Here again, we are dealing with an area of 'adult' life from which children have largely been excluded. If children have traditionally been protected from material that some adults believe might harm or corrupt them, they have also been prevented from having any involvement in the political decisions that influence key areas of their lives. Policies that directly concern them – in areas such as education, family welfare and leisure provision – are generally devised with little attempt to consult or gather the views of children. By and

large, politics is conducted over their heads. It is only at the legal or
biological *end* of childhood that political maturity is seen to begin.

This exclusion of children from the public sphere of politics has
largely been sustained on the basis of arguments about their essential inadequacies. As in the debates about violence and commercialism, children's lack of the critical maturity apparently possessed by
adults is seen to place them particularly at risk. In effect, their inherent lack of rationality and responsibility renders them permanently
incapable of meaningful participation.

Here again, I shall argue that these assumptions about children's
inadequacies are highly questionable. Yet, at the same time, it is necessary to make some distinctions here on the grounds of age. Even
the most fervent advocates of children's rights are bound to recognize that younger children do not possess the intellectual capacities
or the knowledge to make fully informed decisions about political
matters.[1] Yet the logic for denying political rights to *teenagers* on these
grounds is hard to justify, and it is primarily this age group that I am
concerned with in this chapter.

However, my aim here is not simply to demonstrate young people's competence, but to suggest ways in which it could be extended
and developed. As in the other areas I have considered, arguments
about children's 'innate' incompetence give rise to a circular logic.
Children may well appear incompetent (and indeed uninterested)
because they have not been encouraged to develop the skills or knowledge that would enable them to appear otherwise. Yet it is possible
to reverse the direction of this argument. Children will only be likely
to become 'active citizens', capable of exercising thoughtful choice
in political matters, if they are presumed to be capable of doing so.[2]

The media inevitably play a crucial role here. It is something of a
truism to assert that the electronic media are now at the very heart of
the political process: they are the primary means through which contemporary politics is conducted. This may perhaps be self-evident in
the era of 'spin-doctoring', but it has been widely recognized for several decades. The techniques employed in the 'selling of the President' in US elections in the 1960s have increasingly come to
characterize all political campaigning, and indeed political discourse
more widely, both at a national and a local level.[3] For adults and
children alike, the media thus represent the primary means of access
to the public world of social and political debate.

Here again, the question to be addressed is not so much to do with
whether we should *protect* children from the harm that the media
might inflict on them. On the contrary, it is to do with how the media
might more effectively *prepare* children for the responsibilities of adult

citizenship – or indeed enable them to intervene in the political decisions that govern their lives as children.

Young people, politics and the media

Debates about young people's relationship with politics have often
reached pessimistic conclusions. The evidence from social surveys
consistently points to declining levels of political knowledge, interest and participation, and to a growing distrust of politicians among
the young. While these are not new phenomena, they have significantly intensified in the past two decades.

This is most marked in the United States, where there is rising
public concern about young people's ignorance of basic political information, despite the significant rise in college attendance. Between
1947 and 1988, for instance, the percentage of young people who
could locate Europe on a world map fell from 45 per cent to 25 per
cent; while the numbers who were able to recognize prominent
political figures or answer test questions about recent political events
were significantly lower than those in older age groups. Meanwhile,
there has been a historic decline in the proportion of young voters
(aged eighteen to twenty-four) who bother to turn out at national
elections, from around 50 per cent in the 1970s to around 40 per cent
in the 1990s, although the reverse is the case for the oldest age group
of voters (sixty-five and over).[4]

This pattern is repeated in other countries. In their book *Freedom's
Children*, Helen Wilkinson and Geoff Mulgan point to a 'historic political disconnection' among the younger generation both in the UK
and across Europe.[5] Surveys in Britain, France and Germany over
the past decade show that young people under twenty-five are significantly less likely to be registered to vote, to turn out at elections,
and to be politically active than they were in earlier generations. Membership of political parties and related organizations (*including* environmental pressure groups and women's groups) is increasingly
confined to the middle aged and the elderly; while the 'alternative',
'do-it-yourself' politics of eco-campaigns is very much a minority
pursuit.[6] While this disconnection from conventional forms of politics is particularly marked among women, ethnic minorities and the
poor, young people are consistently more alienated than adults.[7] This
is also the case in countries like Australia, where voting is compulsory: a 1994 poll in that country registered very high agreement with
various negative statements about politicians, and showed that young
people placed greater trust in pop musicians.[8] Even in the 1997 gen-

eral election in Britain, where the Labour Party swept to power with a modernizing rhetoric about the 'young country', the proportion of young people voting remained almost unaffected at well under half.[9]

The place of the mass media in these debates is somewhat double-edged. On the one hand, the media – and 'commercialized' youth culture more broadly – are often seen to be primarily to blame for this perceived decline in political awareness. These arguments are perhaps most familiar on the political right, although they are also a significant theme in the 'communitarian' rhetoric which currently inspires left-liberal policy-makers in both Britain and the United States.[10] Traditional notions of citizenship are, it is argued, no longer relevant as viewers zap distractedly between commercial messages and superficial entertainment, substituting vicarious experience for authentic social interaction and community life.[11]

On the other hand, there is growing concern about young people's declining interest in news media. Particularly in the United States, readership of broadsheet newspapers and ratings for 'flagship' television news broadcasts are in steep decline among this age group; and this is compounded by what some critics see as their growing interest in 'tabloid' news, a genre frequently condemned for its 'sensationalism' and its lack of serious political information.[12] Likewise, research in the UK suggests that young people's use of and interest in news media are minimal. Only 6 per cent of young people's viewing of television comes into this category, while their reading of newspapers focuses largely on entertainment, features and sports pages.[13] Research repeatedly finds that young people express a low – and declining – level of interest in media coverage of political affairs.[14]

These developments clearly reflect much broader shifts in society, which cannot be easily reversed or rectified. Young people's rejection of the moral authority both of politicians and of the news media could be seen as symptomatic of a more general decline in the legitimacy of government and of many of the 'intermediate' institutions of civil society.[15] For some critics, this tendency has been seen as a consequence of a more general 'depoliticization' of political debate, as political parties tend to converge and questions about the management of the economy assume priority;[16] for others, it has lent support to a broader lament for the apparent collapse of traditional social networks, and the public sphere of political and social debate which they sustain.[17]

Yet these findings are also often taken to confirm a view of young people as merely ignorant, apathetic and cynical. From this perspective, it is not democratic politics – or indeed news journalism, or the relationship between them – that is the problem, but young people's lack of interest in those things. If kids don't read the broadsheet newspapers or watch serious current affairs programmes on TV, then it's their fault for being so ignorant. Young people are thus implicitly condemned for being lazier and less socially responsible than their parents; and if there have been 'undesirable' changes in the media, such as the advent of 'tabloid television', these too can be laid at the door of the young, with their love of superficiality and sensationalism.[18]

Nevertheless, it is possible to turn this argument around. Young people's apparent rejection of politics and of news media could also be seen to reflect their sense of *exclusion* from the domain of politics, and from dominant forms of political discourse. In this situation, politics and government remain at best an abstraction, and young people's lack of interest in politics is merely a rational response to their own powerlessness. Why should they bother to learn about something when they have no power to influence it, and when it makes no effort to address itself to them? From this perspective, young people are seen, not as apathetic or irresponsible, but as positively *disenfranchised*.[19]

Thus, critics have argued that mainstream news journalism has failed to keep pace with the changing cultural styles and enthusiasms of young people. Jon Katz, for example, suggests that young people have a very different orientation to information from that of older generations, and that they prefer the more 'informal' and 'ironic' style of new media to the 'monotonously reassuring voice' of conventional news journalism.[20] According to Katz, it is the failure of the established news media to connect with the forms of 'everyday politics' that are most important for this generation that accounts for their declining audience. Far from being seen as mere 'sensationalism', the emergence of more popular forms of news journalism – such as 'tabloid television' and 'faction' shows – could be seen as an attempt to engage more fully with the changing cultural competencies of the younger audience.

Here again, Katz establishes a polemical opposition between 'young people' and the 'baby boomers' which is far too generalized (see chapter 3). Nevertheless, his argument finds many echoes in recent academic work on the media. Critics have increasingly challenged the idea that young people's lack of interest in news is somehow symptomatic of laziness or irresponsibility. On the contrary, it is argued that conventional forms of news journalism have proven signally ineffective in enabling them to 'translate' broader political events into the context of their own everyday lives.[21] Likewise, Katz's rejection of the 'monotonously reassuring voice' of the established news media, and his call for more popular forms of news journalism, are increasingly common in academic Cultural Studies.[22] Even comparatively mainstream critics are acknowledging the need to move beyond the 'classical' model of news journalism in the wake of the 'crisis in public communication'.[23]

Nevertheless, this does not mean that news journalism is simply redundant. On the contrary, the news media represent a significant means of 'informal' political education, both for young people and for adults. However indifferent they may appear to be, young people often have little option but to watch the news; and they may absorb a great deal of political information from the media accidentally, or in the course of other activities, albeit often in a fragmented form. In so far as young people *are* being informed about politics and about current events, it seems reasonable to conclude that the news media are likely to constitute one of their most significant sources.

Previous research

In fact, the findings of previous research on these issues are somewhat contradictory. While the classic early studies of political socialization barely mentioned the media,[24] research conducted in the 1970s tended to make very strong claims about their significance.[25] At this stage, exposure to news media was seen to determine political attitudes and political participation to a much greater extent than other influences such as parents, gender or education.

Subsequent research has qualified some of these claims, however. As with the research on advertising discussed in the previous chapter, attention has increasingly been drawn to the significance of other variables, and to the relationships between them, in the political communication process. Thus, studies have considered factors such as family communication patterns[26] and their relationship with ethnicity[27] in mediating political communications. In general, high levels of news media use are correlated with high levels of political participation, although the influence of parents, older siblings, peers and community factors is recognized as more significant.[28]

Like the research on the effects of advertising, this research has steadily moved away from a simple cause-effect approach. Nevertheless, it continues to rely on a notion of political socialization that is highly functionalist: ultimately, children are seen as passive recipients of adults' attempts to mould them into their allotted social roles. From this perspective, young people's disaffection from politics is seen as a kind of psychological dysfunction caused by lack of information, rather than a result of the shortcomings of the political system itself: all we have to do is provide the information and disaffection will disappear.

Meanwhile, more detailed studies of viewers' 'information processing' of television news tell a rather different story. Broadly speaking, this research suggests that viewers understand and learn comparatively little from what they watch.[29] The reasons for this are typically seen to involve a combination of textual factors (such as the brevity of news items, or the frequent lack of connection between visual and verbal material) and audience factors (such as viewers' lack of attention or knowledge of background information). In general, TV news appears to be more effective in imparting information about key personalities than in communicating details about the main stories; and even when viewers can recall what happened or who was involved, they are much less able to retain information about the causes and consequences of events.

This research suggests that viewers typically invest little cognitive effort in viewing: they frequently fail to concentrate, and are easily distracted. Doris Graber, for example, argues that people are generally 'cognitive misers' – that is, they opt for an approach to new information which they believe will involve the least mental effort on their part.[30] In their attempts to make sense of the vast amount of news material they encounter, viewers typically decide to pay attention to only a small amount of the available information. However, Graber argues that viewers' failure to recall particular items of information does not necessarily mean that they have not learnt anything. They may forget the detail, but they may nevertheless have grasped the meaning.

This research paints a fairly consistent picture of the *extent* of viewers' learning from news. It is a picture which is outwardly quite at odds with the view of news media as a major source of political information – and indeed with the self-image of news journalism. At least on this evidence, news (and television news in particular) appears to be a very long way from fulfilling its historic mission of producing an informed citizenry – not only among young people, but also among the population at large.

Ultimately, however, all these studies conceive of learning from news as an essentially psychological process. Their focus is on individual cognition, and on the internal 'processing' of information. As such, they reproduce the 'cognitive bias' that also characterizes studies of the effects of advertising: the social and emotional dimensions of viewers' responses are typically ignored. News is seen here as merely a form of *information transfer*;[31] and what viewers learn from it is assessed primarily in terms of their recall of disembodied 'facts', assessed through multiple-choice tests.

Peter Dahlgren offers an important critique of such 'rationalistic' arguments about the reception of news, suggesting that they may leave 'central elements of the TV news process lingering in the shadows'.[32] The key questions here, Dahlgren suggests, are to do with how news establishes its own credibility and coherence, and thereby creates 'forms of consciousness' and 'structures of feeling', rather than how accurately it communicates particular items of information. This more 'culturalist' approach to television news helps to explain some of the motivations of viewing, and the pleasures it involves. It also suggests a rather different approach to questions about the nature of citizenship. Rather than attempting to measure the effectiveness of news in communicating political information, we should be asking how it enables viewers to construct and define their relationship with the public sphere. How do news programmes 'position' viewers in relation to the social order – for example, in relation to the sources of power in society, or in relation to particular social groupings? How do they enable viewers to conceive of the relations between the 'personal' and the 'political'? How do they invite viewers to make sense of the wider national and international arena, and to make connections with their own direct experience? How, ultimately, do they establish what it *means* to be a 'citizen'?

The making of citizens

In my own research, I have explored these issues both through analysing television news programmes aimed specifically at the younger audience and through detailed studies of how children make sense of particular news items.[33] This research was conducted both in Britain and in the US, using programmes from both countries; and it involved children aged between eleven and seventeen. Here again, my interest is in how children construct and define their identities – in this case 'political identities' – in talking with others about what they have seen. Instead of judging children in terms of their perceived inadequacies in relation to 'adult' norms, my aim is to investigate how they interpret and negotiate the meanings of television in their own terms.

The young people I interviewed were, on one level, extremely cynical about politics as conventionally defined – that is, about the

actions of *politicians*. While they were sometimes irreverent or dis-
missive, they could also be distinctly bitter and forceful. Politicians
were often condemned, not merely as boring, but also as corrupt,
uncaring, insincere and self-interested; and politics was widely dismissed as a kind of dishonest game, which had little relevance to
their everyday lives and concerns. The children explained the reasons for these views in terms of their own inability to intervene or
participate: since they could not make any difference to what happened, why should they make the effort to find out about it? When
pushed, they acknowledged that political changes (for example, at
an election) might well have implications for themselves or their
families; and yet the fact that they could not vote meant that they
could only observe this process with passive detachment. Somehow,
a lack of interest in politics appeared to be perceived as part of the
condition of being a child.

   In my research, this cynical stance became more prevalent with
age, a fact which can be explained in various ways. To some extent,
of course, it can be seen a consequence of cognitive development: as
they become more able to 'decentre', children begin to hypothesize
about (and to analyse critically) the motivations of others. To some
degree, this change is also a matter of access to information: in general, the older children here simply knew and understood much
more about politics – and hence about issues such as corruption and
media manipulation – and were therefore able to provide more concrete evidence in support of their views. However, this increasing
cynicism can also be seen as a result of young people's growing
awareness of their own powerlessness. Older teenagers are frequently
caught between adult injunctions to behave 'responsibly' and adult
prohibitions and controls: they are ceaselessly urged to be 'mature'
and constantly reminded that they are not. It is not surprising that
they are often so keen to challenge what they perceive as inconsistency, complacency or hypocrisy on the part of adults – and not only
politicians.

   The notion of 'cynical chic' which emerges from similar research
with adults[34] captures something of what is taking place here. According to this argument, such expressions of cynicism serve as a
valuable – and indeed pleasurable – way of rationalizing one's own
sense of powerlessness, and even of claiming a degree of superiority
and control. Certainly, there is a sense in which the children's expressions of lack of interest should be seen as superficial. Many
expressed the view that politics as a whole was simply 'boring', and
that it was of no interest to them; and yet they were able to engage
in some extremely complex and sophisticated debates about key

political issues. In this respect, it would seem important to distinguish between cynicism and apathy: as Kum-Kum Bhavnani argues, cynicism may in fact be a necessary prerequisite for certain forms of political activity, and is not necessarily incompatible with the development of political expertise or efficacy.[35]

In attempting to understand what is taking place here, it is necessary to adopt a broader definition of politics, which is not confined to the actions of politicians or political institutions. As Cedric Cullingford points out,[36] children develop 'political' concepts at a very early stage, through their everyday experiences of institutions such as the school and the family: notions of authority, fairness and justice, rules and laws, power and control, are all formed long before they are required to express their views in the form of voting. The choice available at school lunches, the attempt to introduce compulsory uniforms, or even the organization of the school playground – which were among the topics discussed with considerable passion by the children in my interviews – are, in this respect, just as 'political' as what goes on in parliament. One might well make a similar case about sports or entertainment: the success of Tiger Woods or the Spice Girls can clearly be interpreted as 'political' phenomena, as they implicitly were by some of the children here.

Indeed, at several points in our interviews, the children were clearly struggling to connect the 'political' dimensions of their own everyday experiences with the official discourse of politics encountered through the media. Their discussions of youth crime, for example, or of environmental issues demonstrated both a cynicism about those in authority and a genuine attempt to think through the advantages and disadvantages of particular policies, both in the light of the evidence presented on television and in the light of personal experience. Several children possessed very clear commitments on these issues, and few were prepared to support the introduction of curfews or the despoliation of the natural environment; and yet their discussions were characterized by a careful concern for the validity of the evidence, a willingness to consider the consequences of particular policies, and an attempt to imagine alternative solutions. On this level, most of these children possessed a well-developed conceptual understanding of 'political' issues, even if they lacked information on specific topics.

In many instances, however, the preoccupations of national politics were dismissed in favour of the more immediate concerns of the local (for example, the local environment, crime in the neighbourhood, family histories, schooling or consumer behaviour). In the process, the potential *connections* between the two were often lost. This was most apparent in discussions of welfare spending, and to some extent of racial politics. The children were effectively discussing the same issues as the politicians, although they positively refused to recognize this when I pointed it out to them. This was partly symptomatic of the principled rejection identified above; although the extent to which news might be capable of making politics *relevant* to their lived experience also depended on the formal strategies of programmes themselves (as we shall see below).

On one level, of course, the 'personal' is unavoidably 'political'. Yet it is important to avoid any premature collapse of the distinction between them. The personal can *become* political, but this requires a fundamental shift in how issues are framed or defined. At the most general level, 'political thinking' implies a view of the individual self in collective or social terms. This is not an automatic or guaranteed process, but one which may positively require certain kinds of information to be made available, or certain kinds of connections to be explicitly made. The point here is not to replace the 'political' with the 'personal', but to find ways of building bridges between the two.

The growth of this kind of 'political thinking' can partly be explained in developmental terms, of course. Particularly among some of the middle age group in this research (age thirteen to fourteen), it was possible to detect the emergence of a broadly consistent and even 'logical' political world-view, relating partly to other developmental shifts – for instance, the ability to relate parts to wholes (for example, in seeing individuals as representative of broader social categories), or the ability to view the world from perspectives other than one's own (for example, in hypothesizing about why the experiences of members of other generations or cultures might have led them to adopt particular beliefs). Like many previous studies, this research significantly challenges the view that teenagers are inherently lacking in the intellectual or critical abilities that might be seen to constitute political 'maturity'.[37]

Nevertheless, there were also some clear social differences in terms of the children's orientations both towards politics and towards news. Broadly speaking, the middle-class or upwardly mobile children were more likely to express a positive interest in and/or knowledge about political issues (as conventionally defined); and there was some evidence that this reflected their own perceptions of their potential futures, as powerful figures or at least as 'stakeholders' in society. By contrast, the working-class children, particularly in the US schools, appeared to be less well informed and more comprehensively alienated. Likewise, the domain of politics (as conventionally defined) frequently seemed to be perceived by children of both genders, both implicitly and explicitly, as masculine. Girls were more likely to dwell on the 'human interest' aspects of political issues, and to express generalized alienation from or apathy towards institutionalized political activity. There was some variation here according to issues, however: ecology was implicitly seen – and explicitly claimed – as more of a 'girls' issue', while the machinations of elections and party politics were more enthusiastically addressed by boys.

This definition of a 'political self' is, however, a highly self-conscious process, in which social identities are claimed and negotiated in the course of discussion. In the case of gender, there were several instances here in which girls actively resisted 'masculine' values, and chose to assert the authority of what they perceived as 'feminine' values, most overtly in the case of environmentalism. By contrast, 'race' was a much more problematic dimension of identity, particularly in the context of ethnically mixed groups; and the explicit 'race politics' represented in some of the news items we discussed placed further obstacles in the way of claiming a positive 'black' identity. As these examples suggest, claiming membership of a collective is not always a straightforward achievement.

In summary, then, this research confirms the view that young people's alienation from, and cynicism about, the actions of politicians and political parties is a result of exclusion and disenfranchisement, rather than ignorance or immaturity. By the time they reach their teenage years, young people have a well-developed understanding of key political concepts; yet in attempting to identify the development of political understanding, we need to adopt a broader definition of politics which recognizes the *potentially* political dimensions of 'personal' life and of everyday experience. In the process, it is important to recognize that 'political thinking' is not merely an intellectual or developmental achievement, but an interpersonal process which is part of the construction of a collective, social identity.

Teaching through television

What difference does television itself make to this process? Four contrasting programmes were used in this research: *Nick News* and *Channel One News* from the US, and *First Edition* and *Wise Up* from Britain. Broadly speaking, *Channel One News* and *First Edition* are significantly more conventional than *Nick News* and *Wise Up*: in several respects, they are much closer to the style and presentational format of mainstream news. Their aim is essentially to *make news accessible* to a younger audience. This does entail some departures from the conventions of mainstream news, for example in terms of the balance between 'foreground' and 'background', the kind of language used and the style of presentation. To some extent (particularly in the case of *Channel One News*), this could be seen as a kind of superficial 'window dressing', although *First Edition* also uses young people as interviewers (albeit in a rather limited way), and has begun to experiment with a viewers' access slot. Nevertheless, neither programme significantly challenges what is seen to *count* as 'news'; and both appear to position the viewer as a deferential pupil – an empty vessel waiting to be filled – rather than as an active or questioning reader.

By contrast, *Nick News* and *Wise Up* depart more radically from the conventions of the genre. On one level, neither programme should strictly be seen as 'news', in the sense that neither is immediately topical: *Nick News* is essentially a news magazine programme, while *Wise Up* is a young people's access show. Nevertheless, this is implicitly to accept a conventional definition of what counts as news in the first place, and indeed to imply that news should be weighted towards 'foreground' rather than 'background'. In fact, both programmes do cover issues which feature in mainstream news, and which are matters of debate within the political domain (that is, which are of concern to politicians). In terms of their style of teaching and their address to the viewer, however, they offer a distinctly different conception of what might count as 'news', and what form it might take. While this has a particular relevance to the younger audience, the more widespread turn away from news media in recent years suggests that it might also have implications for the audience at large.

Among the children interviewed here, there was very little doubt about the approach they preferred. For the US children, *Nick News* was almost universally perceived to be more interesting and effective than *Channel One News*. In this respect, the issue of the programmes' address to the younger audience was a particular focus of concern. The older children here perceived both programmes to be aimed at a younger audience, although *Channel One News* was particularly singled out for criticism on the grounds that it was patronizing. The programme was repeatedly accused of trying (and failing) to be 'cool' or 'hip'. By contrast, *Nick News* was congratulated for not 'talking down' to its audience; and some explicitly praised it for taking a 'mature' approach. There was also praise for the fact that it presented new information 'about things that you probably don't already know about' rather than just presenting a simplified version of the mainstream news, as was seen to be the case with *Channel One News*. *Nick News* was also judged to be more 'kid centred', in that it included more young people rather than simply 'the person sitting at the desk'. It was praised for its inclusion of 'ordinary' people rather than the 'stuck-up' people who are normally 'all over the news'. According to one thirteen-year-old girl, '*Channel One News* tells you about the President and his home and his wife and the election and stuff, but this [*Nick News*] tells you about real life, the one you have to worry about.'

Responses to the British programmes were even more unanimous. *Wise Up* was universally preferred to *First Edition*, on the grounds both of its style and its address to young people. There was considerable praise for its graphics, camerawork and editing, which were variously described as 'rough', 'cool', 'catchy', 'effective' and 'attention-grabbing'. By contrast, *First Edition* was described as 'just like boring news', and condemned for its 'stupid newsreaders . . . sitting at a desk'. Its approach was seen as much more 'formal', and the young people included on the programme were perceived to be 'stiff' and 'uncomfortable'. Here again, the issue of the programmes' address to the younger audience was a particular focus of concern. There was some scepticism about *Wise Up*'s implicit claim to be providing unmediated access for children's voices: several children suspected that the programme had been 'made to look' as though it had been produced by children, when in fact it had not. Nevertheless, as with *Nick News*, there was considerable praise for its attempt to present 'kids' point of view', and (more broadly) for its focus on 'ordinary people'. By contrast, *First Edition* was seen by many to be 'too adult' and 'not really anything to do with children'. It was pointed out that the dominant voices in the items were those of adults, and that the young interviewers were not allowed to put across their own points of view. Like *Channel One News*, *First Edition* was condemned for its emphasis on 'politics' rather than on 'things that matter to kids'.

On one level, these conclusions appear to confirm commonsense wisdom among television producers who work for this age group. Being patronizing and being boring are obviously to be avoided; although this is easier said than done. For obvious reasons, young people are very sensitive to age differences, and are particularly scathing about programmes that appear to underestimate or 'talk down' to them. They also want programmes that are relevant to their own everyday concerns, which are largely marginalized in mainstream news. Yet while they condemned the more conventional approach of *Channel One News* and *First Edition*, these children did not simply want to be entertained. On the contrary, they *also* wanted to be informed and made to think; and the more adventurous approaches of *Nick News* and *Wise Up* were praised in so far as they achieved this.

The use of direct address and the 'personal view' – which will be considered in more detail below – were particularly significant here.

In this respect, my research clearly confirms the need for innovation if news is to reawaken the interest of younger audiences, and indeed of the large majority of the population. News is undeniably one of the most conservative of media genres, and the horrified charges of 'dumbing down' that typically greet even the most marginal changes in its approach attest to the enormous symbolic importance that seems to be invested in its curiously limited forms and rituals. Yet, as I have shown, research has consistently pointed to its fairly dismal record as a means of communication; and as societies in general invest less and less significance in political authority, it is hardly surprising that its audience is in decline.

There is a need, therefore, for a radically new approach. This is partly a matter of developing new formal strategies, but it also implies a much more fundamental rethinking of what is seen to *count* as news in the first place. The deferential stance which is invited and encouraged by mainstream news formats needs to be abandoned in favour of an approach which invites scepticism and active engagement. Much greater efforts need to be made not merely to explain the causes and the context of news events, but also to enable viewers to perceive their relevance to their own everyday lives. News can no longer afford to confine itself to the words and actions of the powerful, or to the narrow and exclusive discourses which currently dominate the public sphere of social and political debate.

The avoidance of 'entertainment' in favour of a narrow insistence on seriousness and formality which characterizes dominant forms of news production systematically alienates and excludes substantial sectors of the audience. And yet, as I have implied, the answer is not simply to add sugar to the pill. News clearly does have a great deal to learn from the genres which are most successful in engaging the younger audience, such as music videos and talk shows. Obviously, such approaches can be a recipe for superficiality, but they can also offer new ways for news to fulfil its traditional mission to educate and to inform – a mission which it is performing far from adequately at the present time.

Critical viewers?

Generally speaking, these children knew a great deal about how news programmes were put together; they were alert to the potential for misleading information, inadequate evidence and 'bias'; and they were often very prepared to argue with what they had seen, both in terms of its own consistency and logic, and by drawing on contrary evidence of their own. Their debates about these issues focused not only on the selection of information, but also on its presentation: they repeatedly drew attention to aspects of editing, camerawork and visual design which they felt were designed to persuade them to accept a particular reading of the issues. Of course, this is not to say that these young people were therefore immune to media influence: the news clearly sets agendas and 'frames' issues in particular ways, and these inevitably exert constraints on how they can be interpreted. Nevertheless, as William Gamson argues,[38] readers and viewers negotiate meaning in complicated ways that vary from issue to issue; and they draw on other resources, including their general knowledge of television as a medium, in doing so.

As in the children's discussions of politics, there was a clear developmental dimension here, which is partly about access to information, and partly a function of broader cognitive achievements. Unsurprisingly, the older children here knew much more than the younger ones about television as a medium, both in terms of the 'language' and characteristic techniques of television texts and in terms of the operations of the industry. They were also more inclined to 'decentre' (for example, to perceive that a particular message might have persuasive intentions) and to apply criteria to do with logical consistency (for example, to point out the contradictions between verbal commentary and visual evidence).

In general, the more overtly 'biased' approach of *Wise Up* and *Nick News* was preferred to the attempts at bland impartiality adopted by the other programmes; although that is not to say that the views represented were any more likely to be accepted. Indeed, the 'in-your-face' personal views contained in *Wise Up* frequently proved quite counterproductive, even for children who were predisposed to agree with them; while the children did not necessarily accept that the apparently more even-handed debate format of *Nick News* was necessarily giving them a balanced view.

Nevertheless, there are significant difficulties in identifying and evaluating evidence of 'critical viewing'. As in the research described in chapter 6, critical discourses about the media seemed to emerge as a function of the interview context – as a response to what children believe the interviewer wants to hear. From this perspective, critical discourse may be little more than a socially desirable response, a way of distancing oneself from the 'uncritical viewer' who is implicitly invoked, and condemned, in so much academic and public debate about the media. Like that of the 'wise consumer', the position of the 'independent-minded citizen' is one which carries a considerable social status.

Furthermore, as in the case of 'cognitive defences' against advertising (chapter 8), the fact that viewers are capable of being 'critical' – or, more accurately, of mobilizing critical discourses – does not necessarily mean that they are not influenced. In fact, there were some clear indications in several cases here of at least short-term influence. In some instances, *visual* evidence appeared to carry a particular persuasive force, whether or not this might have been the intention of the producers. In others, the provision of new information appeared to change some children's attitudes to the topic. Even here, however, the children were often self-reflexively aware of this process: they drew attention to the influence of visual 'evidence' even as they accepted its validity; and while they rarely challenged the accuracy of new information, they often suspected that other information which might undermine the argument was not being provided.

The perception of 'bias', which is obviously a key dimension of critical viewing, is thus a highly complex phenomenon. It might be logical to expect that viewers who already know more about a particular issue (for example, those who have direct personal experience of it) will be more likely to detect bias than those who know less. Likewise, one would expect viewers who feel strongly about a given topic to be more likely to perceive bias in an item which presents an opposing view to their own. In fact, the situation in these interviews was rather more ambiguous: while there were certainly instances which conformed to this pattern, a significant majority did not. The children's level of emotional 'investment' in the issues often proved more significant in this respect than their capacities as rational critics.

At the same time, analysing perceptions of media bias raises further questions. Is bias something inherent in the text, or is it in the eye of the reader? How are readers' judgements to be evaluated, and what status do they have? On the one hand, there were instances in these discussions where children had clearly *misinterpreted* what they had seen, or just failed to understand it – and in some cases, they themselves directly acknowledged this, or accepted it when it was pointed out to them. Some of these misinterpretations can be traced more or less directly to particular properties of the text: its confusing use of metaphor, its failure to provide sufficient background information or explanation, or the contradictions between verbal and visual evidence. Yet others were clearly a result of inattention, or the fact that children had mistakenly emphasized (or been distracted by) comparatively marginal elements of the text, or reached false conclusions from them.

On the other hand, there were significant mismatches between the way I read particular items (in my privileged capacity as the academic analyst) and the way the children did so, which cannot be put down simply to misinterpretation. These divergent responses can partly be explained in terms of the different knowledge and competencies that readers bring to the text; and in this respect, at least some of the differences result from the fact that as a white, male adult – and, in the case of the US study, as British rather than American – I was bound to apply or invoke different frames in making sense of the material from those of some of the children I interviewed.

These differences point to the limitations of objectivism – that is, to the view that texts contain fixed meanings which can be recovered with lesser or greater degrees of accuracy. Equally, they cannot simply be sidestepped by an appeal to relativism. Empirically, texts do not mean whatever readers want them to mean, and all readings are *not* equally valid. However unfashionable it may be in academic circles, 'bias' is a key conceptual category in viewers' everyday responses to television news, and to other texts that purport to be factual. Yet we cannot begin to evaluate such judgements without some notion of accuracy – that is, without some way of appealing to a set of facts about the text against which particular responses can be compared and assessed.

To sum up, this research confirms the view that young people develop a set of critical competencies, a form of 'media literacy', which they are able to apply to their readings even of relatively unfamiliar texts or genres. In the case of news and factual programming, judgements about bias are a central concern, although they are not simply a matter of 'detecting' something which is or is not immanent in the text. In practice, the emotional, personal or social identifications which viewers have *invested* in a particular political issue may be more important in determining how they interpret texts than any purely cognitive or rationalistic process of critical judgement. To this extent, there may be limitations in any model of critical viewing which is based merely on a cynical rejection of the medium, or indeed on the dispassionate pursuit of information.

Rethinking politics?

Young people's relationship with the public sphere of politics is often taken as an index of the future health of our society. As I have indicated, the prognosis here is generally far from positive: young people's apparent apathy and cynicism are seen to bode ill for the survival of democracy. In responding to these concerns, more optimistic commentators tend to point to the apparent success of 'alternative politics' and 'new social movements' among the young. In fact, however, active involvement in these new forms of politics is still confined to a small minority. More fundamentally, this optimistic emphasis on single-issue campaigns appears to leave the central institutions of politics untouched. There may indeed be a case for redefining politics, or for changing dominant forms of political culture, but 'politics as usual' will continue to exercise a fundamental influence on people's lived experiences, despite all the claims about its 'irrelevance'. The challenge, as Wilkinson and Mulgan put it,[39] is not so much to develop alternatives to conventional politics as to find ways of 'reconnecting politics', by making it more accessible and meaningful to young people.

Likewise, for all its shortcomings, news journalism remains the primary means of access to the public sphere of political debate and activity. Even for those who wish to become involved in 'single issue' events and campaigns – Live Aid, for example, or Greenpeace – the need for information remains. Indeed, it could be argued that public action of the kind espoused by these new social movements requires *greater* access to information, precisely because such information is less likely to appear in the mainstream media.[40] To reject news as simply irrelevant to such forms of 'everyday politics', as some critics have come close to doing,[41] is thus to ignore the continuing need for knowledge. Indeed, it is hard to see how everyday lived experience can be conceptualized in 'political' terms without the ability to connect it to the wider world of collective action – and hence without access to *information* about that wider world.

In both areas, there is certainly a need for some fresh thinking about the relationship between the 'personal' and the 'political', and about the potential of popular cultural forms in this respect. Jon Katz's call for news journalists to adopt less formal and conservative modes of address is certainly supported by the responses of the children reported here. Nevertheless, there is a need for some fairly traditional thinking also. Calls for formal innovation and for more 'popular' approaches in the news need to be balanced with calls for a more informative, less superficial approach to political communication. In relation to young people in particular, news has distinctive *educational* responsibilities, which could and should be fulfilled much more effectively than they are at present.

There are crucial challenges here for media producers; yet there are also particular implications for schools. The notion of citizenship has been the focus of a considerable amount of educational rhetoric in recent years, not least in response to young people's perceived disaffection with politics. Yet the aims and methods of 'citizenship education' have often been inadequately defined. During the late 1980s and early 1990s, the Conservatives in Britain promoted a form of citizenship education which came close to a modern version of 'civics': it was largely about encouraging young people to take on the necessary tasks that are left undone by the welfare state, such as picking up litter, fund-raising for charity or visiting the elderly, rather than encouraging any more active and informed participation in politics. Indeed, 'political education' was condemned by the Conservatives as tantamount to an opportunity for indoctrination[42] – even though they were keen to use the National Curriculum to promote a highly 'political' and socially divisive notion of national identity, in subjects such as History and English.[43] Yet in seeking to avoid political controversy, educational policy-makers implicitly assume that children are incapable of making sophisticated political judgements, that they are easy targets for 'indoctrination'. As Cedric Cullingford argues, this effectively leaves the business of political education to other sources, not least the media. In the process, children may be left inadequately prepared: 'On the one hand, we expect children to have developed enough social literacy to make political judgments by the age of 18 [when they are allowed to vote]. On the other hand, we avoid giving them the means of acquiring such knowledge and analytical skills.'[44]

However, it is important to avoid a view of political education as simply a matter of making good the apparent deficits in young people's political knowledge. The more difficult challenge for teachers, as for news journalists, is to find ways of establishing the *relevance* of politics, and of *connecting* the 'micro-politics' of personal experience with the 'macro-politics' of the public sphere. This will not be accomplished simply by dumping information on young people, or indeed by issuing them with implicit injunctions to do their civic duty; and it will require a definition of politics that goes well beyond the formal operations of political institutions.

Furthermore, this emphasis on relevance necessarily implies a context in which such information will be *used* – in other words, that it will feed into people's *political actions* in real life. This in turn suggests that young people need to be provided with opportunities to engage in political activity, rather than simply observing it from a distance – in other words, that they are entitled to be political actors in their own right.

In this chapter, I have argued that young people's alienation from the domain of politics should not be interpreted as merely a form of apathy or ignorance. On the contrary, it needs to be seen as a result of their positive exclusion from that domain – in effect, as a response to *disenfranchisement*. Yet the notion that young people are 'disenfranchised' necessarily implies that they should have some kinds of political rights. There is a similar implication in the assertion that young people are (or should be) 'citizens' – not potential citizens, or citizens-in-the-making, but *actual* citizens.

Such arguments implicitly challenge the assumptions on which most contemporary conceptions of citizenship or political rights are based. Citizenship is predominantly perceived to be a function of rationality: it requires a fundamental distinction between public and private, a free flow of undistorted communication, and a dutiful subjection to the public good. In these respects, enfranchisement, political rights and citizenship are defined in opposition to all the things that children and young people are traditionally seen to represent.

These arguments about 'children's rights' will be taken up more directly in my conclusion. In this context, however, it is important to assert that 'cultural rights' – for example in relation to the media – must necessarily be related to *political* rights. As Rob Gilbert argues,[45] the political and the cultural are not synonymous; and if rights of access to cultural expression are to be realized, more traditional forms of civil and political rights must also inevitably be at stake, not least for young people.

While there clearly are problems with the more romantic notions of 'children's liberation' espoused by some in the 1970s, it is hard to see why adult rights and responsibilities in this field should not be extended at least to contemporary teenagers. As Richard Lindley suggests,[46] many of the restrictions society currently places on younger children are unnecessary for teenagers, and actively undermine their efforts to take control of their own lives. In relation to politics, it is certainly debatable whether teenagers in general are any more ignorant than the majority of adults. My own research is by no means alone in suggesting that teenagers are at least *capable* of understanding complex political concepts and issues, and of making sophisticated judgements about them, provided they are given the means to do so.[47] Here again, there seems to be little justification for excluding them from what is seen to be a purely 'adult' domain – in effect, for perpetually disenfranchising them merely on the grounds of their biological age.

Conclusion

10

Children's Media Rights

What will be the fate of childhood in the twenty-first century? Will children increasingly be living 'media childhoods', dominated by the electronic screen? Will their growing access to 'adult' media help to abolish the distinctions between childhood and adulthood? Or will the advent of new media technologies widen the gaps between the generations still further? And what are the implications of these developments in terms of social, cultural and educational policy?

In the first part of this book, I reviewed two contrasting responses to these questions. On the one hand, there are critics who have held the media – and particularly television – responsible for the 'death of childhood'; while on the other, there are those who see the media – and particularly computers – as a means of children's liberation. From both perspectives, the media are seen to have a central role, not only in reflecting broader social and cultural changes, but also in producing them.

As I have indicated, there is some truth in both positions, but there are also some significant problems with each of them. Much of the evidence on which they rely is very limited, and their rhetorical claims are frequently exaggerated. Both perspectives reflect essentialist views, both of childhood and of communications media; and they are based on a deterministic analysis of the relationships between them. In terms of policy, the solutions they provide appear highly unrealistic. To call for a return to traditional notions of childhood, or alternatively to place all our faith in the power of technology, is ultimately to ignore the complexity of the changes that are taking place.

My own analysis of these developments, contained in the second part of this book, was somewhat more cautious. Despite the rhetoric of complete and irreversible change, there are significant continuities between the experiences of contemporary children and those of their parents' generation. Our children are not yet the alien creatures – or indeed the premature adults – some have imagined them to be. Nevertheless, I too have tended to emphasize changes rather than continuities. Indeed, I have perhaps focused too readily on risk and insecurity than on the stability and authority of historical tradition.

However, I have also argued that the pattern of change is more complex and ambiguous. Contemporary changes in childhood pull in different directions at the same time. Thus, in some respects, children are becoming 'empowered', while in others they are becoming more institutionalized and subject to adult control: in some areas, the boundaries between adults and children are blurring, but in others they are being powerfully reinforced. Furthermore, I have argued that these developments affect different groups of children in different ways. Thus, childhood is indeed becoming commercialized, but there are also growing inequalities in material and cultural capital that make it difficult to talk about 'childhood' in such generalized terms.

These broader changes – both in ideas about childhood and in the realities of children's lives – have been echoed and to some extent reinforced by changes in the media environment of children. Here again, traditional distinctions are being eroded, while new gaps are opening up. Children are increasingly gaining access to 'adult' media, and being 'empowered' as consumers in their own right; yet the commercialization and privatization of the media (and of leisure provision more broadly) are also contributing to the growth of inequalities. If children are indeed now living 'media childhoods', the media environments they inhabit have become increasingly diverse.

These changes are further reflected in changing views of the child audience, albeit in some quite ambivalent and contradictory ways. If public debates are increasingly dominated by anxieties about the need for control (and hence by a notion of children as powerless), the media industries themselves have enthusiastically championed the child as a sovereign consumer (and hence as *already* powerful). While laments for the 'death of childhood' have become commonplace in the press and in political debate, media producers are now much more likely to indulge in a heady optimism about the sophistication of the 'electronic generation'.

Meanwhile, academic research in this field has been engaging in a parallel debate: the traditional view of children as passive and vulnerable has increasingly been challenged by the more recent view of them as 'media-wise' and innately competent. While my sympathies are evidently with the latter perspective, I have also argued that it can lead to a kind of sentimentality and an unwarranted optimism. By contrast, I have attempted to move beyond these either/or alternatives. I have argued that we need to situate the activities of child audiences within their social contexts – in relation to other social forces in children's lives, and in relation to the changing nature of media technologies, texts and institutions.

In the final part of the book, I attempted to develop this approach in relation to three areas. In different ways and for different reasons, each of these areas is one in which children are typically excluded from what is seen to be the proper domain of adults. In choosing to focus on violence, commercialism and politics, I have reflected the concerns of my own previous research; although similar questions could undoubtedly be raised about issues such as sexuality and cultural identity that have also been in the forefront of contemporary debates about children and the media.

Each of these issues clearly raises different questions, and they should not be collapsed into each other. Nevertheless, what underlies my analysis here is a more general concern about the terms under which children are gaining, or should be given, access to the 'adult' world – at least as this is made available via the electronic media. As I have argued, some of the anxieties that are typically raised here are quite misplaced. We need to do more than simply bemoan the negative consequences of children's increasing experience of 'adult' life, or indeed than celebrating it as a form of liberation. On the contrary, we need to understand the extent – and the limitations – of children's competence as *participants* in the adult world. In relation to the media, we need to acknowledge children's ability to evaluate the representations of that world which are made available to them; and to identify what they might need to know in order to do so more productively and effectively.

In different ways, these are all issues of *public policy*, and they require us to think about the principles that should guide and inform such policies. Cultural Studies has recently been accused, with some justification, of neglecting questions of policy in favour of empty political rhetoric.[1] This is not, I would argue, a meaningful option when it comes to children and the media – an issue which, as I have indicated, has been a constant focus of public concern and anxiety.

In this brief concluding chapter, therefore, I will explore some of the implications of these arguments in terms of cultural and educational policy. If children are increasingly using the media to gain access to aspects of the 'adult' world, how do we respond to this? Is a defensive, protectionist stance either desirable or realistic? Alternatively, can we resort to a liberationist argument, asserting children's freedom to choose? Do we look to 'privatized' solutions which place responsibility in the hands of individuals – families, parents or children themselves? Or can we also imagine more explicitly *political* responses, in the public sphere of social and cultural institutions?

Children's rights

In particular, I want to examine whether and in what ways it might be possible to address these questions by talking about children's *rights* in relation to the media. Over the past decade there has been a significant revival of interest in children's rights, which has been reflected in academic and philosophical debates,[2] in public campaigns and in new legislation.[3] The United Nations Convention on the Rights of the Child, adopted by the General Assembly in 1989, is perhaps the most visible aspect of this phenomenon, and it has been echoed by legislation in many countries. Needless to say, there has also been considerable debate about whether the rhetoric has been matched by reality; and the United Kingdom has in fact been castigated by the UN for its failure to implement the Convention fully, particularly in the field of schooling.[4]

Philosophically, the clearest position here is the liberationist one, whose recent origins may be found in the work of Shulamith Firestone, Richard Farson and John Holt, published in the early 1970s.[5] In broad terms, the liberationists argue that the separation between children and adults is arbitrary and oppressive of children; and that it is sustained by an ideology of childhood which defines 'childishness' in terms of vulnerability and helplessness. Liberating children from this oppression will mean giving them access to adult privileges. Thus, Holt and others argue that children should be allowed to vote, to undertake paid employment and to engage in sexual activity; and that they should be able to choose whether or not to go to school, where and with whom they want to live, and so on.

However, it is important to distinguish here between different *types* of rights. Thus, the early liberationists make a distinction between rights which are to do with guaranteeing a certain kind or level of treatment by adults (for example, in health care or education) and rights of self-determination, which children can exercise if they so choose (for example, the right to vote, work or travel).[6] These might broadly be seen as 'passive' and 'active' rights respectively. Bob and Annie Franklin make a related distinction between rights to *provi-*

sion and *protection* on the one hand (in my terms, 'passive' rights), and rights to *participation* on the other ('active' rights). They suggest that the latter, which implicitly define children as political actors in their own right, have for the most part yet to be realized.[7]

Statements on children's rights typically combine – if not conflate and confuse – these different types of rights. The UN Convention, for example, contains an uneven mixture of protectionism and an emphasis on autonomous participation.[8] Thus, on the one hand, it is argued that children should be protected *against* exploitation, neglect and abuse; while on the other, they are to be given rights *to* education, privacy and freedom of association and expression. It is not hard to imagine situations in which these different kinds of rights might come into conflict. Ironically, as Mary John points out, the Convention's emphasis on children's right to have their voices heard is somewhat belied by the fact that children were not actually involved in drafting it. In practice, she suggests, the Convention largely excludes the possibility of children having *political* rights.[9]

In addition, there is often an awkward balance here between the emphasis on children's autonomy and the emphasis on the rights of *parents*. In the case of the UN Convention, this is particularly apparent in debates about cultural identity.[10] The Convention declares that children have rights to a cultural identity, but in practice this seems to be equated with the cultural identity of their parents. Some critics have argued that there is a danger of cultural imperialism here, that the universalizing approach of rights discourse tends to ignore cultural differences.[11] Yet this argument seems to deny the possibility that some cultures are more oppressive of children than others. Ultimately, in this as in other areas, the UN Convention resolves this dilemma by locating children's rights within the context of the family, and hence placing its central emphasis on sustaining the rights of parents.

As this implies, the notion of children's rights is far from politically straightforward. Some apparently radical authors argue that children's rights must involve a reassertion of childhood as a sacred space, one that is somehow outside politics, the market and global culture – a position which aligns quite easily with the conservatism of the 'death of childhood' thesis.[12] On the other hand, as I have indicated, arguments for children's rights can easily be elided with a notion of children as 'sovereign consumers' – in which case the exercise of rights is directly related to the ability to buy.

Moreover, the actual involvement of children in debates and campaigns for children's rights has in general been minimal. Of course, there are significant practical obstacles to securing children's involvement in such movements, and there is a distinct danger of tokenism.

Nevertheless, there is a sense in which, even here, the *idea* of 'child-hood' becomes a vehicle for other adult concerns, just as it has been in much more conservative social campaigns.

Rights and competence

One significant difficulty in these debates is the tendency to general-ize about children, as though they constituted a homogeneous group. Proposals for the wholesale extension of 'adult' rights to very young children – of the kind suggested by John Holt, for example – stretch the credulity of most observers. This is particularly the case with *participation* rights, where the practical obstacles to 'empowering' young children would seem to be immense.

As David Archard suggests, the key issue here is how we estab-lish whether or not children are sufficiently *competent* to exercise rights.[13] Archard agrees with the liberationists that the distinction between children and adults is to some extent arbitrary; yet he ar-gues that in practice there are significant correlations between bio-logical age and the possession of capacities that are relevant to the possession of rights. Distinctions between adults and children are thus not *wholly* arbitrary or ideological. Age does provide some broad indications about competence; and not least for legal reasons, there is a need for indisputable dividing lines between those who are seen to be competent to make choices (and hence to exercise rights) in certain contexts and those who are not.

Of course, the rationales that are used in drawing these lines are quite diverse. For example, there are legal rationales (according to which children are seen to be not responsible for their actions); epis-temological or psychological ones (in which children are seen to be incapable of adult reasoning); and political ones (in which children are seen to be incapable of participating in the running of society).[14] As I have indicated, there are some significant contradictions in terms of the age at which these different lines are drawn. For example, the age of criminal responsibility in the UK has recently been lowered to ten: children can thus be prosecuted under the law, but they are not seen to be mature enough to play a part in the process whereby laws are formed and validated. Likewise, as Archard points out, it seems illogical for a country to deny the franchise to those who can, as en-listed soldiers, die in its service.[15]

In practice, however, even the most 'extreme' advocates of chil-dren's liberation tend to draw the line somewhere. From his more moderate position, Archard seeks to distinguish between *teenagers*

and younger children in these terms. He argues that there is no justi-
fiable reason for denying rights to self-determination – for example,
in voting or sexual activity – to teenagers. He asserts that teenagers
possess both the intellectual competency and the degree of knowledge to make informed decisions about these matters – or at least as
much as adults do.[16] Likewise, Richard Lindley argues that there are
good reasons for restricting the liberties of younger children: for example, they are not necessarily sufficiently informed of the dangers
of the world, or aware of the consequences of their actions. But he
asserts that these reasons do not apply to teenagers: empirical evidence suggests that teenagers can make responsible decisions and
live autonomously, particularly if they are given the level of education that will help them to do so.[17]

This last point is very important. Children may be more competent than they are typically credited with being, but the fact remains
that they acquire this competence gradually. As I have argued, there
is a self-confirming process here: how we think about children leads
us to act in particular ways towards them, which tends to produce
the behaviour that confirms our own thinking about what children
are like. Children may be unable to act in any other way simply because they have not had the opportunity to do so. It is in this sense
that discourse in general can be said to produce behaviour rather
than simply reflecting it. One implication of this, of course, is that
children will only be able to *become* competent if they are treated as
though they *are* competent. Indeed, it is hard to see how they might
become competent if they are not at some stage given the chance to
engage in the activity in question.

Thus, for example, authors like Archard and Lindley argue (as I
have done in the previous chapter) that there is no reason why teenagers should not have the right to vote. There is no evidence that
they are *intellectually* unable to understand political issues, although
some may lack the *knowledge* to make informed decisions. But the
differences between teenagers and most adults in these respects are
not sufficient to justify teenagers being permanently disenfranchised.
For both groups, there is a need for political education here – in which,
as I have suggested, the media (as well as schools) may have an important role to play.

Towards media rights

What would it mean to talk about children's rights in relation to the
media? Such issues are by no means neglected by the UN Conven-

tion. Article 13, for example, asserts children's right to freedom of expression; Article 17 proclaims their rights of access to a range of media; while Article 31 identifies broader rights to leisure and to participation in cultural life. Here again, however, this assertion of 'positive' rights is somewhat qualified by the emphasis on what is 'appropriate to the age of the child', or conducive to 'his or her social, spiritual and moral well-being', and on the need to 'protect the child from material injurious to his or her well-being'. Quite how, and by whom, these things are to be defined is left conveniently vague.

This ambivalence is reflected in other documents inspired by the UN Convention. The Children's Television Charter, for example,[18] originally drawn up at the 1995 World Summit on Children and Television in Australia, illustrates some of these continuing tensions. The Charter's primary motivation is to defend traditional public service principles. Quality, diversity and universal access are thus among its key concerns: it asserts, for example, that children's programmes should be made to 'the highest possible standards'; they should be 'wide-ranging in genre and content'; and they should be 'aired in regular slots when children are available to view and/or distributed via other widely available media or technologies'. At the same time, there are clear protectionist principles here, for example in references to avoiding 'gratuitous scenes of violence and sex', and the need to protect children from programmes that might 'exploit' them. As in the UN Charter itself, it is in its implicit response to the global commercialization of children's media, and the resulting concerns about cultural identity, that some of the tensions are most apparent. Thus, the Children's Television Charter argues that programmes should 'affirm [children's] sense of community and place', while simultaneously promoting 'an awareness and appreciation of other cultures in parallel with the child's own cultural background'. Here again, it is not hard to imagine circumstances in which these different principles might come into conflict.

To return to Bob and Annie Franklin's distinctions, the types of rights that are primarily emphasized here are those of *provision* and *protection*. These are undeniably important, and (as I have argued) there may be good reasons why they should be reasserted at this time. By contrast, however, there is comparatively little mention of children's rights to *participation*, whether in terms of the actual production of programmes or in terms of a more general public involvement in the making of broadcasting policy. In this respect, the Charter suffers from the problem of all such documents: it ascribes views, needs and interests to children without organizing the kind of dialogue which would allow children's own perspectives to be heard. However, in a key passage, the Charter urges producers, companies and governments to affirm that 'children should hear, see and *express themselves*, their culture, their languages and their life experiences' (my emphasis). It is at this point, in its emphasis on the right to expression alongside rights in relation to consumption, that the document most clearly admits the child to a kind of citizenship.

Nevertheless, participation rights cannot simply be bestowed on children: if they are to develop the abilities to exercise such rights, they need to be equipped to do so. To this extent, therefore, we need to add a fourth term to our set of media rights, namely that of *education*. This form of education will not be one that seeks primarily to defend children from the influence of the media, or indeed to persuade them to conform to the teacher's 'critical consciousness'. On the contrary, it will seek to extend their active and informed participation in the media culture that surrounds them.

Finally, there is a danger that the discourse of rights can be seen as an individualizing one, as an assertion of the powers of autonomous individuals, or indeed of 'consumers'. By contrast, I want to argue for a more *social* conception of rights. In each of the four areas above – of protection, provision, participation and education – and particularly in the latter two, my proposals are primarily for initiatives in the *public* sphere. This is not to imply a simplistic or a necessary distinction between the 'public' and the 'private', or indeed between the 'citizen' and the 'consumer'. Nevertheless, as in many of the more specific areas addressed in this book, my argument is generally in favour of increasing children's access to the public sphere and against a further privatization or domestication of childhood. Rather than attempting to reinforce the boundaries between childhood and adulthood, and to confine children more securely within them, we need to face the fact that those boundaries are increasingly being crossed and blurred in all sorts of ways. And rather than leaving children isolated in their encounters with the 'adult' world of the contemporary media, we need to find ways of preparing them to cope with it, to participate in it, and if necessary to change it.

Protection

I want to conclude, therefore, with a brief – and somewhat polemical – discussion of each of the four aspects of children's media rights identified above. The assertion that children need *protection* from harm is the most familiar of these; and, as we have seen, it is strongly emphasized in the UN Convention and in most similar definitions of children's rights. In relation to the media, this is an emphasis that it is difficult to question, at least in general terms. Children (like adults) should not be subjected to material that they themselves have not knowingly chosen to experience, or that might (in the words of the Convention) prove 'injurious to their well-being'. At least in the UK, there is already a high degree of regulation in this respect. For example, there are existing laws against child pornography, 'indecent displays' and the incitement to racial hatred; as well as strict codes of practice relating to false claims in advertising, the invasion of privacy and depictions of violence in film and television.

However, as I have implied, arguments about children's vulnerability also tend to be used as a justification for denying them access to knowledge and power. In practice, there is a considerable room for debate – not least between parents and children – about what *counts* as 'appropriate to the age of the child', or 'injurious to his or her well-being' (to quote the UN Convention), let alone as a form of 'exploitation'. Furthermore, the growing accessibility of new distribution technologies significantly undermines the possibility of regulation, both at the level of government and (increasingly) in the home. On both philosophical and pragmatic grounds, therefore, we need to move towards a system that provides for and supports *self-regulation* – not just by parents, but also by children themselves.

In fact, the evidence that children in general are more vulnerable to harm – or less competent in their dealings with the media – than the majority of adults is in many respects very questionable (see chapter 7). While there may be a case for special protection for the very young, most such restrictions based on age seem quite anachronistic. The existence in Britain of an '18' certificate in film and video classification, for example, is an absurd denial of what the majority of teenagers (and many younger children) know about the media – and indeed about the world in general. In my view, there is no justification for *legally preventing* teenagers from gaining access to material that is available to adults, on the grounds that it is morally harmful or a negative influence on their behaviour. There is certainly a case for *classification*, and indeed for informing consumers much more effectively than is the case at present. However, to define the suitability or appropriateness of particular categories of media content in terms of age is both misleading and potentially counterproductive; and there is no case for making such a system legally enforceable, or for censoring (that is, physically removing) material on the grounds that it might be seen by children, as is currently the case with film and video classification in the UK.

At present, such questions appear more complex in relation to the internet than in relation to film and television. This is partly because of the sheer volume of material that is available, and the difficulty of monitoring or controlling it; but it is also because some of it is undeniably offensive to the majority of people, in a way that broadcast television is not. Existing laws should in principle provide protection against child pornography or incitement to racial hatred, for example, although the complexity of the situation suggests that it may at least be some time before this becomes effective. Here again, I would argue that the solution to this situation is not to be found in stricter centralized control, particularly of the crude variety that is likely to be available. Like Jon Katz,[19] I would see the V-chip and blocking software as fundamental infringements of children's liberty; and like him, I take comfort from the fact that they are unlikely to have much effect. Children who are determined to find hard-core pornography or racist propaganda are likely to be able to find it in any case, irrespective of technological constraints.

Here too, there is an urgent need for much more effective provision of information, both of a negative variety (in the form of warnings) and of a positive one (in the form of recommending valuable sites). In my view, this is too important and too controversial to be left to commercial providers. Along with public information of this kind, there is also a need for education. On the most basic level, children obviously need to be encouraged to take steps to protect themselves on the internet, and to take care about the information they provide, not least to commercial companies; although experience suggests that they quickly become aware of this. On a more complex level, there are questions about how children learn to evaluate the information they find, although these apply just as much to adults. Traditional questions about the ownership and control of information, and about representation and persuasion, are just as relevant to these new media as they are to more established ones. Here again, issues of child protection will need to be rethought as issues of *education*.

Provision

The pace of technological and economic change in the media industries has raised new questions about the adequate provision of media for children. In the case of broadcasting, for example, these changes have had ambiguous consequences. The notion that children will simply lose out in the new commercial media environment is one that cannot be sustained: the sheer quantity of new media being made available to children – or at least to those who have access to technologies such as cable and satellite – has massively increased. Of course, quantity does not necessarily imply quality or diversity, and the emphasis on these contained in the Children's Television Charter is one that should be supported. The temptation to target children with inexpensive, poor quality material is ever present, as is the assumption that they will watch anything they are given. There should continue to be regulation of both public and commercial providers in order to ensure the availability of a range of material *specifically designed for children* – and indeed for the full diversity of children. The fact that older children are overwhelmingly interested in 'adult' media should not be taken as a reason to deny the fact that they too have specific needs, interests and concerns.

As I have indicated, the proliferation of material on new commercial channels has been positive, albeit in a limited range of genres (see chapter 5). Yet there is a continuing need to fund and support the kinds of material that would not immediately appear to be profitable, to encourage innovation, and to counterbalance the dominance of US producers in the world market. Material produced by children themselves should also be funded and made available via these new channels. In this respect, the UK could build on the public access requirement imposed on cable operators in the US, and seek to extend this specifically to children and other underrepresented groups. Nevertheless, these developments will not be achieved merely via quotas or other 'negative' forms of regulation: there also needs to be a more proactive attempt to fund the production of material that children will actually want to seek out, and to enable children to produce such material themselves.

Equally significant here is the Charter's emphasis on universal access – its assertion that programmes for children should be 'aired in regular slots when children are available to view and/or distributed via other widely available media or technologies'. These issues are perhaps clearest in relation to broadcasting, which (at least in the UK) has traditionally been subject to a considerable level of state regulation. As I have noted, privatization is resulting in significant inequalities of access, inequalities that are already much more apparent in relation to media where provision is wholly or largely subject to the laws of the market, such as film, books and now computers.

The emphasis on extending and equalizing access is a key theme in government cultural policy in the UK, although it sits awkwardly with its emphasis on the economic value of the cultural industries and its generally enthusiastic approach to global media corporations.[20] Schools, libraries and other state-funded cultural institutions can undoubtedly play a significant role here, by providing access at a community or neighbourhood level; and in this respect, there is scope for imaginative collaborations with the private sector (as in the recent emergence of free internet cafés in supermarkets, for example). However, it should be emphasized that access is not simply about technology: it is also about the cultural and educational capital that is needed if technology is to be used creatively and effectively. Investing in technological infrastructures – 'wiring up' schools, for example – is a merely cosmetic gesture if it is not sustained by an investment in specialist staff and in training.

At the same time, much greater efforts should be made to take account of children's own perspectives on these issues. As I have noted, arguments about children's cultural and psychological needs frequently serve as a justification of adults' vested interests and a defence against change (see chapter 8). In broadcasting, as in other areas of cultural policy, there is a need to create a dialogue in which children's voices will be heard, and to extend the accountability of cultural producers to the audiences they purport to serve. In this respect too, arguments about provision begin to feed in to arguments about the need for *education*.

Participation

To argue for children's right to *participation* in the media is to move from 'passive' rights to 'active' rights. The emphasis here is not so much on what should be provided for children (or alternatively kept away from them), but on their active involvement in shaping and producing the media environment that surrounds them. Two broad types of participation can be identified here: participation in production itself, and participation in the formation of media policy and the management of media institutions.

As I have noted, the proliferation of new means and channels of distribution offers significant opportunities for the democratization of media production. This is most obviously the case in relation to the internet, although there is no reason in principle why it should not also be the case with cable and digital broadcasting. Here again, what is needed is a positive requirement on the part of governments to ensure that public access to production is provided as a condition of the granting of licences.

Past attempts at providing access to production for children have, perhaps inevitably, been somewhat tokenistic. In practice, such opportunities have largely been dominated by teenagers, and there has been little attempt to draw the attention of a wider audience to such material. On some occasions it would seem that (despite appearances) children have had very little involvement in editorial decision-making. Nevertheless, there have been some important achievements here also. On British television, Channel 4's *Wise Up* and *Look Who's Talking* or the BBC's *As Seen on TV* have contained some excellent and innovative material produced by young people; although only *Look Who's Talking* was scheduled for a more general audience. These kinds of initiatives are often perceived as merely a matter of 'do-gooding'; yet from the point of view of new digital and cable channels, programmes of this kind would provide a fairly inexpensive way of generating original, domestically produced material – material which, in my view, they should be positively required to provide.

Production opportunities for children in other media will need to be made available in different ways. Media corporations could be encouraged by means of specific tax breaks to sponsor and invest in community access facilities. In the light of the inequalities of access, such projects should be primarily targeted at low-income areas; and they need to be supported by providing access to distribution, for example through community websites, publications, exhibition spaces and so on.

Participation also implies a more general form of accountability in the functioning of media institutions. Of course, there have always been pressure groups which seek to define the interests of children, and to speak for them; but there is a strong need to establish means by which children themselves can speak more directly, collectively and loudly to producers and policy-makers. Institutions such as citizens' juries or consumer councils, which are sometimes proposed in this context,[21] are perhaps less useful for children. This is not so much because children are immature, as because their status as students, as people involved in a process of organized learning, could enable them to develop and articulate a deeper understanding of media issues than could ever be achieved in the brief meetings of a jury, or in the small space that an adult-dominated consumer council would allow. A regular series of regional conferences, preceded by website debates and linked to the media education curriculum of primary and secondary schools, would give children the opportunities to make a well-prepared, persistent contribution to debates about media policy. Likewise, resources could be given to create forums on the internet for critical dialogue between young people, in the form of webzines or chat rooms. This kind of support for a public 'media culture' would enable children to think of themselves as citizens in more general terms, and in turn encourage adults to re-evaluate their view of children's capacities.

In both areas, my earlier arguments about children's competence clearly apply: children will only develop the competence to produce meaningful statements in the media, or to make their views known, if they are given sustained and well-supported opportunities to do so. Here again, opportunities for participation need to be seen as part of a wider set of *educational* initiatives.

Education

As the preceding observations imply, education is very much the key to the whole process. Educational institutions, broadly conceived, can play a vital role in equalizing children's access, both to media technologies and to the kinds of cultural capital that are needed to use them most productively. They can provide the means and the necessary support for participation in the media, of both the kinds identified above. And they can develop children's ability to protect themselves from – or, more positively, to understand and to deal effectively with – the broader media environment.

Like access, education has been identified as a key theme in the British government's cultural policy; although the emphases of its *educational* policy are generally much more traditional and utilitarian. Amid attempts to return to a nineteenth-century curriculum, media education – teaching *about* the media – has largely remained on the margins of formal schooling. It seems quite extraordinary that the school curriculum should continue to neglect the forms of culture and communication that have so thoroughly dominated the twentieth century, and will continue to dominate the twenty-first.

Historically, media education has largely been characterized by forms of defensiveness: it has been motivated by the desire to protect children from what are seen to be the moral, cultural or political shortcomings of the media. In recent years, however, this approach has come to be questioned, not least as a result of research on children's learning, and on classroom practice.[22] There is a great deal more that needs to be known here, particularly about the ways in which students progress in their learning, and how their understandings of the media might transfer to other areas of the curriculum. Nevertheless, we do now possess a rigorous and coherent model of media education, which has been highly influential internationally.[23] From this contemporary perspective, media education is not confined to analysing the media – much less to some rationalistic notion of 'critical viewing skills'. On the contrary, it seeks to encourage young people's critical participation as cultural producers in their own right.

Like many of its advocates, I would see media education as a very significant site in defining future possibilities for citizenship. If, as Rob Gilbert suggests, the struggle for citizenship is partly a struggle over the 'means and substance of cultural expression'[24] – and particularly over those which are made available by the electronic media – it is essential that the curriculum should equip young people to become actively involved in the media culture that surrounds them. Apart from its broader social and cultural benefits, such a curriculum would encourage children to have high expectations of the media themselves.

As I have indicated, some critics have argued that such developments are emerging in any case. The new digital media are seen by some of their advocates as bringing about precisely the kind of active, participatory citizenship that I have called for here. Jon Katz, for example, argues that the internet provides children with opportunities to escape from adult control, and to create their own autonomous cultures and communities.[25] My own analysis has been somewhat more sceptical, both of the evidence for such claims and of the technological determinism on which they are often based. Certainly, the new forms of cultural expression envisaged by enthusiasts for digital media will not simply arise of their own accord, or as a guaranteed consequence of technological change: we will need to devise imaginative forms of cultural policy that will foster and support them, and ensure that their benefits are not confined to a narrow elite.

Nevertheless, these developments point towards the possibility of forms of media education that move beyond the traditional classroom. These will involve new types of dialogue between parents and children, and between producers, policy-makers and audiences. They may well involve the creation of new public sphere institutions which provide all sections of the population with opportunities for access to and participation in a whole range of 'old' and 'new' media. And in any event, they will represent a broader form of education about culture and communication than is currently envisaged by the majority of educational policy-makers.

Finally, it is important to emphasize that media or cultural rights should not be seen in isolation from broader questions about the social and political status of children. In this sense, the call for cultural rights must inevitably entail a call for political rights. In the process, traditional questions about power and access – about who owns the means of production, who has the right to speak, and whose voices can be heard – must remain at the top of the policy agenda.

We cannot return children to the secret garden of childhood, or find the magic key that will keep them forever locked within its walls. Children are escaping into the wider adult world – a world of dangers and opportunities, in which the electronic media are playing an ever more important role. The age in which we could hope to protect children from that world is passing. We must have the courage to prepare them to deal with it, to understand it, and to become active participants in their own right.

Notes

1   In Search of the Child

1   Andersen (1995), p. 10.
2   For representative instances of this argument, see James, Jenks and Prout
    (1998), James and Prout (1990), Jenks (1996), Jordanova (1989) and
    Stainton Rogers and Stainton Rogers (1992).
3   The theoretical underpinnings of this approach are of course derived
    from the works of Michel Foucault: see, for example, Foucault (1980,
    1981).
4   Useful accounts of these developments can be found in Cunningham
    (1991), Davin (1996), Hendrick (1997) and Steedman (1990).
5   Hendrick (1990).
6   Cunningham (1991), p. 152.
7   See Archard (1993), pp. 32–6.
8   See Rose (1984); and for a more celebratory account, Wullschlager (1995).
9   See Kline (1993), Fleming (1996).
10 See Forgacs (1992).
11 Holland (1992), pp. 12–13.
12 Archard (1993), p. 39.
13 Holland (1992), p. 14.
14 For useful cross-cultural studies of childhood, see Amit-Talai and Wulff
    (1995) and Stephens (1995).
15 This formulation is derived from Thompson (1990).
16 Jenkins (1992).
17 This is particularly apparent in Steedman's (1990) analysis of the work
    of the socialist reformer Margaret Macmillan.
18 Our research suggests that this is one way in which children them-
    selves perceive and define 'children's television': see Kelley, Bucking-
    ham and Davies (1999).

19 For critiques of psychological theories of child development along these
   lines, see Burman (1994), Henriques et al. (1984), Rose (1985) and
   Stainton Rogers and Stainton Rogers (1992).
20 For a discussion, see Ivy (1995).

2 The Death of Childhood

1 Elkind (1981), p. 73.
2 Ibid., p. xii.
3 Winn (1984), p. 71.
4 Ibid., p. 42.
5 Winn (1977).
6 Winn (1984), p. 13.
7 Ibid., p. 95.
8 Ibid., p. 47. This is one of many assertions that would be significantly
   challenged by child historians: see, for example, Cunningham (1995).
9 Winn (1984), p. 73.
10 Elkind (1981), p. 22.
11 Ariès (1962).
12 Postman (1983), p. xii.
13 Ibid., p. 46.
14 For example, Innis (1951), McLuhan (1964).
15 Postman (1983), p. 99.
16 Ibid., p. 45.
17 Ibid., p. 152. For a useful critique of Postman's conservatism, see
   Hoikkala et al. (1987).
18 Meyrowitz (1985), p. 363.
19 Ibid., pp. 231–5.
20 Ibid., p. 242.
21 Ibid., p. 266.
22 Sanders (1995), p. xii.
23 Ibid., p. xii.
24 Ibid., p. 178.
25 Ibid., pp. 39–44.
26 Steinberg and Kincheloe (1997), p. 16.
27 Ibid., p. 46.
28 See Swingewood (1977).
29 Steinberg and Kincheloe (1997), p. 22.
30 Ibid., pp. 11–12.
31 Ibid., p. 9.
32 For a critique of this approach, see Buckingham (1996a).
33 For a discussion of questions of modernity and postmodernity in relation to childhood, see Jenks (1996).
34 Ariès (1962).
35 See, most notably, Pollock (1983); and for further discussion, Luke (1989)
   and Hendrick (1997), pp. 27–8.

36   Steedman (1995).
37   Cunningham (1991).
38   Walkerdine (1997).
39   Holland (1992).
40   For an important critique of the uses of such data, see Gusfield (1981).
41   De Mause (1976).
42   Luke (1989).
43   Cunningham (1991).
44   See Lavalette (1994).
45   See Hunter (1994).
46   Luke (1989).
47   As Kubey (1992) points out.
48   See De Castell, Luke and Egan (1986).
49   For a comprehensive review of this research, see S. Neuman (1991).
50   There is, of course, an enormous body of literature here. For a critical review, see Gauntlett (1995). These issues are dealt with at greater length in chapter 7.
51   See Street (1984).
52   Again, there is considerable debate here: for contrasting views, see Dorr (1986) and Messaris (1995).
53   The term 'cultural literacy' derives from the work of the conservative educator E. D. Hirsch (1987). I am using it here in a more neutral, and much less prescriptive, way.

3   The Electronic Generation

1   For example, Ohmae (1995).
2   Postman (1983, 1992).
3   See Melody (1973).
4   For example, Moir (1967). For parallel analyses in relation to 'older' technologies, see Dovey (1996a) and F. Johnson (1996).
5   See Oswell (1995) and Spigel (1992).
6   See, for example, Provenzo (1991).
7   See Griffiths (1996).
8   For a more positive analysis, see Tobin (1998).
9   Alloway and Gilbert (1998), Orr Vered (1998), Provenzo (1991).
10   Wallace and Mangan (1996).
11   Papert (1980, 1993, 1996).
12   Lanham (1993).
13   For a review of these arguments, see Sefton-Green and Buckingham (1996). Some pointed critiques of this broader utopian rhetoric can be found in Dovey (1996b).
14   See Nixon (1998).
15   For a definitive discussion of technological determinism, see Williams (1974). See also Webster (1995).
16   Tapscott (1998), Papert (1996), Katz (1997), Rushkoff (1996). Some of

the material here draws on Buckingham (1998a).
17 Tapscott (1998), p. 17.
18 Ibid., p. 3.
19 Ibid., p. 218.
20 Ibid., p. 50.
21 Papert (1996), p. x and cover blurb.
22 Papert (1993).
23 Papert (1996), p. 1.
24 Katz (1997), pp. 173–4.
25 Ibid., ch. 10.
26 Ibid., p. 10.
27 Rushkoff (1996), p. 8.
28 Ibid., p. 65. 'Pogs' are small disks made of cardboard, plastic or metal, collected by younger children: they were originally bottle tops from fruit drinks. A 'mosh pit' is the central 'dancing' area at a punk or grunge concert.
29 Ibid., p. 246.
30 Ibid., p. 268.
31 For less sanguine analyses of these developments, see Goodson and Mangan (1996), Sefton-Green (1998b), Webster (1995).
32 For some evidence on these points, see Healy (1998) and Sefton-Green (1998b).
33 Tapscott (1998), p. 305.
34 Appropriately (and amazingly) enough, *Kinderculture* is dedicated to 'John, Paul, George and Ringo'.

4 Changing Childhoods

1 See Stainton Rogers and Stainton Rogers (1992).
2 Unless otherwise indicated, statistics in this chapter are taken from official government publications. My primary source is *Social Trends* 28 (Pullinger, 1998). Further data comes from Bothing (1995), Fry (1994), Office of National Statistics (1997, 1998) and Newman and Smith (1997). I have also drawn on the National Children's Homes 'Factfile' (Dunn and Clusky, 1997), and on the studies included in Mayall (1994), Pilcher and Wagg (1996) and Scraton (1997).
3 Useful comparative data on several of these points can be found in Qvortrup et al. (1994).
4 For a parallel account relating to the US, see Corsaro (1997).
5 See James, Jenks and Prout (1998), pp. 126–8.
6 The potential conflict between these different ways of analysing childhood is considered, if not fully resolved, by James, Jenks and Prout (1998), esp. ch. 10.
7 See Burman (1994), ch. 5.
8 A review of research on this issue can be found in Dunn and Clusk (1997), ch. 5. See also Burman (1994), ch. 7.

9   Reported in the *Times Educational Supplement*, 18 Dec. 1998.
10 For discussions of the ideological import of the family in social policy, see David (1986) and Coppock (1997).
11 According to a report in the *Daily Telegraph*, 4 Nov. 1996.
12 See Corsaro (1997), ch. 10.
13 See Kline (1993) and Seiter (1993); and the further discussion in chapters 5 and 8 below.
14 These figures are drawn from the Family Expenditure Survey, reported in the 1998 *Social Trends*; the Youth Target Group Index (TGI) market research survey; and the Broadcasters Audience Research Board and the British Video Association annual reports for 1996. More detail is provided below and in chapter 5.
15 There are parallels here with the 'valorization' of the child that took place in the early years of the century: see Zelizer (1985).
16 See Ennew (1994).
17 See Burman (1994), esp. ch. 4.
18 For critical perspectives on this 'explosion of discourses', see Urwin (1985) and Burman (1994).
19 Humphries, Mack and Perks (1988), p. 59.
20 See Hendrick (1997), ch. 3.
21 James, Jenks and Prout (1998), p. 44; Burman (1994).
22 See, among many others, Campbell (1988), Davis and Bourhill (1997), Jenkins (1992), Parton (1996). Critical questions about the construction of 'abuse' are raised by Archard (1993) and Ivy (1995).
23 For analyses of recent education policy, see Haydon (1997), Jones (1990), Jones and Hatcher (1996) and Wagg (1996).
24 See Bridges and McLaughlin (1994) and Kenway and Fitzclarence (1999).
25 See Ennew (1994) for an analysis of how children's 'free time' has been steadily 'curricularized'.
26 See Epstein et al. (1998) and Jones and Hatcher (1996).
27 Since sixteen-year-olds can no longer register as unemployed, there is no official figure for this.
28 Brinkley (1998).
29 Rutherford (1998), p. 19.
30 Ibid., pp. 23, 16.
31 See Lavalette (1994, 1996), Morrow (1994).
32 James, Jenks, and Prout (1998), p. 121.
33 For a review, see Hendrick (1997), ch. 6. A contemporary cross-cultural analysis is provided by Ennew (1994).
34 Livingstone (1998).
35 Ward (1994).
36 See Hood et al. (1996).
37 Research by CAVIAR (Cinema and Video Industry Audience Research). Other figures here are taken from the journal *Cultural Trends*, 1996–8.
38 Opie and Opie (1984).
39 Figures in this section are taken from the National Children's Homes report by Dunn and Clusky (1997).

40 See Newburn (1996) and Scraton (1997). The fact that there has been a striking increase in the incidence of crime in general is difficult to dispute, however: see Jenkins (1992), ch. 4.
41 Hodgkin (1998).
42 See Qvortrup et al. (1994) for international comparisons here.
43 For the broader argument, see Giddens (1991) and Beck (1992); and for a measured application to contemporary childhood, see Hood et al. (1996).
44 Again, see Qvortrup et al. (1994). An account of the children's rights movement can be found in Franklin and Franklin (1996). This issue is discussed more fully in chapter 10 below.
45 See Winter and Connolly (1996).
46 These issues are discussed in more detail in chapters 5 and 6 below. See also Buckingham et al. (1999).
47 This is very much the emphasis of the contributors to Scraton (1997).
48 Rutherford (1988), p. 20.
49 See Oppenheim and Lister (1996); also Hendrick (1997). These issues are even more acute in the United States: see Corsaro (1997), ch. 10.

5 Changing Media

1 Some of the material in this chapter draws on Buckingham (1993b).
2 I would see this approach as characteristic of Cultural Studies: see Du Gay et al. (1997) and R. Johnson (1986–7).
3 See Adorno and Horkheimer (1979); and for a useful critique of this approach, Swingewood (1977).
4 The most controversial exponent of this approach is John Fiske (e.g. 1987, 1989). There are countless critiques, not all of them strictly fair or accurate: see, for example, Morris (1988) and McGuigan (1992). For an application of the argument to young people, see Willis (1990), and the critique by Buckingham (1993d).
5 Useful accounts of the implications of new media technologies may be found in Dovey (1996b), Hayward and Wollen (1993), Morley and Robins (1995) and Webster (1995).
6 See Cupitt and Stockbridge (1996), Murdock, Hartman and Gray (1992) and Sefton-Green (1998b).
7 See Nixon (1998).
8 Statistics here are from the BARB (Broadcasters' Audience Research Board) and British Video Association annual reports, and from the National Household Survey.
9 See Pasquier et al. (1998).
10 'Sampling' is a means of digitally 'quoting' extracts from an existing piece of music (for example, a bass line or a vocal refrain).
11 See Sefton-Green and Buckingham (1996).
12 Van der Voort et al. (1998).
13 Wartella et al. (1990).

14   See Buckingham (1996b).
15   For contemporary accounts of changes in the media industries, see Collins and Murroni (1996). For a broader picture, see Harvey (1989).
16   For a definitive discussion of the relationship between media and globalization, see Morley and Robins (1995).
17   See Melody (1973).
18   Buckingham et al. (1999), ch. 2.
19   Ibid., ch. 3.
20   Ibid., ch. 6. This issue is taken up in more detail in chapter 6 below.
21   See Buckingham et al. (1999), ch. 5
22   See, for example, Collins (1995).
23   See Bazalgette and Buckingham (1995), Kinder (1991).
24   See Bell, Hass and Sells (1995), Bryman (1995), Project on Disney (1995); and for a critical review, Buckingham (1997).
25   Kinder (1991).
26   See Rosen (1997).
27   See Buckingham et al. (1999), ch. 3.
28   E.g. Barker and Brooks (1998), Collett and Lamb (1986), Hermes (1995).
29   See W. R. Neuman (1991).
30   Buckingham et al. (1999), ch. 5.
31   Michael Fallon, former Tory schools minister, in the *Sun*, 14 May 1991; Stephen Byers, former Labour schools minister, in the *Guardian*, 29 July 1997.
32   E.g. Phillips and Robie (1988).
33   Professor Michael Barber of London University, reported in the *Guardian*, 1 June 1996; Mike Presdee of Sunderland University, on 'The consumption and enjoyment of crime as popular pleasure', reported in the *Daily Telegraph*, 4 Apr. 1997.
34   Research conducted by the Professional Association of Teachers in 1994; press responses to the computer game *Grand Theft Auto* in 1997.
35   20 June 1996.
36   See, for example, Abrams (1956).
37   For example, 'Dangers of the internet', *What PC?*, May 1998, pp. 94–101. A survey in 1998 reported that a majority of teachers were unwilling to give pupils access to the internet not because of the complexity of the technology but because of fears about pornography.
38   On the former, see Home (1993). Parliamentary questions have in fact been asked about the latter: see McRobbie (1994).
39   The material here is drawn from Buckingham, et al. (1999), ch. 6.
40   See, for example, Laybourne (1993); and Buckingham et al. (1999).
41   For a discussion of this contrary situation, see Davies, Buckingham and Kelley (2000).
42   See Frith (1993).
43   See Sefton-Green (1998a).
44   See Buckingham (1998c).
45   Kinder (1995).
46   Ibid., p. 77.

47 This issue is discussed in relation to the question of children's taste in Davies, Buckingham and Kelley (2000).

6 Changing Paradigms

1 See Jenkins (1992), pp. 18–22.
2 Hartley (1987).
3 Ang (1991).
4 Despite these assertions, this insecurity does not seem to be widely shared in the industry: see Kent (1994); and specifically in relation to children, Buckingham et al. (1999), ch. 5.
5 This would seem to be the position taken by Hartley (1987).
6 See Buckingham (1998b); and for more general reviews, Gauntlett (1995) and Gunter and McAleer (1997).
7 This work is reviewed by Young (1990).
8 For an excellent review of effects research in this area, see Durkin (1985).
9 See S. Neuman (1991).
10 See Bryant and Anderson (1983), Dorr (1986).
11 For an early example, see Noble (1975).
12 See Davies (1997), Dorr (1983), Hawkins (1977) and, for a recent review, Chandler (1997).
13 See (for example) Burman (1994), Edwards and Potter (1992), Henriques et al. (1984), Walkerdine (1988).
14 Hodge and Tripp (1986).
15 See Rudd (1992).
16 See Buckingham (1987, 1993c, 1993f, 1996b, 2000). For further examples, see Gauntlett (1997), Howard (1998), M. Robinson (1997), and Sefton-Green (1998b).
17 This approach is derived from the work of authors such as Billig (1991), Edwards and Potter (1992), Potter and Wetherell (1987) and their associates.
18 See Buckingham (1993a) and (1993c, ch. 3) respectively.
19 E.g. P. Palmer (1986), Lindlof (1987), Richards (1993).
20 E.g. Willis (1990), Wood (1993).
21 Gillespie (1995).
22 E.g. Buckingham and Sefton-Green (1994), Buckingham, Grahame and Sefton-Green (1995), Buckingham (1998d), Richards (1998).
23 For an overview of this approach in audience research, see Moores (1993).
24 The following section is based on Buckingham (1993c), esp. ch. 9.
25 Bourdieu (1984).
26 See Livingstone (1990).
27 See Buckingham (1993c), ch. 7; and Nava and Nava (1990).
28 For an example of this kind of argument, see Caputo (1995); and for a more developed critique, see Buckingham (1993c), ch. 3.
29 For a general discussion, see Buckingham (1993c), chs 3 and 4.

30 For a recent discussion of these issues, see Barker and Brooks (1998). These issues are also taken up in my discussion of 'bias' in chapter 9.
31 There are exceptions here, notably Buckingham and Sefton-Green (1994) and Gillespie (1995).
32 See James and Prout (1990).
33 This is a striking absence in the work reviewed in James, Jenks and Prout (1998) and in the studies in Qvortrup et al. (1994), for example.
34 Livingstone (1998), p. 438.
35 Murdock (1989), p. 227.

7 Children Viewing Violence

1 The term 'moral panic' derives from the work of Stan Cohen (1972). For a later reconsideration, see Cohen (1985).
2 This analogy is pursued in the notorious report by Elizabeth Newson (1994) which fuelled the controversy surrounding the James Bulger case: see Barker (1997).
3 See Buckingham (1996b), ch. 2; and Petley and Franklin (1996).
4 This was acknowledged by a Parliamentary Select Committee in July 1994.
5 The so-called Campaign for Christian Democracy played a vital behind-the-scenes role in the debates that followed the Bulger case, for example.
6 Plato (1987), Book II, pp. 377–8. For a discussion, see Buckingham (1993e).
7 For representative discussions, see Jenkins (1992), Pearson (1983) and Starker (1989). This issue is also considered by Murdock (1997), Petley (1997) and other contributors to the collection by Barker and Petley (1997).
8 See Starker (1989).
9 Jenkins (1992).
10 See A. Walker (1996).
11 See Buckingham (1996b), ch. 2.
12 See, for example, Barker (1984a, 1984b) and Starker (1989).
13 For some hypotheses on this, see McRobbie (1994).
14 Studies in the UK suggest that TV violence in fact declined following the peak of the 1970s: see Cumberbatch and Howitt (1989).
15 Amis (1996).
16 For studies of children's readings of these texts, see Christian-Smith and Erdman (1997) and Sarland (1994a, 1994b).
17 Medved (1992). The evidence that the presence or absence of 'violence' is in fact a key criterion in audience tastes is, however, very unreliable.
18 Gerbner (1997).
19 For a selection of such arguments, see French (1996).
20 See Barker (1997), pp. 27–8.
21 See Kirby (1988) and Gerrard (1996) respectively.

22 See Andrews (1996).

23 The large-scale National Television Violence Study (1997–8) in the United States represents the first significant attempt by researchers in this tradition to develop a more 'contextual' approach to media violence; although accounts of this research are inclined to use content analysis as a means of supporting a whole range of unsubstantiated assertions about 'effects'.

24 Representative examples include Cumberbatch and Howitt (1989), Gauntlett (1995) and Vine (1997).

25 Recent work in this field has shown some recognition of the social and cognitive dimensions of viewers' responses, but these have largely been conceptualized as 'intervening variables' which mediate between the stimulus and the behavioural response. See, for example, Geen (1994).

26 See Cohen (1985).

27 See Rowland (1983, 1997).

28 Gerbner (1997). For a European perspective, see Linné (1998).

29 This is undoubtedly the central motivation for Barker and Petley (1997).

30 See, for example, Taylor (1988) and Philo (1997).

31 Dorr and Kovaric (1980).

32 Gunter (1985).

33 Ibid.

34 Van der Voort (1986).

35 See Herz (1997).

36 See Barker and Brooks (1998), ch. 12.

37 The account which follows is based on Buckingham (1993c), ch. 5, and Buckingham (1996b), esp. chs 3 and 8. I am grateful to the Broadcasting Standards Council for funding the latter research, and to Mark Allerton for his assistance.

38 For example, Holman and Braithwaite (1982), Buckingham (1993c).

39 In 1987, Michael Ryan murdered sixteen people in the English town of Hungerford, having allegedly been inspired by the film *Rambo* – which it later transpired he had never seen. For an account of the debates surrounding the case, see Webster (1989).

40 See Buckingham (1996b), ch. 2.

41 The material here is based on Buckingham (1996b).

42 See Messaris (1986).

43 For a discussion in relation to action movies, see Andrews (1996); on horror, see Kermode (1997).

44 Of all the popular hypotheses about the effects of television violence, this is the one that is least effectively supported by the available evidence: see Buckingham and Allerton (1996).

45 This issue of children's perceptions of reality in television has been widely researched: see my discussion in chapter 6. My own research in this area can be found in Buckingham (1993c), ch. 9, and Buckingham (1996b), ch. 7.

46 See the contributions to French (1996), particularly those by Martin Amis, Poppy Z. Brite and John Waters. For some empirical work on this issue,

see Barker and Brooks (1998).
47 For an empirical investigation of this process, see Hill (1997).
48 On the latter, see Self (1996).
49 In Carroll (1990).
50 Clover (1992).
51 See J. Wood (1993).
52 See, for example, R. Wood (1985). An obvious alternative here would be to see the genre as a kind of psychological 'safety valve' (Docherty, Morrison and Tracey, 1987).
53 This was the explicit charge of some of the press coverage in the Bulger case: see Buckingham (1996b), ch. 2.
54 See Buckingham (1994) and Davies, Buckingham and Kelley (1999).
55 There is a parallel here with debates around pornography, for example surrounding the Report of the Committee on Obscenity and Film Censorship in the late 1970s: Williams Report 1979.
56 For indications of this in the comments of the UK's film censor, see Bragg and Grahame (1997); and, for a more general discussion, Buckingham and Sefton-Green (1997).
57 The Department of National Heritage in Britain acknowledged as much in a report on the matter produced in 1997.
58 In this respect as in several others, the British system is much stricter than in most other developed countries.
59 Holland (1996), p. 55.

8 Children as Consumers

1 Jenkins (1992).
2 A much earlier instance may be found in Goldsen (1977).
3 Jordanova (1989), p. 20.
4 See Lury (1996), pp. 29–36.
5 Estimates of this kind are reported by Gunter and Furnham (1998), ch. 1.
6 Ibid., ch. 7. For a thoughtful analysis of the rise of marketing in schools, see Kenway and Fitzclarence (1999).
7 See Center for Media Education (1997) and Sefton-Green (forthcoming).
8 Kline (1993), p. 350.
9 This phrase appears to be a Nickelodeon company motto. See Laybourne (1993).
10 These arguments can be found, for example, in Berger (1972), Marcuse (1964) and Williams (1980).
11 The most notorious exponent of this argument is Vance Packard (1957).
12 Williams (1980).
13 Leiss, Kline and Jhally (1990), p. 365.
14 For a review of research (albeit dating mainly from the 1970s and early 1980s) see Gunter and Furnham (1998), chs 5 and 6.

15 Young (1986). See also Goldstein (1992).
16 For reviews, see Dorr (1986), Gunter and Furnham (1998), Palmer and Dorr (1980) and Young (1990). Key primary texts would include Rossiter and Robertson (1974), Esserman (1981) and Jaglom and Gardner (1981).
17 The account here is drawn from Buckingham (1993c), ch. 10.
18 Nava and Nava (1990).
19 Gunter and Furnham (1998), p. 168.
20 However, Kenway and Fitzclarence (1999) provide some interesting insights into students' understandings of the marketization of schooling.
21 See also Buckingham, Fraser and Mayman (1990).
22 This and the following section draw on Buckingham (1995a).
23 These series were almost exclusively US in origin, although they also appear to involve Japanese animators, and in some cases Japanese co-production.
24 Kinder (1991) provides a valuable analysis of the *Ninja Turtles* phenomenon in these terms.
25 The more recent success of the live-action series *Mighty Morphin' Power Rangers* represents the exception that proves the rule here: the extensive action sequences involve robots, monsters or humanoid characters in masks, clearly obviating the problem of dubbing – in this case partly from the Japanese.
26 For examples of these criticisms, see Carlsson-Paige and Levin (1990), Engelhardt (1986), Greenfield et al. (1993), Kline (1989, 1993, 1995), E. L. Palmer (1988). For more positive views, see Kinder (1991), Myers (1995) and Seiter (1995). See also Fleming's (1996) analysis of children's TV-related toys; and for analyses of their use in children's play, see Barrs (1988) and Richards (1995).
27 See De Cordova (1994).
28 Gomery (1994), Bryman (1995).
29 See Kline (1995).
30 Kunkel (1988).
31 Fleming (1996) offers some interesting hypotheses here, although they are not backed up by audience research.
32 See Wagg (1992), Kress and Davies (forthcoming).
33 See the contributions to *Metro Education* 5, World Summit Edition, 1995.
34 Kline (1993), p. 12.
35 Ibid, p. 13.
36 See, for example, S. Neuman (1991), D. F. Roberts et al. (1993).
37 Kline (1993), pp. 313–14.
38 Ibid, p. 261.
39 For example, it is interesting to contrast Kline's glowing account of Fisher-Price 'educational' toys with Seiter's much more sceptical view. A brief glance at the Fisher-Price catalogue would suggest that the sexism Kline condemns in commercial television is far from confined to the 'bottom end' of the market.
40 For a parallel analysis, see Walkerdine and Lucey (1989).

41 This position is strongly argued by McDonnell (1994). For a fuller dis-
    cussion of the question of children's taste, see Davies, Buckingham and
    Kelley (2000); and for an account of the difficulties inherent in *adult*
    judgements of *children's* tastes, see Buckingham (1995b).
42 For examples, see Featherstone (1991), Lury (1996) and Nava (1992).
43 This broad shift is particularly apparent in two chronologically organ-
    ized collections of work in this area: McRobbie (1991) and Nava (1992).
    Similar changes are apparent in the work of Willis (e.g. 1977, 1990): for
    a discussion, see Buckingham (1993d).
44 Variants of this argument can be found in Fiske (1989) and Willis (1990).
45 See Lury (1996), ch. 8.
46 See Gunter and Furnham (1998), pp. 92–4.
47 As it is in the International Children's Television Charter. The Charter
    is reprinted in Buckingham et al. (1999), and discussed in more detail
    in chapter 10 below.

9 Children as Citizens

1   See Archard (1993), and the discussion in the following chapter.
2   For a discussion, see Archard (1993), ch. 6.
3   For a symptomatic analysis, see B. Franklin (1994).
4   These statistics are taken from the Times Mirror Center (1990) and Pew
    Research Center (1996) reports.
5   Wilkinson and Mulgan (1995).
6   See Gartside (1998).
7   See also Kenny (1998).
8   Hartley (1996), p. 73.
9   Rutherford (1998), pp. 17–18.
10 For example, Etzioni (1993).
11 For a particularly grandiose example, see Wexler (1990).
12 See Times Mirror Center (1990).
13 Harcourt and Hartland (1992).
14 For example, Buckingham (1996b), ch. 6; Cullingford (1992); D. Walker
    (1996).
15 See Kenny (1998).
16 See Bewes (1997) and Gartside (1998).
17 See, for example, Hart (1994) and Putnam (1995).
18 This argument is at least implicit in several of the studies referenced
    here, notably the Times Mirror Center study (1990) and the work of
    Hart (1994).
19 See Bhavnani (1991).
20 Katz (1993, 1997).
21 See Barnhurst (1998), Barnhurst and Wartella (1991).
22 See particularly Fiske (1989, 1992).
23 For example, Blumler and Gurevitch (1995), Dahlgren (1995).
24 For example, Greenstein (1965), Hess and Torney (1967).

25 For example, Atkin and Gantz (1978), Chaffee, Ward and Tipton (1970), Conway et al. (1981), Dominick (1972), Drew and Reeves (1980), Rubin (1976). For useful reviews, see Chaffee and Yang (1990) and Comstock and Paik (1991).
26 Dennis (1986), Liebes (1992).
27 Austin and Nelson (1993), Chaffee and Yang (1990).
28 Andreyenkov, Robinson and Popov (1989), Chaffee and Yang (1990), Robinson, Chivian and Tudge (1989).
29 See Graber (1988), Gunter (1987), Robinson and Levy (1986).
30 Graber (1988); see also Just, Neuman and Crigler (1992).
31 See Robinson and Levy (1986).
32 Dahlgren (1986); see also Dahlgren (1995).
33 The research summarized here is reported in full in Buckingham (2000). See also Buckingham (1996b), ch. 6.
34 See Eliasoph (1990), Gamson (1992).
35 Bhavnani (1991).
36 Cullingford (1992); see also Barnhurst (1998).
37 See also the studies by Connell (1971) and Stevens (1982).
38 Gamson (1992).
39 Wilkinson and Mulgan (1995).
40 See Gamson (1992), D. Walker (1996).
41 For example, Fiske (1989).
42 See Scruton, Ellis-Jones and O'Keefe (1985).
43 Harber (1992), Kerr (1997).
44 Cullingford (1992), p. 16.
45 Gilbert (1992, 1996).
46 Lindley (1989).
47 For similar studies, see Connell (1971), Cullingford (1992) and Stevens (1982).

10   Children's Media Rights

1 See Bennett (1998) and McQuail (1997).
2 See, for example, Archard (1993) and Scarre (1989).
3 See, for example, B. Franklin (1995), Franklin and Franklin (1996) and Stephens (1995).
4 See Scraton (1997). As noted in chapter 4, 'consumer rights' in education are not typically extended to children, and children's involvement in policy-making even at school level is often negligible.
5 Farson (1974), Firestone (1971), Holt (1975).
6 See Archard (1993), p. 47.
7 Ibid., pp. 101–2, 111.
8 For a commentary, and a reprint of the Convention itself, see Stephens (1995).
9 John (1995), pp. 105–6, 114.
10 For a discussion, see Hall (1995).

11 See Stephens (1995), pp. 36–9.
12 For example, Stephens (1995); and cf. Kline (1993), Steinberg and Kincheloe (1997).
13 Archard (1993), ch. 5.
14 Ibid., p. 25.
15 Ibid., p. 72.
16 Ibid., pp. 66–9.
17 Lindley (1989); and for a contrasting view, see Hughes (1989).
18 See Buckingham et al. (1999), ch. 6, for a more extensive discussion.
19 Katz (1997).
20 See Smith (1998).
21 See Collins and Murroni (1996).
22 See Buckingham and Sefton-Green (1994), Buckingham, Grahame and Sefton-Green (1995) and Buckingham (1998d).
23 For a useful introductory account of media education, see Bazalgette (1992).
24 Gilbert (1992).
25 Katz (1997).

References

Abrams, M. 1956: Child audiences for television in Great Britain. *Journalism Quarterly* 33, 35–41.

Adorno, T. and Horkheimer, M. 1979: *Dialectic of Enlightenment*. London: Verso.

Alloway, N. and Gilbert, P. 1998: Video game culture: playing with masculinity, violence and pleasure. In S. Howard (ed.), *Wired Up: Young People and the Electronic Media*, London: University College London Press.

Amis, M. 1996: Blown away. In K. French (ed.), *Screen Violence*, London: Bloomsbury.

Amit-Talai, V. and Wulff, H. (eds) 1995: *Youth Cultures: A Cross-Cultural Perspective*. London: Routledge.

Andersen, C. 1995: *Michael Jackson Unauthorized*. New York: Pocket Books.

Andrews, N. 1996: Muscle wars. In K. French (ed.), *Screen Violence*, London: Bloomsbury.

Andreyenkov, V., Robinson, J. P. and Popov, N. 1989: News media use and adolescents' information about nuclear issues: a Soviet–American comparison. *Journal of Communication* 39(2), 95–104.

Ang, I. 1991: *Desperately Seeking the Audience*. London: Routledge.

Archard, D. 1993: *Children: Rights and Childhood*. London: Routledge.

Ariès, P. 1962: *Centuries of Childhood*. London: Cape.

Atkin, C. K. and Gantz, W. 1978: Television news and political socialization. *Public Opinion Quarterly* 42(2), 183–97.

Austin, E. W. and Nelson, C. L. 1993: Influence of ethnicity, family communication, and media on adolescents' socialization to US politics. *Journal of Broadcasting and Electronic Media* 37(4), 419–35.

Barker, M. 1984a: *A Haunt of Fears*. London: Verso.

Barker, M. (ed.) 1984b: *The Video Nasties*. London: Pluto.

Barker, M. 1997: The Newson Report: a case study in 'common sense'. In M. Barker and J. Petley (eds), *Ill Effects: The Media/Violence Debate*, London:

Routledge.

Barker, M. and Brooks, K. 1998: *Knowing Audiences: Judge Dredd, its Friends, Fans and Foes*. Luton: University of Luton Press.

Barker, M. and Petley, J. (eds) 1997: *Ill Effects: The Media/Violence Debate*. London: Routledge.

Barnhurst, K. G. 1998: Politics in the fine meshes: young citizens, power and media. *Media, Culture and Society* 20(2), 201–18.

Barnhurst, K. G. and Wartella, E. 1991: Newspapers and citizenship: young adults' subjective experience of newspapers. *Critical Studies in Mass Communication* 8(2), 195–209.

Barrs, M. 1988: Maps of play. In M. Meek and C. Mills (eds), *Language and Literacy in the Primary School*, London: Falmer.

Bazalgette, C. 1992: *Media Education*. London: Hodder and Stoughton.

Bazalgette, C. and Buckingham, D. (eds) 1995: *In Front of the Children: Screen Entertainment and Young Audiences*. London: British Film Institute.

Beck, U. 1992: *Risk Society: Towards a New Modernity*. London: Sage.

Bell, E., Hass, L. and Sells, L. (eds) 1995: *From Mouse to Mermaid: The Politics of Film, Gender, and Culture*. Bloomington and Indianapolis: Indiana University Press.

Bennett, T. 1998: *Culture: A Reformer's Science*. London: Sage.

Berger, J. 1972: *Ways of Seeing*. Harmondsworth: Penguin.

Bewes, T. 1997: *Cynicism and Postmodernity*. London: Verso.

Bhavnani, K.-K. 1991: *Talking Politics: A Psychological Framing for Views from Youth in Britain*. Cambridge: Cambridge University Press.

Billig, M. 1991: *Ideology and Opinions: Studies in Rhetorical Psychology*. London: Sage.

Blumler, J. and Gurevitch, M. 1995: *The Crisis of Public Communication*. London: Routledge.

Bothing, M. (ed.) 1995: *The Health of our Children: Decennial Supplement*. London: Office of Population Censuses and Surveys.

Bourdieu, P. 1984: *Distinction: A Social Critique of the Judgment of Taste*. London: Routledge and Kegan Paul.

Bragg, S. and Grahame, J. 1997: Does it hurt when they fall downstairs? An interview with James Ferman of the BBFC. *English and Media Magazine* 36, 33–6.

Bridges, D. and McLaughlin, T. 1994: *Education and the Market Place*. London: Falmer.

Brinkley, I. 1998: Underworked and underpaid. In J. Rutherford (ed.), *Young Britain: Politics, Pleasures and Predicaments*, London: Lawrence and Wishart.

Bryant, J. and Anderson, D. R. (eds) 1983: *Children's Understanding of Television*. New York: Academic Press.

Bryman, A. 1995: *Disney and his Worlds*. London: Routledge.

Buckingham, D. 1987: *Public Secrets: 'EastEnders' and its Audience*. London: British Film Institute.

Buckingham, D. 1993a: Boys' talk: television and the policing of masculinity. In D. Buckingham (ed.), *Reading Audiences: Young People and the Media*, Manchester: Manchester University Press.

Buckingham, D. 1993b: *Changing Literacies: Media Education and Modern Culture*. London: Tufnell Press.

Buckingham, D. 1993c: *Children Talking Television: The Making of Television Literacy*. London: Falmer.

Buckingham, D. 1993d: Conclusion: re-reading audiences. In D. Buckingham (ed.), *Reading Audiences: Young People and the Media*, Manchester: Manchester University Press.

Buckingham, D. 1993e: Introduction: young people and the media. In D. Buckingham (ed.), *Reading Audiences: Young People and the Media*, Manchester: Manchester University Press.

Buckingham, D. (ed.) 1993f: *Reading Audiences: Young People and the Media*. Manchester: Manchester University Press.

Buckingham, D. 1994: Television and the definition of childhood. In B. Mayall (ed.), *Children's Childhoods Observed and Experienced*, London: Falmer Press.

Buckingham, D. 1995a: The commercialisation of childhood? The place of the market in children's media culture. *Changing English* 2(2), 17–40.

Buckingham, D. 1995b: On the impossibility of children's television: the case of Timmy Mallett. In C. Bazalgette and D. Buckingham (eds), *In Front of the Children: Screen Entertainment and Young Audiences*, London: British Film Institute.

Buckingham, D. 1996a: Critical pedagogy and media education: a theory in search of a practice. *Journal of Curriculum Studies* 28(6), 627–50.

Buckingham, D. 1996b: *Moving Images: Understanding Children's Emotional Responses to Television*. Manchester: Manchester University Press.

Buckingham, D. 1997: Dissin' Disney: critical perspectives on children's media culture. *Media, Culture and Society* 19(2), 285–93.

Buckingham, D. 1998a: Children of the electronic age? Digital media and the new generational rhetoric. *European Journal of Communication* 13(4), 557–65.

Buckingham, D. 1998b: Children and television: a critical overview of the research. In R. Dickinson, O. Linné and R. Harindranath (eds), *Approaches to Audiences*, London: Edward Arnold.

Buckingham, D. 1998c: Telly trouble. *English and Media Magazine* 39, 14–18.

Buckingham, D. (ed.) 1998d: *Teaching Popular Culture: Beyond Radical Pedagogy*. London: University College London Press.

Buckingham, D. 2000: *The Making of Citizens: Young People, News and Politics*. London: Routledge.

Buckingham, D. and Allerton, M. 1996: *Fear, Fright and Distress: A Review of Research on Children's Emotional Responses to Television*. London: Broadcasting Standards Council.

Buckingham, D. and Sefton-Green, J. 1994: *Cultural Studies Goes to School: Reading and Teaching Popular Media*. London: Taylor and Francis.

Buckingham, D. and Sefton-Green, J. 1997: From regulation to education. *English and Media Magazine* 36, 28–32.

Buckingham, D., Fraser, P. and Mayman, N. 1990: Stepping into the void: beginning classroom research in media education. In D. Buckingham (ed.), *Watching Media Learning: Making Sense of Media Education*, London: Falmer.

Buckingham, D., Grahame, J. and Sefton-Green, J. 1995: *Making Media: Practical Production in Media Education*. London: English and Media Centre.

Buckingham, D., Davies, H., Jones, K. and Kelley, P. 1999: *Children's Television in Britain: History, Discourse and Policy*. London: British Film Institute.

Burman, E. 1994: *Deconstructing Developmental Psychology*. London: Routledge.

Campbell, B. 1988: *Unofficial Secrets: Child Sexual Abuse – The Cleveland Case*. London: Virago.

Caputo, V. 1995: Anthropology's silent 'others': a consideration of some conceptual and methodological issues for the study of youth and children's cultures. In V. Amit-Talai and H. Wulff (eds), *Youth Cultures: A Cross-Cultural Perspective*, London: Routledge.

Carlsson-Paige, N. and Levin, D. E. 1990: *Who's Calling the Shots? How to Respond Effectively to Children's Fascination with War Play and War Toys*. Santa Cruz: New Society.

Carroll, N. 1990: *The Philosophy of Horror: Or Paradoxes of the Heart*. London: Routledge.

Center for Media Education 1997: *Web of Deception: Threats to Children from Online Marketing*. Washington DC: Center for Media Education.

Chaffee, S. H. and Yang, S.-M. 1990: Communication and political socialization. In O. Ichilov (ed.), *Political Socialization, Citizenship Education and Democracy*, New York: Teachers College Press.

Chaffee, S. H., Ward, L. S. and Tipton, L. P. 1970: Mass communication and political socialization. *Journalism Quarterly* 47, 647–59 and 666.

Chandler, D. 1997: Children's understanding of what is 'real' on television: a review of the literature. *Journal of Educational Media* 23(1), 65–80.

Christian-Smith, L. K. and Erdman, J. I. 1997: 'Mom, it's not real!' Children constructing childhood through reading horror fiction. In S. R. Steinberg and J. L. Kincheloe (eds), *Kinderculture: The Corporate Construction of Childhood*, Boulder: Westview.

Clover, C. 1992: *Men, Women and Chainsaws: Gender in the Modern Horror Film*. London: British Film Institute.

Cohen, S. 1972: *Folk Devils and Moral Panics: The Creation of the Mods and Rockers*. Oxford: Blackwell.

Cohen, S. 1985: *Visions of Social Control*. Cambridge: Polity.

Collett, P. and Lamb, R. 1986: *Watching People Watching Television*. Report to the Independent Broadcasting Authority. London: IBA.

Collins, J. 1995: *Architectures of Excess*. London: Routledge.

Collins, R. and Murroni, C. 1996: *New Media: New Policies*. Cambridge: Polity.

Comstock, G. and Paik, H. 1991: *Television and the American Child*. San Diego: Academic Press.

Connell, R. W. 1971: *The Child's Construction of Politics*. Melbourne: University of Melbourne Press.

Conway, M. M., Wyckoff, M. L., Feldbaum, E. and Ahern, D. 1981: The news media in children's political socialization. *Public Opinion Quarterly* 45(2), 164–78.

Coppock, V. 1997: 'Families' in 'crisis'?. In P. Scraton (ed.), *'Childhood' in 'Crisis'*, London: University College London Press.
Corsaro, W. A. 1997: *The Sociology of Childhood*. Thousand Oaks: Pine Forge Press.
Cullingford, C. 1992: *Children and Society: Children's Attitudes to Politics and Power*. London: Cassell.
Cumberbatch, G. and Howitt, D. 1989: *A Measure of Uncertainty: The Effects of the Mass Media*. London: John Libbey.
Cunningham, H. 1991: *The Children of the Poor: Representations of Childhood since the Seventeenth Century*. Oxford: Blackwell.
Cunningham, H. 1995: *Children and Childhood in Western Society since 1500*. London: Longman.
Cupitt, M. and Stockbridge, S. 1996: *Families and Electronic Entertainment*. Sydney: Australian Broadcasting Authority and the Office of Film and Literature Classification.
Dahlgren, P. 1986: Beyond information: TV news as cultural discourse. *Communications* 12(2), 125–36.
Dahlgren, P. 1995: *Television and the Public Sphere*. London: Sage.
David, M. 1986: *Moral and maternal: the family in the Right*. In R. Levitas (ed.), *The Ideology of the New Right*, Cambridge: Polity.
Davies, H., Buckingham, D. and Kelley, P. 1999: Kids' time: childhood, television and the regulation of time. *Journal of Educational Media* 24(1), 25–42.
Davies, H., Buckingham, D. and Kelley, P. 2000: In the worst possible taste: children, television and cultural value. *European Journal of Cultural Studies* 3(1).
Davies, M. M. 1997: *Fact, Fake and Fantasy*. Mahwah, N.J.: Lawrence Erlbaum.
Davin, A. 1996: *Growing Up Poor*. London: Rivers Oram.
Davis, H. and Bourhill, M. 1997: 'Crisis': the demonization of children and young people. In P. Scraton (ed.), *'Childhood' in 'Crisis'*, London: University College London Press.
De Castell, S., Luke, A. and Egan, K. (eds) 1986: *Literacy, Society and Schooling*. Cambridge: Cambridge University Press.
De Cordova, R. 1994: The Mickey in Macy's window: childhood, consumerism and Disney. In E. Smoodin (ed.), *Disney Discourse*, London: British Film Institute.
De Mause, L. (ed.) 1976: *The History of Childhood*. London: Souvenir.
Dennis, J. 1986: Preadult learning of political independence: media and family communication effects. *Communication Research* 13, 401–33.
Docherty, D., Morrison, D. and Tracey, M. 1987: *The Last Picture Show: Britain's Changing Film Audience*. London: British Film Institute.
Dominick, J. R. 1972: Television and political socialization. *Educational Broadcasting Review* 6(1), 48–56.
Dorr, A. 1983: No shortcuts to judging reality. In J. Bryant and D. Anderson (eds), *Children's Understanding of Television*, New York: Academic Press.
Dorr, A. 1986: *Television and Children: A Special Medium for a Special Audience*. Beverly Hills: Sage.

228 *References*

Dorr, A. and Kovaric, P. 1980: Some of the people some of the time – but which people? In E. L. Palmer and A. Dorr (eds), *Children and the Faces of Television: Teaching, Violence, Selling*, New York: Academic Press.

Dovey, J. 1996a: The revelation of unguessed worlds. In J. Dovey (ed.), *Fractal Dreams: New Media in Social Context*, London: Lawrence and Wishart.

Dovey, J. (ed.) 1996b: *Fractal Dreams: New Media in Social Context*. London: Lawrence and Wishart.

Drew, D. and Reeves, B. 1980: Learning from a television news story. *Communication Research* 7(1), 121–35.

Du Gay, P., Hall, S., Janes, L., Mackay, H. and Negus, K. 1997: *Doing Cultural Studies: The Story of the Sony Walkman*. London: Sage.

Dunn, M. and Clusky, J. 1997: *National Children's Homes Action for Children Factfile*. London: National Children's Homes.

Durkin, K. 1985: *Television, Sex Roles and Children*. Milton Keynes: Open University Press.

Edwards, D. and Potter, J. 1992: *Discursive Psychology*. London: Sage.

Eliasoph, N. 1990: Political culture and the presentation of a political 'self'. *Theory and Society* 19(3), 465–94.

Elkind, D. 1981: *The Hurried Child: Growing Up Too Fast Too Soon*. Reading, Mass.: Addison Wesley.

Engelhardt, T. 1986: Children's television: the shortcake strategy. In T. Gitlin (ed.), *Watching Television*, New York: Pantheon.

Ennew, J. 1994: Time for children or time for adults? In J. Qvortrup, M. Bardy, G. Sgritta and H. Wintersberger (eds), *Childhood Matters: Social Theory, Practice and Politics*, Aldershot: Avebury.

Epstein, D., Ellwood, J., Hey, V. and Leonard, D. (eds) 1998: *Failing Boys? Issues in Gender and Achievement*. Milton Keynes: Open University Press.

Esserman, J. F. (ed.) 1981: *Television Advertising and Children*. New York: Child Research Service.

Etzioni, A. 1993: *The Spirit of Community: The Reinvention of American Society*. New York: Simon and Schuster.

Farson, R. 1974: *Birthrights*. London: Collier Macmillan.

Featherstone, M. 1991: *Postmodernism and Consumer Culture*. London: Sage.

Firestone, S. 1971: *The Dialectic of Sex: The Case for Feminist Revolution*. London: Cape.

Fiske, J. 1987: *Television Culture*. London: Methuen.

Fiske, J. 1989: *Reading the Popular*. London: Unwin Hyman.

Fiske, J. 1992: Popularity and the politics of information. In P. Dahlgren and C. Sparks (eds), *Journalism and Popular Culture*, London: Sage.

Fleming, D. 1996: *Powerplay: Toys as Popular Culture*. Manchester: Manchester University Press.

Forgacs, D. 1992: Disney animation and the business of childhood. *Screen* 33(4), 361–74.

Foucault, M. 1980: *Power/Knowledge*, ed. C. Gordon. Brighton: Harvester.

Foucault, M. 1981: *The History of Sexuality*, vol. 1. Harmondsworth: Penguin.

Franklin, A. and Franklin, B. 1996: Growing pains: the developing children's rights movement in the United Kingdom. In J. Pilcher and S. Wagg (eds),

Thatcher's Children: Politics, Childhood and Society in the 1980s and 1990s, London: Falmer.

Franklin, B. 1994: *Packaging Politics*. London: Edward Arnold.

Franklin, B. (ed.) 1995: *The Handbook of Children's Rights: Comparative Policy and Practice*. London: Routledge.

French, K. (ed.) 1996: *Screen Violence*. London: Bloomsbury.

Frith, S. 1993: Youth/music/television. In S. Frith, A. Goodwin and L. Grossberg (eds), *Sound and Vision: The Music Video Reader*, London: Routledge.

Fry, D. 1994: *Social Focus on Children*. London: Central Statistical Office.

Gamson, W. A. 1992: *Talking Politics*. New York: Cambridge University Press.

Gartside, P. 1998: Bypassing politics? A critical look at DIY culture. In J. Rutherford (ed.), *Young Britain: Politics, Pleasures and Predicaments*, London: Lawrence and Wishart.

Gauntlett, D. 1995: *Moving Experiences: Understanding Television's Influences and Effects*. Luton: John Libbey.

Gauntlett, D. 1997: *Video Critical: Children, the Environment and Media Power*. Luton: John Libbey.

Geen, R. G. 1994: Television and aggression: recent developments in research and theory. In D. Zillmann, J. Bryant and A. C. Huston (eds), *Media, Children and the Family*, Hillsdale, N.J.: Erlbaum.

Gerbner, G. 1997: Violence in TV drama. *News on Children and Violence on the Screen* 3, 6–7.

Gerrard, N. 1996: In front of the children. In K. French (ed.), *Screen Violence*, London: Bloomsbury.

Giddens, A. 1991: *Modernity and Self-Identity: Self and Society in the Late Modern Age*. Cambridge: Polity.

Gilbert, R. 1992: Citizenship, education and postmodernity. *British Journal of Sociology of Education* 13(1), 51–68.

Gilbert, R. 1996: Identity, culture and environment: education for citizenship in the twenty-first century. In J. Demaine and H. Entwistle (eds), *Beyond Communitarianism: Citizenship, Politics and Education*, London: Macmillan.

Gillespie, M. 1995: *Television, Ethnicity and Cultural Change*. London: Routledge.

Goldsen, R. 1977: *The Show and Tell Machine*. New York: Dial.

Goldstein, J. 1992: Television advertising and children: a review of research. Paper prepared for Toy Manufacturers of Europe.

Gomery, D. 1994: Disney's business history: a reinterpretation. In E. Smoodin (ed.), *Disney Discourse*, London: British Film Institute.

Goodson, I. and Mangan, M. 1996: Computer literacy as ideology. *British Journal of Sociology of Education* 17(1), 65–79.

Graber, D. 1988: *Processing the News: How People Tame the Information Tide*, 2nd ed. New York: Longman.

Greenfield, P. M., Yut, E., Chung, M., Land, D., Kreider, H., Pantoja, M. and Horsley, K. 1993: The program-length commercial: a study of the effects of television/toy tie-ins on imaginative play. In G. L. Berry and J. K.

Asamen (eds), *Children and Television*, London: Sage.

Greenstein, F. I. 1965: *Children and Politics*. New Haven: Yale University Press.

Griffiths, M. 1996: Computer game playing in children and adolescents: a review of the literature. In T. Gill (ed.), *Electronic Children: How Children are Responding to the Information Revolution*, London: National Children's Bureau.

Gunter, B. 1985: *Dimensions of Television Violence*. Aldershot: Gower.

Gunter, B. 1987: *Poor Reception: Misunderstanding and Forgetting Broadcast News*. Hillsdale, N.J.: Erlbaum.

Gunter, B. and Furnham, A. 1998: *Children as Consumers: A Psychological Analysis of the Young People's Market*. London: Routledge.

Gunter, B. and McAleer, J. 1997: *Children and Television*, 2nd edn. London: Routledge.

Gusfield, J. 1981: *The Culture of Public Problems*. Chicago: University of Chicago Press.

Hall, K. 1995: 'There's a time to act English and a time to act Indian': the politics of identity among British-Sikh teenagers. In S. Stephens (ed.), *Children and Politics of Culture*, Princeton: Princeton University Press.

Harber, C. 1992: *Democratic Learning and Learning Democracy*. Ticknall, Derbyshire: Education Now.

Harcourt, K. and Hartland, S. 1992: *Discovering Readers*. Tunbridge Wells: Newspapers in Education.

Hart, R. 1994: *Seducing America: How Television Charms the Modern Voter*. New York: Oxford University Press.

Hartley, J. 1987: Invisible fictions: television audiences, paedocracy, pleasure. *Textual Practice* 1(2), 121–38.

Hartley, J. 1996: *Popular Reality: Journalism, Modernity, Popular Culture*. London: Edward Arnold.

Harvey, D. 1989: *The Condition of Postmodernity*. Oxford: Blackwell.

Hawkins, R. P. 1977: The dimensional structure of children's perceptions of television reality. *Communication Research* 4(3), 299–320.

Haydon, D. 1997: 'Crisis' in the classroom. In P. Scraton (ed.), *'Childhood' in 'Crisis'*, London: University College London Press.

Hayward, P. and Wollen, T. (eds) 1993: *Future Visions: New Technologies of the Screen*. London: British Film Institute.

Healy, J. 1998: *Failure to Connect: How Computers Affect our Children's Minds – For Better and Worse*. New York: Simon and Schuster.

Hendrick, H. 1990: Constructions and reconstructions of British childhood: an interpretive survey, 1800 to the present. In A. James and A. Prout (eds), *Constructing and Reconstructing Childhood: Contemporary Issues in the Sociological Study of Childhood*, London: Falmer.

Hendrick, H. 1997: *Children, Childhood and English Society, 1880–1990*. Cambridge: Cambridge University Press.

Henriques, J., Hollway, W., Urwin, C., Venn, C. and Walkerdine, V. 1984: *Changing the Subject: Psychology, Social Regulation and Subjectivity*. London: Methuen.

Hermes, J. 1995: *Reading Women's Magazines*. Cambridge: Polity.

Herz, J. C. 1997: *Joystick Nation: How Video Games Gobbled our Money, Won our Hearts and Rewired our Minds*. London: Abacus.

Hess, R. D. and Torney, J. V. 1967: *The Development of Political Attitudes in Children*. Chicago: Aldine.

Hill, A. 1997: *Shocking Entertainment: Viewer Response to Violent Movies*. Luton: University of Luton Press.

Hirsch, E. D. 1987: *Cultural Literacy: What Every American Needs to Know*. Boston: Houghton Mifflin.

Hodge, B. and Tripp, D. 1986: *Children and Television: A Semiotic Approach*. Cambridge: Polity.

Hodgkin, R. 1998: Crime and disorder bill. *Children and Society* 12, 66–8.

Hoikkala, T., Rahkonen, L., Tigerstedt, C. and Tuormaa, J. 1987: Wait a minute, Mr Postman! Some critical remarks on Neil Postman's childhood theory. *Acta Sociologica* 30(1), 87–99.

Holland, P. 1992: *What is a Child? Popular Images of Childhood*. London, Virago.

Holland, P. 1996: 'I've just seen a hole in the reality barrier!' Children, childishness and the media in the ruins of the twentieth century. In J. Pilcher and S. Wagg (eds), *Thatcher's Children: Politics, Childhood and Society in the 1980s and 1990s*, London: Falmer.

Holman, J. and Braithwaite, V. A. 1982: Parental lifestyles and children's television viewing. *Australian Journal of Psychology* 34(3), 375–82.

Holt, J. 1975: *Escape from Childhood: The Needs and Rights of Children*. Harmondsworth: Penguin.

Home, A. 1993: *Into the Box of Delights*. London: BBC Books.

Hood, S., Kelley, P., Mayall, B. and Oakley, A. 1996: *Children, Parents and Risk*. London: Social Science Research Unit, Institute of Education, University of London.

Howard, S. (ed.) 1998: *Wired Up: Young People and the Electronic Media*. London: University College London Press.

Hughes, J. 1989: Thinking about children. In G. Scarre (ed.), *Children, Parents and Politics*, Cambridge: Cambridge University Press.

Humphries, S., Mack, J. and Perks, R. 1988: *A Century of Childhood*. London: Sidgwick and Jackson.

Hunter, I. 1994: *Rethinking the School*. Sydney: Allen and Unwin.

Innis, H.A. 1951: *The Bias of Communication*. Toronto: University of Toronto Press.

Ivy, M. 1995: Have you seen me? Recovering the inner child in late twentieth century America. In S. Stephens (ed.), *Children and the Politics of Culture*, Princeton: Princeton University Press.

Jaglom, L. M. and Gardner, H. 1981: The preschool television viewer as anthropologist. In H. Kelly and H. Gardner (eds), *Viewing Children through Television*, San Francisco: Jossey-Bass.

James, A. and Prout, A. (eds) 1990: *Constructing and Reconstructing Childhood: Contemporary Issues in the Sociological Study of Childhood*. London: Falmer.

James, A., Jenks, C. and Prout, A. 1998: *Theorizing Childhood*. Cambridge: Polity.

Jenkins, P. 1992: *Intimate Enemies: Moral Panics in Contemporary Great Britain.* New York: Aldine de Gruyter.

Jenks, C. 1996: *Childhood.* London: Routledge.

John, M. 1995: Children's rights in a free-market culture. In S. Stephens (ed.), *Children and the Politics of Culture*, Princeton: Princeton University Press.

Johnson, F. 1996: Cyberpunks in the White House. In J. Dovey (ed.), *Fractal Dreams: New Media in Social Context*, London: Lawrence and Wishart.

Johnson, R. 1986–7: What is Cultural Studies anyway? *Social Text* 16, 38–80.

Jones, K. 1990: *Right Turn: The Conservative Revolution in Education.* London: Hutchinson.

Jones, K. and Hatcher, R. (eds) 1996: *Education after the Conservatives: The Response to the New Agenda of Reform.* Stoke-on-Trent: Trentham Books.

Jordanova, L. 1989: Children in history; concepts of nature and society. In G. Scarre (ed.), *Children, Parents and Politics*, Cambridge: Cambridge University Press.

Just, M. R., Neuman, W. R. and Crigler, A. 1992: An economic theory of learning from news. Research Paper R-6, Harvard College, Cambridge, Mass.

Katz, J. 1993: The media's war on kids. *Rolling Stone*, 25 Nov., 47–9 and 130.

Katz, J. 1997: *Virtuous Reality: How America Surrendered Discussion of Moral Values to Opportunists, Nitwits and Blockheads like William Bennett.* New York, Random House.

Kelley, P., Buckingham, D. and Davies, H. 1999: Talking dirty: children, sexual knowledge and television. *Childhood* 6(2), 221–42.

Kenny, M. 1998: 'That's entertainment . . . ' Generation X in the time of New Labour. In J. Rutherford (ed.), *Young Britain: Politics, Pleasures and Predicaments*, London: Lawrence and Wishart.

Kent, R. (ed.) 1994: *Measuring Media Audiences.* London: Routledge.

Kenway, J. and Fitzclarence, L. 1999: *Selling Education: Consumer Kids, Consuming Cultures.* Milton Keynes: Open University Press.

Kermode, M. 1997: I was a teenage horror fan: or, 'How I learned to stop worrying and love Linda Blair'. In M. Barker and J. Petley (eds), *Ill Effects: The Media/Violence Debate*, London: Routledge.

Kerr, D. 1997: *Citizenship Education Revisited*, IEA Civic Education Project: Abbreviated Phase 1: National Case Study: England. Slough, Berkshire: National Foundation for Educational Research.

Kinder, M. 1991: *Playing with Power in Movies, Television and Video Games: From Muppet Babies to Teenage Mutant Ninja Turtles.* Berkeley: University of California Press.

Kinder, M. 1995: Home alone in the 90s: generational war and transgenerational address in American movies, television and presidential politics. In C. Bazalgette and D. Buckingham (eds), *In Front of the Children: Screen Entertainment and Young Audiences*, London: British Film Institute.

Kirby, L. 1988: Male hysteria and early cinema. *Camera Obscura* 17, 112–31.

Kline, S. 1989: Limits to the imagination: marketing and children's culture. In I. Angus and S. Jhally (eds), *Cultural Politics in Contemporary America*, New York: Routledge.

Kline, S. 1993: *Out of the Garden: Toys and Children's Culture in the Age of TV Marketing*. London: Verso.

Kline, S. 1995: The empire of play: emergent genres of product-based animations. In C. Bazalgette and D. Buckingham (eds), *In Front of the Children*, London: British Film Institute.

Kress, G. and Davies, H. (forthcoming): That's edu-tainment: Saturday morning magazine programmes from *Swapshop* to *Live and Kicking*. In D. Buckingham (ed.), *Small Screens: Television for Children*. London: Continuum.

Kubey, R. 1992: A critique of *No Sense of Place* and the homogenization theory of Joshua Meyrowitz. *Communication Theory* 2, 259–71.

Kunkel, D. 1988: From a raised eyebrow to a turned back: the FCC and children's product-related programming. *Journal of Communication* 38(4), 90–108.

Lanham, R. 1993: *The Electronic Word: Democracy, Technology and the Arts*. Chicago: University of Chicago Press.

Lavalette, M. 1994: *Child Employment in the Capitalist Labour Market*. Basingstoke: Avebury.

Lavalette, M. 1996: Thatcher's working children: contemporary issues of child labour. In J. Pilcher and S. Wagg (eds), *Thatcher's Children: Politics, Childhood and Society in the 1980s and 1990s*, London: Falmer.

Laybourne, G. 1993: The Nickelodeon experience. In G. L. Berry and J. K. Asamen (eds), *Children and Television*, London: Sage.

Leiss, W., Kline, S. and Jhally, S. 1990: *Social Communication in Advertising*. London: Routledge.

Liebes, T. 1992: Television, parents and the political socialization of children. *Teachers College Record* 94(1), 73–86.

Lindley, R. 1989: Teenagers and other children. In G. Scarre (ed.), *Children, Parents and Politics*, Cambridge: Cambridge University Press.

Lindlof, T. (ed.) 1987: *Natural Audiences*. Newbury Park: Sage.

Linné, O. 1998: What do we know about European research on violence in the media? In U. Carlsson and C. von Feilitzen (eds), *Children and Media Violence*, Goteborg: UNESCO.

Livingstone, S. 1990: *Making Sense of Television: The Psychology of Audience Interpretation*. Oxford: Pergamon.

Livingstone, S. 1998: Mediated childhoods: a comparative approach to young people's changing media environment in Europe. *European Journal of Communication* 13(4), 435–56.

Luke, C. 1989: *Pedagogy, Printing and Protestantism: The Discourse on Childhood*. Albany, N.Y.: SUNY Press.

Lury, C. 1996: *Consumer Culture*. Cambridge: Polity.

McDonnell, K. 1994: *Kid Culture: Children and Adults and Popular Culture*. Toronto: Second Story.

McGuigan, J. 1992: *Cultural Populism*. London: Routledge.

McLuhan, M. 1964: *Understanding Media*. New York: New American Library.

McQuail, D. 1997: Policy help wanted: willing and able media culturalists please apply. In M. Ferguson and P. Golding (eds), *Cultural Studies in Question*, London: Sage.

234 *References*

McRobbie, A. 1991: *Feminism and Youth Culture: From 'Jackie' to 'Just Seventeen'*. London: Macmillan.
McRobbie, A. 1994: *Postmodernism and Popular Culture*. London: Routledge.
Marcuse, H. 1964: *One Dimensional Man*. Boston: Beacon.
Mayall, B. (ed.) 1994: *Children's Childhoods Observed and Experienced*. London: Falmer.
Medved, M. 1992: *Hollywood vs America: Popular Culture and the War on Traditional Values*. New York: HarperCollins.
Melody, W. 1973: *Children's Television: The Economics of Exploitation*. New Haven: Yale University Press.
Messaris, P. 1986: Parents, children and television. In G. Gumpert and R. Cathcart (eds), *Inter Media: Interpersonal Communication in a Media World*, New York: Oxford University Press.
Messaris, P. 1995: *Visual 'Literacy': Image, Mind and Reality*. Boulder: Westview.
Meyrowitz, J. 1985: *No Sense of Place: The Impact of Electronic Media on Social Behaviour*. Oxford: Oxford University Press.
Moir, G. (ed.) 1967: *Teaching and Television: ETV Explained*. Oxford: Pergamon.
Moores, S. 1993: *Interpreting Audiences: The Ethnography of Media Consumption*. London: Sage.
Morley, D. and Robins, K. 1995: *Spaces of Identity*. London: Routledge.
Morris, M. 1988: Banality in Cultural Studies. In P. Mellencamp (ed.), *Logics of Television: Essays in Cultural Criticism*, London: British Film Institute.
Morrow, V. 1994: Responsible children? Aspects of children's work and employment outside school in contemporary UK. In B. Mayall (ed.), *Children's Childhoods Observed and Experienced*, London: Falmer.
Murdock, G. 1989: Critical inquiry and audience activity. In B. Dervin, L. Grossberg, B. J. O'Keefe and E. Wartella (eds), Rethinking Communication, vol. 2: *Paradigm Exemplars*, London: Sage.
Murdock, G. 1997: Reservoirs of dogma: an archaeology of popular anxieties. In M. Barker and J. Petley (eds), *Ill Effects: The Media/Violence Debate*, London: Routledge.
Murdock, G., Hartman, P. and Gray, P. 1992: Contextualising home computing: resources and practices. In R. Silverstone and E. Hirsch (eds), *Consuming Technologies: Media and Information in Domestic Spaces*, London: Routledge.
Myers, G. 1995: 'The power is yours': agency and plot in *Captain Planet*. In C. Bazalgette and D. Buckingham (eds), *In Front of the Children: Screen Entertainment and Young Audiences*, London: British Film Institute.
Nava, M. 1992: *Changing Cultures: Feminism, Youth and Consumerism*. London: Sage.
Nava, M. and Nava, O. 1990: Discriminating or duped? Young people as consumers of advertising/art. *Magazine of Cultural Studies* 1, 15–21.
Neuman, S. 1991: *Literacy in the Television Age*. Norwood, N.J.: Ablex.
Neuman, W. R. 1991: *The Future of the Mass Audience*. New York: Cambridge University Press.
Newburn, T. 1996: Back to the future? Youth crime, youth justice and the

rediscovery of 'authoritarian populism'. In J. Pilcher and S. Wagg (eds), *Thatcher's Children? Politics, Childhood and Society in the 1980s and 1990s*, London: Falmer.

Newman, P. and Smith, A. 1997: *Social Focus on Families*. London: Central Statistical Office.

Newson, E. 1994: Video violence and the protection of children. *The Psychologist*, June, 272–4.

Nixon, H. 1998: Fun and games are serious business. In J. Sefton-Green (ed.), *Digital Diversions: Youth Culture in the Age of Multimedia*, London: University College London Press.

Noble, G. 1975: *Children in Front of the Small Screen*. London: Constable.

Office of National Statistics 1997: *Family Spending: A Report on the 1996–7 Family Expenditure Survey*. London: Office of National Statistics.

Office of National Statistics 1998: *Living in Britain: Results from the 1996 General Household Survey*. London: Office of National Statistics.

Ohmae, K. 1995: *The End of the Nation State*. New York: HarperCollins.

Opie, I. and Opie, P. 1984: *Children's Games in Street and Playground* (first published 1969). Oxford: Oxford University Press.

Oppenheim, C. and Lister, R. 1996: The politics of child poverty 1979–1995. In J. Pilcher and S. Wagg (eds), *Thatcher's Children? Politics, Childhood and Society in the 1980s and 1990s*, London: Falmer.

Orr Vered, K. 1998: Blue group boys play *Incredible Machine*, girls play hopscotch: social discourse and gendered play at the computer. In J. Sefton-Green (ed.), *Digital Diversions: Youth Culture in the Age of Multimedia*, London: University College London Press.

Oswell, D. 1995: Watching with mother: a genealogy of the child television audience. Ph.D. thesis, Open University.

Packard, V. 1957: *The Hidden Persuaders*. Harmondsworth: Penguin.

Palmer, E. L. 1988: *Television and America's Children: A Crisis of Neglect*. New York: Oxford University Press.

Palmer, E. L. and Dorr, A. (eds) 1980: *Children and the Faces of Television: Teaching, Violence, Selling*. New York: Academic Press.

Palmer, P. 1986: *The Lively Audience: A Study of Children around the TV Set*. Sydney: Allen and Unwin.

Papert, S. 1980: *Mindstorms: Children, Computers and Powerful Ideas*. New York: Basic Books.

Papert, S. 1993: *The Children's Machine: Rethinking School in the Age of the Computer*. New York: Basic Books.

Papert, S. 1996: *The Connected Family: Bridging the Digital Generation Gap*. Atlanta: Longstreet.

Parton, N. 1996: The new politics of child protection. In J. Pilcher and S. Wagg (eds), *Thatcher's Children? Politics, Childhood and Society in the 1980s and 1990s*, London: Falmer.

Pasquier, D., Buzzi, C., d'Haenens, L. and Sjoberg, U. 1998: Family lifestyles and media use patterns: an analysis of domestic media among Flemish, French, Italian and Swedish children and teenagers. *European Journal of Communications* 13(4), 503–19.

Pearson, G. 1983: *Hooligan: A History of Respectable Fears*. London: Macmillan.

Petley, J. 1997: Us and them. In M. Barker and J. Petley (eds), *Ill Effects: The Media/Violence Debate*, London: Routledge.

Petley, J. and Franklin, B. 1996: Killing the age of innocence: newspaper reporting of the death of James Bulger. In J. Pilcher and S. Wagg (eds), *Thatcher's Children? Politics, Childhood and Society in the 1980s and 1990s*, London: Falmer.

Pew Research Center 1996: TV news viewership declines. News release, Pew Research Center for the People and the Press, Washington DC.

Phillips, P. and Robie, J. H. 1988: *Horror and Violence: The Deadly Duo in the Media*. Lancaster, Pa.: Starburst.

Philo, G. 1997: *Children and Film/Video Violence*. Glasgow: Glasgow University Media Group.

Pilcher, J. and Wagg, S. (eds) 1996: *Thatcher's Children: Politics, Childhood and Society in the 1980s and 1990s*. London: Falmer.

Plato 1987: *The Republic*, trans. D. Lee. Harmondsworth: Penguin.

Pollock, L. A. 1983: *Forgotten Children: Parent–Child Relations from 1500 to 1900*. Cambridge: Cambridge University Press.

Postman, N. 1983: *The Disappearance of Childhood*. London: W. H. Allen.

Postman, N. 1992: *Technopoly: The Surrender of Culture to Technology*. New York: Knopf.

Potter, J. and Wetherell, M. 1987: *Discourse and Social Psychology*. London: Sage.

Project on Disney (Karen Klugman, Jane Kuenz, Shelton Waldrep and Susan Willis) 1995: *Inside the Mouse: Work and Play at Disney World*. Durham, N.C. and London: Duke University Press.

Provenzo, E. 1991: *Video Kids: Making Sense of Nintendo*. Cambridge: Harvard University Press.

Pullinger, J. (ed.) 1998: *Social Trends 28*. London: Office of National Statistics.

Putnam, R. D. 1995: Tuning in, tuning out: the strange disappearance of social capital in America. Paper delivered to the American Political Science Association, Oct.

Qvortrup, J., Bardy, M., Sgritta, G. and Wintersberger, H. (eds) 1994: *Childhood Matters: Social Theory, Practice and Politics*. Aldershot: Avebury.

Richards, C. 1993: Taking sides? What young girls do with television. In D. Buckingham (ed.), *Reading Audiences: Young People and the Media*, Manchester: Manchester University Press.

Richards, C. 1995: Room to dance: girls' play and *The Little Mermaid*. In C. Bazalgette and D. Buckingham (eds), *In Front of the Children*, London: British Film Institute.

Richards, C. 1998: *Teen Spirits: Music and Identity in Media Education*. London: University College London Press.

Roberts, D. F., Henriksen, L., Voelker, D. H. and van Vuuren, D. P. 1993: Television and schooling: displacement and distraction hypotheses. *Australian Journal of Education* 37(2), 198–211.

Robinson, J. P. and Levy, M. R. 1986: *The Main Source: Learning from Television News*. Beverly Hills: Sage.

Robinson, J. P., Chivian, E. and Tudge, J. 1989: News media use and adolescents' attitudes about nuclear issues: an American–Soviet comparison. *Journal of Communication* 39(2), 105–13.

Robinson, M. 1997: *Children Reading Print and Television*. London: Falmer.

Rose, J. 1984: *The Case of Peter Pan: On the Impossibility of Children's Fiction*. London: Macmillan.

Rose, N. 1985: *The Psychological Complex*. London: Routledge.

Rosen, M. 1997: *Junk* and other realities: the tough world of children's fiction. *English and Media Magazine* 37, 4–6.

Rossiter, J. R. and Robertson, T. S. 1974: Children's TV commercials: testing the defenses. *Journal of Communication* 24(4), 137–44.

Rowland, W. 1983: *The Politics of TV Violence: Policy Uses of Communication Research*. Beverly Hills: Sage.

Rowland, W. 1997: Television violence redux: the continuing mythology of effects. In M. Barker and J. Petley (eds), *Ill Effects: The Media/Violence Debate*, London: Routledge.

Rubin, A. M. 1976: Television in children's political socialization. *Journal of Broadcasting* 20(1), 51–9.

Rudd, D. 1992: *Children and Television*: A critical note on theory and method. *Media, Culture and Society* 14(2), 313–20.

Rushkoff, D. 1996: *Playing the Future: How Kids' Culture Can Teach Us to Thrive in an Age of Chaos*. New York: HarperCollins.

Rutherford, J. 1998: Introduction. In J. Rutherford (ed.), *Young Britain: Politics, Pleasures and Predicaments*, London: Lawrence and Wishart.

Sanders, B. 1995: *A is for Ox: The Collapse of Literacy and the Rise of Violence in an Electronic Age*. New York: Vintage.

Sarland, C. 1994a: Attack of the teenage horrors: theme and meaning in popular series fiction. *Signal* 73, 48–62.

Sarland, C. 1994b: Revenge of the teenage horrors: pleasure, quality and canonicity in (and out of) popular series fiction. *Signal* 74, 113–31.

Scarre, G. (ed.) 1989: *Children, Parents and Politics*. Cambridge: Cambridge University Press.

Scraton, P. (ed.) 1997: *'Childhood' in 'Crisis'?* London: University College London Press.

Scruton, R., Ellis-Jones, A. and O'Keefe, D. 1985: *Education and Indoctrination*. Harrow, Middlesex: Education Research Centre.

Sefton-Green, J. 1998a: Introduction: being young in the digital age. In J. Sefton-Green (ed.), *Digital Diversions: Youth Culture in the Age of Multimedia*, London: University College London Press.

Sefton-Green, J. (ed.) 1998b: *Digital Diversions: Youth Culture in the Age of Multimedia*. London: University College London Press

Sefton-Green, J. (forthcoming): From watching with mother to surfing with father: children's television and digital media. In D. Buckingham (ed.), *Small Screens: Television for Children*. London: Continuum.

Sefton-Green, J. and Buckingham, D. 1996: Digital visions: children's 'creative' uses of multimedia technologies. *Convergence* 2(2), 47–79.

Seiter, E. 1993: *Sold Separately: Parents and Children in Consumer Culture*. New Brunswick: Rutgers University Press.

Seiter, E. 1995: Toy-based video for girls: *My Little Pony*. In C. Bazalgette and D. Buckingham (eds), *In Front of the Children*, London: British Film Institute.

Self, W. 1996: The American vice. In K. French (ed.), *Screen Violence*, London: Bloomsbury.

Smith, C. 1998: *Creative Britain*. London: Faber.

Spigel, L. 1992: *Make Room for TV: Television and the Family Ideal in Postwar America*. Chicago: University of Chicago Press.

Stainton Rogers, R. and Stainton Rogers, W. 1992: *Stories of Childhood: Shifting Agendas of Child Concern*. Toronto: University of Toronto Press.

Starker, S. 1989: *Evil Influences: Crusades against the Mass Media*. New Brunswick: Transaction.

Steedman, C. 1990: *Childhood, Culture and Class in Britain: Margaret Macmillan 1860–1931*. London: Virago.

Steedman, C. 1995: *Strange Dislocations: Childhood and the Idea of Human Interiority, 1780–1930*. London: Virago.

Steinberg, S. and Kincheloe, J. (eds) 1997: *Kinderculture: The Corporate Construction of Childhood*. Boulder: Westview.

Stephens, S. (ed.) 1995: *Children and the Politics of Culture*. Princeton, NJ: Princeton University Press.

Stevens, O. 1982: *Children Talking Politics: Political Learning in Childhood*. Oxford: Martin Robertson.

Street, B. 1984: *Literacy in Theory and Practice*. Cambridge: Cambridge University Press.

Swingewood, A. 1977: *The Myth of Mass Culture*. London: Macmillan.

Tapscott, D. 1998: *Growing Up Digital: The Rise of the Net Generation*. New York: McGraw Hill.

Taylor, I. 1988: Video violence: a social democratic approach. In P. Drummond and R. Paterson (eds), *Television and its Audience*, London: British Film Institute.

Thompson, J. B. 1990: *Ideology and Modern Culture*. Cambridge: Polity.

Times Mirror Center 1990: *The Age of Indifference: A Study of Young Americans and How They View the News*. Washington DC: Times Mirror Center for the People and the Press.

Tobin, J. 1998: An American *otaku*: or, a boy's virtual life on the net. In J. Sefton-Green (ed.), *Digital Diversions: Youth Culture in the Age of Multimedia*, London: University College London Press.

Urwin, C. 1985: Constructing motherhood: the persuasion of normal development. In C. Steedman, C. Urwin and V. Walkerdine (eds), *Language, Gender and Childhood*, London: Routledge and Kegan Paul.

Van der Voort, T. 1986: *Television Violence: A Child's Eye View*. Amsterdam: North-Holland.

Van der Voort, T., Beentjes, J., Bovill, M., Gaskell, G., Koolstra, C., Livingstone, S. and Marseille, N. 1998: Young people's ownership of new and old forms of media in Britain and the Netherlands. *European Journal of Communication* 13(4), 457–77.

Vine, I. 1997: The dangerous psycho-logic of media 'effects'. In M. Barker and J. Petley (eds), *Ill Effects: The Media/Violence Debate*, London: Routledge.

Wagg, S. 1992: One I made earlier: media, popular culture and the politics of childhood. In D. Strinati and S. Wagg (eds), *Come on Down? Popular Media Culture in Post-war Britain*, London: Routledge.

Wagg, S. 1996: 'Don't try to understand them': politics, childhood and the new education market. In J. Pilcher and S. Wagg (eds), *Thatcher's Children? Politics, Childhood and Society in the 1980s and 1990s*, London: Falmer.

Walker, A. 1996: Suffer the little children. In K. French (ed.), *Screen Violence*, London: Bloomsbury.

Walker, D. 1996: Young people, politics and the media. In H. Roberts and D. Sachdev (eds), *Young People's Social Attitudes*, Ilford: Barnardos.

Walkerdine, V. 1988: *The Mastery of Reason*. London: Routledge.

Walkerdine, V. 1997: *Daddy's Girl: Young Girls and Popular Culture*. Cambridge: Harvard University Press.

Walkerdine, V. and Lucey, H. 1989: *Democracy in the Kitchen: Regulating Mothers and Socialising Daughters*. London: Virago.

Wallace, J. and Mangan, M. 1996: *Sex, Laws and Cyberspace*. New York: Henry Holt.

Ward, C. 1994: Opportunities for childhoods in late twentieth century Britain. In B. Mayall (ed.), *Children's Childhoods Observed and Experienced*, London: Falmer Press.

Wartella, E., Heintz, K. E., Aidman, A. J., and Mazzarella, S. R. 1990: Television and beyond: Children's video media in one community. *Communications Research* 17(1), 45–64.

Webster, D. 1989: 'Whodunnit? America did': *Rambo* and post-Hungerford rhetoric. *Cultural Studies* 3(2), 173–93.

Webster, F. 1995: *Theories of the Information Society*. London: Routledge.

Wexler, P. 1990: Citizenship in the semiotic society. In B. S. Turner (ed.), *Theories of Modernity and Postmodernity*, London: Sage.

Wilkinson, H. and Mulgan, G. 1995: *Freedom's Children: Work, Relationships and Politics for 18–34 Year Olds in Britain Today*. London: Demos.

Williams, R. 1974: *Television, Technology and Cultural Form*. Glasgow: Fontana.

Williams, R. 1980: Advertising: the magic system. Originally published 1960. In R. Williams, *Problems in Materialism and Culture*, London: Verso.

Williams Report 1979: Report of the Committee on Obscenity and Film Censorship. Cmnd 7772, London: Her Majesty's Stationery Office.

Willis, P. 1977: *Learning to Labour*. Farnborough: Saxon House.

Willis, P. 1990: *Common Culture: Symbolic Work at Play in the Everyday Cultures of the Young*. Milton Keynes: Open University Press.

Winn, M. 1977: *The Plug-in Drug*. New York: Viking.

Winn, M. 1984: *Children without Childhood*. Harmondsworth: Penguin.

Winter, K. and Connolly, P. 1996: 'Keeping it in the family': Thatcherism and the Children Act 1989. In J. Pilcher and S. Wagg (eds), *Thatcher's Children? Politics, Childhood and Society in the 1980s and 1990s*, London: Falmer.

Wood, J. 1993: Repeatable pleasures: notes on young people's use of video. In D. Buckingham (ed.), *Reading Audiences: Young People and the Media*, Manchester: Manchester University Press.

Wood, R. 1985: An introduction to the American horror film. In B. Nichols (ed.), *Movies and Methods*, vol. 2, Berkeley: University of California Press.

Wullschlager, J. 1995: *Inventing Wonderland*. London: Methuen.

Young, B. 1986: New approaches to old problems: the growth of advertising literacy. In S. Ward, T. Robertson and R. Brown (eds), *Commercial Television and European Children*, Aldershot: Gower.

Young, B. 1990: *Children and Television Advertising*. Oxford: Oxford University Press.

Zelizer, V. 1985: *Pricing the Priceless Child: The Changing Social Value of Children*. New York: Basic Books.

Index